The Merchant Bankers

Illuminating the fabulous world of international high finance, Joseph Wechsberg draws profiles in depth of seven of the world's paramount merchant-banking houses. Their activities include merging great companies, lending huge sums to governments (often averting chaos), underwriting stock and bond issues and, in general, undertaking risks that ordinary banks could never consider.

Wealth and power give them a stunning capacity for the Grand Gesture. When Queen Elizabeth came to lunch at Hambros, a surprise was planned for her——a pile of gold, silver, and platinum worth exactly one million pounds. "It was three feet high, weighed 5322 pounds, and consisted of 400-ounce and 32-ounce gold bars, sovereigns, Dutch guilders and Persian rials; silver minted in Peking, Broken Hill, Australia, Peru, San Francisco and Bunker Hill; and a few Bank of England pound notes placed on top."

"The Queen loved it and graciously accepted a tiny, three-ounce gold bar as a souvenir."
—*The Merchant Bankers*

The Merchant Bankers

Joseph Wechsberg

PUBLISHED BY POCKET BOOKS NEW YORK

POCKET BOOKS, a division of Simon & Schuster, Inc.
1230 Avenue of the Americas, New York, N.Y. 10020

Published by arrangement with Little, Brown and Company

POCKET and colophon are registered trademarks
of Simon & Schuster, Inc.

Printed in the U.S.A.

*To the Memory of
My Father*

Preface: Strictly Personal

I ALMOST became a merchant banker myself. Around the middle of the nineteenth century, an enterprising young man named Albert Wechsberg came to Ostrava, a small town in Moravia, which was then a province of the Habsburg monarchy. Why Grandfather stopped in Ostrava I do not know. Had he continued toward California, he might have arrived there at the height of the gold rush.

Grandfather was born in 1827, the year Beethoven died, and though I have been unable to locate his birthplace, I later heard that he'd arrived "from the East." Not surprising; nearly all grandfathers seem to have come from the East, like the sun.

Grandfather brought sunshine to his family. In every merchant-banking dynasty (as you will read in this book) there is one pioneer who began with nothing and died rich. The Rothschilds started out as coin-changers in the ghetto, the Barings in textiles, the Hambros in foodstuffs, the Warburgs in silver. The Wechsbergs, I would like to add, began in grains. Grandfather arrived in town in style, sitting on top of a haycart loaded high with corn.

He loved to tell the story, often changing minor details and adding embroidery, but always sticking to the main story line. I could almost see him on that haycart. When I knew him, he was a patriarch with great dignity and a beautiful white beard yet without a trace of pomposity. His eyes were twinkling when he told his stories and I had a feeling he was making fun of his listeners. He could laugh at himself. He said people in town used to call him Albert der Gütige (Albert the Benevolent) because he would lend them money at five per cent. I had no idea what that meant. Later I heard that when Albert the Benevolent liked a man he would lend him the money without any collateral—taking a chance on the man's promise to pay him back.

"Under the circumstances," Grandfather would say, thoughtfully stroking his beautiful beard, "I don't think I overcharged him. I should have asked for six per cent interest."

Later Grandfather switched from corn to credit, in the manner of all merchant bankers, and opened a *Wechselstube* (coin-changing office). In the 1890's, which must have been quite gay in our town, according to various family chroniclers, Grandfather extended the firm into the banking house, A. Wechsberg & Co. By that time people no longer crossed the street when they saw him, like some of his former debtors. Instead they took off their hats and greeted the Herr Bankier respectfully.

The "Co." in the name of the firm were, exactly as in the case of most merchant bankers, Grandfather's sons who became his partners. One of them was my father. The bank was doing very well. When Grandfather died, with his perfect sense of timing, in 1913, one year before the outbreak of the First World War, he was eighty-six and the richest man in town, and very much loved. He owned land, mills, factories, houses, distilleries, stocks and bonds. He was dealing with Messrs. Rothschild in Vienna and Messrs. Warburg in Hamburg. He was a junior but esteemed member of the exclusive fraternity of the merchant bankers. The local paper called him "our own Rothschild." It was his great chagrin that the *real* Rothschild controlled the nearby Vitkovice Iron and Steel Works.

I remember Grandfather's funeral, as impressive as a state affair. The whole town was there, including those who had never paid him back, and they cried more than anybody else. Naturally; now they no longer could ask him for money which they had no intention of paying back. A man who had recently gone bankrupt, with Grandfather's backing, made a moving speech. Occasionally a merchant banker puts his money on the wrong debtor (as you will read in this book).

I was six, and I thought it would be nice to have such a funeral.

I've changed my mind about funerals but not about Grandfather Wechsberg. He was not ashamed of his humble beginnings. He never gave us the usual homilies about hard work and the virtue of thrift. When I asked him how he'd become a "millionaire"—I thought "millionaire" was a profession like locomotive engineer, then my favorite profession—he tapped his right temple, pointed his forefinger at me, and said, "I used my head. Don't you ever forget that, my child."

I didn't.

Without doubt, the firm of A. Wechsberg & Co. would still be in business today if certain disasters which the insurance companies call *vis major* hadn't occurred. The First World War and its aftermath swept away most private banks in our part of the world and ruined all decent people who had patriotically invested their money in war bonds. You know what happened later. Even S. M. Rothschild & Söhne in Vienna did not survive the Nazis and the Second World War.

Come to think of it, perhaps it was my good luck that Grandfather Wechsberg settled in Moravia in the 1850's. Had he gone farther west—to Frankfurt, to Hamburg, to London, to Manchester, or even so far as New York—I might now be a third-generation merchant banker.

Contents

The Merchant Bankers

1

The Merchant Bankers: Daylight
Upon Magic

*"We must not let in
daylight upon magic."*
        Walter Bagehot

MEN have always been fascinated by the spectacle of
other men making big money, and there could be no
more colorful setting for that spectacle than the City of London. Even those who criticize, fear, hate or ridicule the City
are secretly intrigued by it.

Ninety-two years ago Walter Bagehot, the brilliant Victorian banker, economist and critic, called the City of London
"by far the greatest combination of economical power and
economical delicacy that the world has ever seen." The world
has changed. Today the City has lost much of its power but
none of its delicacy. It preserves its mystique. Few Englishmen and practically no foreigners understand its intricate
financial mechanism and strange tribal customs.

"More than a million men and women work in the City of
London by day—the night population is only six thousand—
but most of them are merely 'Something in the City' to
friends and neighbors, and in many cases little more to one
another," writes Sir John Benn, an insider.

Outsiders often feel lost in the City's bright labyrinths
where, apart from the production of newspapers on its
western fringe, nothing is made but money. The City has
made the making of money a science, and forever dreams up
new ways of making money. It provides the "invisible earnings," estimated at over one hundred and fifty million pounds
a year, that help to redress Britain's chronically unhealthy
balance of payments. Most outsiders think of the City as a
large gambling den where big fortunes are made or lost.

Actually the City is a vast artist's workshop where people have developed the making of money into a fine, modern art.

The City is also a way of life that has gone on for over five hundred years amidst drama, crisis and panic. The mightiest citadel of money east of Wall Street, it has come dangerously close to chaos and destruction but always survived. The City is dominated by quaint rules and bizarre customs which everybody observes and no one takes seriously. The rules are often useless and archaic, rigid and pretentious, but no one would think of changing them. The Bank of England is still "protected" every night by a detachment of the Brigade of Guards who march there in scarlet and gold with black busbies, to the sound of a drum, an anachronistic Kipling phantom in Technicolor that creates major traffic jams. Why? Because during the Gordon Riots in 1780 the mob attacked the Bank after destroying Newgate Prison. (The Bank of England and the City are always capitalized—on paper and in the minds of all City-dwellers.)

Several years ago the War Office, millions of light-years away from the City, wanted to discontinue the mounting of the Guard. The City rose like one man. The Governor of the Bank protested. The Guards are still there. So are the tall men wearing top hats with golden bands who stand inside the hall of the Bank. And so are the doormen of Lloyd's, wearing red cloaks and high silk hats, reminiscent of the doormen in Mr. Edward Lloyd's coffeehouse in Tower Street, over two hundred and seventy-five years ago.

City people say, "The City is a paradox—but it works." So does "motoring" on the left side of the road and counting in half-crowns, though many young Britons wonder whether it's still practical. The City is a microcosm of England where everything changes except appearances. The pound has long been officially inconvertible but the City is truly an international society, concerned with commercial interdependence. Although the sterling area gets smaller all the time, the City is once again the most smoothly functioning money market in the world. The City is a concentration of power and largely Conservative, but even Labor admits that the City is a great force for political and economic freedom. The capitalists in the City, conscious of their noble traditions, are more modern and progressive than Britain's highly protected industry.

Paradoxes wherever one looks. Lloyd's underwriters still sit on their uncomfortable benches in The Room but elsewhere in the modern building the latest computers are installed— out of sight as though the people were a little embarrassed about using them. Most City men are genuine experts who like to pose as dabbling dilettantes. They talk a strange lingo of their own, like doctors or scientists, hoping that outsiders will not understand it. The deeper meaning of this pretense of amateurism was explained to me a while ago by a great merchant banker.

"Underneath there is always the awareness that one may make a costly mistake," he said. "No one in the City ever stops learning." He added that he himself had often been wrong. He must be more often right though. The assets of his bank have tripled in the past ten years.

No one can fail to notice the sense of detachment that pervades the City. City men refuse to take things seriously because they know how serious things can be. To show concern is "not done." Everybody exudes quiet confidence although the competition is getting worse all the time.

The City is a great place for skilled mind-readers. Few City people seem to think alike though many of them look alike, dressed in black, carrying bowlers, umbrellas and the *Financial Times*. Men in blue uniforms carry shabby brief-cases with millions' worth of securities. Stockjobbers in silk top hats emerge, like characters out of Galsworthy. Young boys with Beatle haircuts do errands. Tomorrow or next year or the year after next, when they are promoted to clerks, the boys will have their hair cut and wear black suits, bowlers and umbrellas, and they will staunchly defend the bizarre traditions that amused them only yesterday.

The City likes to appear eminently respectable and very solid but is secretly fond of gamblers and eccentrics. A young merchant banker and heir to a peerage speaks fondly of his cousin who would brighten up the dull routine of the bank's issuing department by standing on his head for long periods of time. He was much admired by the employees of the dignified, two-hundred-year-old bank.

Between two Dickensian pubs there is a dark, damp cellar where men with "minds that know the margin" and an uncanny ability to calculate infinitesimal gradations of risks, down to one sixty-fourth of one per cent, stand between old barrels and drink half a bottle of champagne before lunch; or instead of it. Brokers lunch hastily on beer and sandwiches. The streets are narrow and have wonderful names—Threadneedle, Bishopsgate, Cheapside, Old Jewry, Lombard, Poultry. At noontime people walk leisurely through dark alleys where no car can get through, greeting each other as in a cozy village. Once the City was indeed a village, the original London that goes back to a Celtic first-century settlement. Tacitus called it "a busy emporium for trade and traders."

The City is indestructible. It was completely destroyed by the great London fire of 1666, rebuilt itself, during the last war was more thoroughly blitzed than any other part of London, rebuilt itself again. The empire was liquidated, sterling went through dire crises, but the City is still there, the financial center of Britain and the Commonwealth.

People in the City are firmly welded together by a practical, unemotional sense of togetherness ("divided we fall") but the various tribes never mix. Bankers, stockbrokers, insurance men, discount brokers, traders, diamond men have their own pubs. It is a masculine world where girls are merely tolerated —somewhat like the computers. The girls are banished at noontime to tea shops and awful little restaurants where they seem to enjoy their own company.

The City still tries to convey the impression that it is a postgraduate course of half a dozen "good" public schools, and many City men display a studied, casual style of speech. Their voices are soft and confident—especially in moments of grave crisis. But the City is no longer their domain. A gradual process of democratization continues, as the City looks for talented outsiders. In the stock-brokerage firms men who began as lowly clerks are now top partners who make fifteen thousand pounds a year. What Bagehot called "the rough and vulgur structure of English commerce" nowadays shows up often behind the staid Victorian façades.

"You won't be made a partner today because you happen to be the son of a rich father," says the merchant banker. "It helps—but first you have to prove your ability."

THEY KNEW THE BEST-KEPT SECRETS

The merchant banks are located in the very heart of what is often but misleadingly called "the Square Mile." (Its length is twice its width.) Economists abroad speak of "the financial district." The London Post Office knows it as E.C. 2. In this small area, wedged between the Bloody Tower and Temple Bar, eighty per cent of the world's gold is marketed and sixty-five per cent of its ship-chartering is done.

Traders from everywhere come to the City's commodity markets. The London Stock Exchange lists over 9500 issues —more than any other exchange on earth. The Exchange, the commodity markets, the big commercial banks (with over five hundred branches in foreign lands), the merchant banks, the Lord Mayor's Mansion House, Lloyd's, and the Bank of England are within a few minutes' walking distance. The City is really a village. No one there ever takes a taxi.

And of all the "institutions" in the City—a favorite City expression—the merchant banks are, by common consent, the most interesting and the least known. The late Sir Oscar Hobson, a twentieth-century economist and critic, a few years ago called the merchant banks "among the more 'mysterious' phenomena of the City ... The names of some of them are almost household words, synonymous with great wealth. But what they actually do, and how they make their money, is a sealed book to most people outside the City and many people in it."

The legend of the merchant bankers immediately makes one think of international intrigue, world power, kings and dictators in need of loans, empire building or empire toppling. "Every loan ... seats a Nation or upsets a Throne," Byron wrote, with only a modicum of poetic license. One remembers sinister stories of revolutions that were financed by the merchant bankers, dramatic coups launched by daring operators—the mysterious atmosphere of "international, big finance" which has remained one of the oldest arguments against "capitalism."

"Old men drunk with power, plotting in dim boardrooms," says the merchant banker, smiling wistfully because he knows it's only a legend today. But in the cool, calculating world of commercial banking the merchant bankers provide an added element of mystery. They prove that romance is still alive in the City.

"The [merchant banks] belong in tales of fog-coated streets and hansom cabs, with tea clippers coming softly up the Thames," writes Paul Ferris, an expert chronicler of the City. "The gas lamps are burning in the banking parlor where all the partners sit together, a rich foreign banker has just been sent away with a flea in his ear, an emissary from a distant king waits by the bright coal fire in the outer hall, a pigeon is arriving on the roof with a dispatch from Dover, and the carriage that is pulling up outside contains the senior partner's beautiful young wife, who is closely related to four Cabinet Ministers and the Archbishop of Canterbury."

The merchant bankers complain that their public image as men of mystery is completely false—but they do little to change it. Merchant banking is a very private business that cannot, and perhaps should not, be defined. The truth is that the merchant bankers don't mind being the mystery men of the City. They love it.

There are sixteen banking establishments in London that are members of the Accepting Houses Committee—the only true merchant bankers. All but two were set up in London before the end of the nineteenth century. They call themselves "merchants" or "bankers" or "merchant bankers" or "merchants and bankers"—or nothing. Nearly all of them started as a family business.

"I know not why commerce in England should not have its old families rejoicing to be connected with commerce from generation to generation," said Gladstone.

Some did it all in one generation. Marcus Samuel evolved from a merchant in shells to one of England's great organizers, in 1897 transforming his trading company into an oil company named after the shells his father had dealt in. In 1907 he consolidated his interests with Royal Dutch Petroleum Company and became head of the powerful Anglo-Dutch oil trust, the rival of Rockefeller's Standard Oil. During the First World War he was commended by the Admiralty for his "services of the utmost importance to the fighting forces." He was one of the first to discover the possibilities of trade with Japan, rose from an obscure alderman in 1891 to a knighthood seven years later, became Lord Mayor of London and was made a Baronet in 1903, raised to the Peerage as Lord Bearsted in 1921, and four years later became Viscount.

The merchant bankers and their merchant banks are uniquely British. "Nowhere in the world is there anything like the London merchant bank," said the late J. H. Hambro, who called the City "one hell of a financial mechanism." The French *banque d'affaire*, the German *Handelsbank*, the American investment bank prior to the New Deal, had some, but not all, of the features of the classic British merchant bank. Closest to it are Japan's big trading companies, which is no accident: both England and Japan are islands and depend on trade for survival.

The merchant bankers go back to the earlier merchant princes in Venice, Genoa, Florence, Augsburg—such as the Medicis and the Fuggers. An early merchant banker was William Caxton (c.1422-1491), a member of the London Mercers' Guild who traded over thirty years in the Low Countries. Nearly all the founders of today's great merchant banks are descendants of seventeenth-century entrepreneurs on "the Continent of Europe." In those days Britons didn't have a knack for international banking. They lacked the knowledge of foreign lands, foreign customs, foreign languages that was needed for the worldwide banking system of the emerging British empire. The gap was filled by immigrants from Germany, Holland, Denmark, France, Russia, Ireland. The Barings, doyens of the small, select fraternity, came from Bremen to Exeter in 1717 and started the London house in 1763. The Rothschilds came from Frankfurt, the Schroders (originally called Schroeders) and the Warburgs came from Hamburg, the Brandts from St. Petersburg, the Browns from Ireland, the Lazards from Alsace. Morgan Grenfell, the parent house of the whole Morgan group, was founded in London in 1838 by George Peabody, an American whose family came from St. Albans, Hertfordshire.

Almost all merchant bankers were merchants before they became bankers. They traded with certain commodities in certain parts of the world, and later found it more profitable to leave the actual trading to others and to deal in credit instead of goods. First they attended to their own affairs, later they financed the transactions of friends and clients. It was easier to sell one's signature than a bale of silk; it was also more profitable. As they grew in stature, they discovered they could borrow more cheaply than could other merchants. They would guarantee a transaction by "accepting" the bill of exchange for which they collected a small commission. If things went wrong—and they did occasionally—they had to pay for the bill themselves.

Such a business demanded boldness and instinct, judgment and knowledge. In spite of wars, revolutions, embargoes, blockades, defaulting governments and slow communications the merchant bankers took audacious risks and made enormous profits, financed Britain's colonial expansion and built up the Empire's credit structure, and in the process organized a worldwide intelligence system and network of agents. They financed the Napoleonic Wars and later financed the peace; they were both war and peace profiteers. They made money when the Continental wars stimulated trade in England. During the Continental blockade they built up a remunerative trade in contraband goods. They dealt in goods as well as in money and news. They knew the best-kept secrets and pulled off coups that astounded their contemporaries but in retrospect turned out to be sound risks.

The early files in an old merchant bank contain fascinating random information on the rice trade in Java, gold shipments from Russia, the China tea trade, the early railroads, exports from Manila, the Amsterdam waterworks, trade in Shanghai, duties imposed on foreign shops in Cuba, sales of Siam sugar, lists of shippers of silk from Japan, prices of textiles in Mexico, tobacco "per London Packet," insolvencies of firms in Austria, sales of Russian goods on consignment, the production of beet sugar in Central Europe, lists of American ships passing the Sound of Copenhagen, exports from Java, prices of the East India Company, memoranda about the cultivation of coffee in Brazil, lists of German wool correspondents, an invoice for 1000 bottles of quicksilver, a statement of probable prices of Bengal and China silk goods, sales of cotton at Le Havre, information on the trade on the Danube, regulations proposed by the Druggists' Club for the weighing and taxing of drugs sold in London. And so on and on. Nothing was too insignificant not to be noted. Today only government agencies could compile such vast files of economic information and political intelligence.

Using their wealth of information and manipulating with skill and daring, the merchant bankers acquired prestige and power, wealth and connections. But of all their assets, integrity and common sense were the most important. In the seventeenth century Nicholas Breton wrote, "The worthy merchant is the heir of adventure, his care his accounts, his comfort his conscience, his wealth his good name." Sixty years ago John Crosby Brown, a partner in Brown Shipley and Company, defined merchant banking as "a sense of commercial honor, an absolute fairness in all dealings, willingness to suffer pecuniary loss, if need be, rather than tarnish by one unworthy act the good name of the firm ... character was prized more than wealth, and it brought its rewards in happy, useful lives. . . . Confidence, absolute confidence, at first between father and son, later between brothers and later still between the partners in different countries, at a time when there was no Atlantic cable and communications by mail were slow."

Communications are no longer slow but the merchant banker's credo has not changed. "The essence of great banking is liability," wrote Walter Bagehot. There have always been several merchant bankers on the board of the Bank of England. None ever took personal advantage of the hot tips and financial secrets which he heard at the Bank.

THE PRINCES OF THE CITY

After the Napoleonic Wars, England emerged as the financially safest country, the only country on earth that never borrowed. The Continent's capitalists in Amsterdam and Frankfurt, Paris and St. Petersburg sent their funds to London, the great clearing house. Consols became *the* gilt-edged securities and sterling *the* world's currency. Britain's financial prestige was closely allied to her maritime power. After Waterloo all governments in need of money—France, Prussia, Austria, Russia, Portugal, Spain—came to the City. The great merchant bankers listened to their propositions and either arranged loans—or didn't. Often they didn't, which made them only more powerful.

Sometimes they made mistakes and gave loans to the wrong country, and lost money. They influenced national economies, backed cities and countries, railroads and utilities, invested in underdeveloped areas, pioneered shipping lines, canals and communications, equipped whole armies, became king-makers and court bankers, and frequently made world history. In 1818 Richelieu said, "There are six great powers in Europe: England, France, Russia, Austria, Prussia, and the Baring Brothers." Richelieu had reason to be grateful to the great merchant bankers who had successfully manipulated the gigantic indemnity loan granted to defeated France, saving the country from chaos and ending the occupation.

During the nineteenth century the City's merchant bankers channeled the capital surplus at home into profitable investments abroad. Gold and currencies were freely transferable, and currency values remained stable. There were no taxes, no restrictions for the bold entrepreneur, almost no public controls. The banker's main problem was to invest fast and well. The Barings were known as the leading "American house" in London; the Rothschilds concentrated on Europe; Lazards was the Far East expert; Marcus Samuel built ships and founded an oil empire; Arbuthnot Latham was active in East Africa; and the Hambros from Scandinavia did business there and on the Continent.

The decades prior to the First World War were the golden days of British foreign investment. The merchant bankers channeled the capital surplus at home into profitable investments abroad. They built proud monuments that still exist: great mines, railroads, utilities. The 1914-1918 war changed all that. The climate for foreign investments deteriorated. Currency devaluation, political tension, then the Depression discouraged people from investing abroad. At home death duties and taxation forced many private enterprises to become public companies. The role of the merchant banker changed from a money lender to the modern financier. The private banker became the intermediary between lender and borrower. He had to look after the lender's interests and had to advise the borrower to use the borrowed funds properly. Basically, the merchant bankers remained freelances and jacks-of-all-financial-trades. The financial press, often irreverent toward wealth and power, continues to call them "the great bankers of London" or "the Princes of the City."

The "Princes" are the City's most exclusive group, its innermost circle, and intricately intermarried. Their power is no longer what it once was but their flexibility and skill in adapting themselves to the changing times has been remarkable. In 1868, when the silk crops failed in France and Italy, the merchant bankers speedily imported silk from Japan. After a famine in India, they chartered ships and sent surplus rice from Siam to Calcutta. They did many other things that only big governments can do today. The merchant bankers still make sensational headlines (against their own will) when they advise giant corporations in dramatic take-over battles or finance international pipeline projects.

They always were, and still are, hard to beat. In the 1930's, when the confused situation on the Continent and restrictions in England killed off the remunerative foreign-law business, and governments, cities and individuals went else-where for credit, the merchant bankers turned around and began to finance British industry. After the war many ob-solescent British enterprises came to the City to raise money for costly modernization projects. The merchant bankers were ready for the task. Putting through a new issue is a highly technical business requiring know-how, instinct and timing. The people in the issuing department know the chilling feeling when there is a small demand for prospec-tuses and no one seems enthusiastic. "It's like being at the theater during a first-night flop," says a merchant banker.

They all have their flops but they always exploit every possible avenue of success. When the American interest equalization tax threatened severe limitations on foreign loans in the United States, London's merchant bankers promptly arranged dollar loans in London. Within several months they had raised over two hundred million dollars in London and found new markets on the Continent.

One of the great financial parlor games is to find the answer to the question, "Who attacks the pound, why and how?" No satisfactory answer has yet been given, which makes the game so intriguing.

Doubtless there are the inevitable speculators who start to float rumors about a certain currency and then try to sell short the rumored currency. It's an old, old game. In 1790 a powerful consortium of bearish bankers made enormous profits by gambling on the fall of *assignats,* the French paper money, and then buying up the money cheaply when one louis d'or would be worth eighteen hundred *assignats.* Since then prominent merchant bankers have often acted as *bais-siers.*

Today's merchant bankers have more severe ethical stand-ards. During the grave sterling crisis, late in 1964, people in finance and industry who had maintained large sterling balances in London withdrew them, but the merchant bankers participated in no speculative maneuvers against the pound. As usual, there were rumors and legends. The sensationalist newspapers began to hint at various "secret organizations," called "the Gnomes of Zurich," "the Club of Basel" and the "Paris Club." The theory was that groups of international financiers might launch an attack against a currency for the sake of profit, or that certain governments might do it through their central banks to gain political advantage. Large amounts of pounds and dollars are in the hands of foreign nations. General de Gaulle's attacks against the dollar gave many people in Washington and elsewhere many sleepless nights.

"The Gnomes of Zurich" are said to be a mysterious league of private bankers in Central and Western Europe. "The Club of Basel" is described as an even more mysterious group around the Bank for International Settlements. The "Paris Club" allegedly consists of private corporations in West Germany, Holland, Italy, Switzerland and Britain. Allegedly it doesn't stick to the ground rule that forbids attack on fellow members. After the sterling crisis was averted by a dramatic intervention of eleven nations that put up three billion dollars in defense of the pound, recriminations ranged far and wide. West German bankers were accused by the British of dumping pounds and in turn accused some British banks of doing just that. Dutch bankers blamed "certain American corporations" for transferring their pounds into dollars. Everybody accused the Swiss, who accused everybody else.

The merchant bankers had their share of the accusations. But no one was able to prove that they were members of any "group," although they have their fingers in every major financial pie. There are many people, in England and elsewhere, who think that the "Establishment" (which includes the merchant bankers) is mostly to blame for the continuing crisis of the pound. The English upper class refuses to face the unpleasant facts of life: that the world has changed, that England is no longer what it used to be, that Britain cannot go on living beyond her means and expecting others to pay for it. A new way of thinking, a new education will be needed to cure the sickness of the pound where it should be cured: at its very source. And the merchant bankers will have to be educators and doctors.

"We must not let in daylight upon magic," Bagehot wrote about the merchant bankers. That is still their motto. Bankers are laconic people who say only ten per cent of what they think. Hereditary merchant bankers say even less. "Much of what merchant bankers do is inevitably never made public," says Kenneth Keith, a member of the silent fraternity.

The Rothschilds, fertile breeding ground of legends, never let any outsider go through their archives. The Barings don't even bother to put their name on their letterhead. To advertise or do anything smacking of publicity-seeking is considered out of the question. Merchant bankers have stricter rules than doctors. A merchant banker doesn't mind seeing his name in the paper in connection with a new issue of a spectacular loan. American newspapers often carry ads, "This announcement appears as a matter of record only, all bonds having been sold." The merchant banker is securely surrounded by his fellow bankers. It's a proud roll call of financial grandeur. But any other mention is taboo.

The City respects this penchant for secretiveness but is delighted when a sudden ray of "daylight upon magic" briefly discloses some mysteries of merchant banking. In 1890 when the Baring crisis might have caused the worst panic in the City's history, the danger was averted in the eleventh hour by a spectacular demonstration of the "Princes'" *esprit de corps*. Barings was saved, there was no run on the banks, but some facts became known, and the "Princes" shuddered audibly. They shuddered again in 1957 when the Bank Rate Tribunal investigated the rumors and goings-on behind that year's sterling crisis. And in 1959, Lord Radcliffe's Committee on the Monetary System investigated the City and brought to light some facts about the sacrosanct merchant bankers.

It was a very thorough investigation but the Radcliffe Report divulged no dark secrets. It said that "several houses have an active trustee business. . . . Several handle insurance. . . . Two founded merchant companies which have successfully developed new export trade to the dollar area. . . . Two still carry on an active merchant business, one being prominent in the London coffee market, the other having its own houses in the Americas, Australia and Africa. . . . Each house has its own characteristics on which it is regarded as an authority. But the granting of acceptance credit to finance the trade of others is a business which they all have in common."

Hardly any sensational disclosures, but the Old Guard merchant bankers were appalled. The younger ones admit, somewhat reluctantly, that "you cannot stop progress." No one will talk about credit, which remains a private matter between banker and customer. But a sensational take-over bid, affecting hundreds of thousands of shareholders, can hardly be called a private matter.

All merchant bankers agree that their activities are based on mutual confidence, that the clan must keep its strict professional ethics, that undignified stunts or a scramble for new business would destroy the very special relationship between customer and banker, who is a sort of family doctor or lawyer or father confessor.

All agree that theirs is a highly competitive business. "We get protection from nothing and nobody has any particular sympathy if we go under," says a prominent member of the fraternity. "And that's good."

That's the spirit!

2

Hambros: The King-Makers

*"Experience and knowledge,
common sense and calm."*
Carl Joachim Hambro

THE popular image of merchant bankers as a group of sinister conspirators is wrong. But there *is* drama in the daily routine of a great merchant bank. One afternoon recently I sat in an office in Bishopsgate, where four great merchant banks have their headquarters—Baring Brothers, the oldest in the City, founded in 1763, when Meyer Amschel Rothschild was still changing money in the ghetto of Frankfurt am Main; Marcus Samuel, who began as an obscure merchant in shells, selling boxes and needle cases decorated with shells; Antony Gibbs, founded in 1808; and Hambros Bank Ltd., the world's largest accepting house, as the merchant bankers call their establishments.

That afternoon I sat across from a blond, young, friendly Norwegian named Otto Norland, then manager of Hambros' Norwegian department. He was there with a young German bank manager who had come to London to spend a few days at Hambros to see how they did it.

It was late Friday afternoon, the hour when the City gets suddenly empty and people make pleasant plans for the weekend. Suddenly the phone rang: the operator told the Norwegian manager it was an urgent, personal call from a big city in Norway. A prominent shipowner was on the line. He needed help, at once. To be exact, he needed two hundred thousand pounds within the next half hour.

He told the manager that one of his ships had undergone repairs at a big Amsterdam shipyard. A few minutes ago he'd had a call from his captain. The Amsterdam yard would not release the ship unless a cash payment was made of £ 200,000. Otherwise the ship would be tied up for the week-end, and the owner would lose at least twenty thousand pounds—the cost of two days of charter and expenses for the crew of twenty-two. Not to mention the loss of profit.

The Hambros man looked at the clock and said, "It's getting late but I'll see whether I can catch anyone at the bank in Amsterdam ... Stay at the phone."

Over a second phone he dictated to a secretary in the bank a telex message to the Amsterdam bank: "PLEASE PAY £ 200,000 TELEPHONICALLY TO [NAME] SHIPYARD ON UNDER-STANDING THAT [NAME OF SHIP] WILL BE RELEASED AT ONCE." This done, he put down the second receiver and told the Norwegian on the long-distance phone to have a little patience.

Within three minutes the second phone rang. Somebody in the bank in Amsterdam confirmed that they had already telephoned to the shipyard that £ 200,000 was at their disposal. The Hambros man said "Thanks," put down the receiver and told the Norwegian over the other phone that payment of £ 200,000 had been arranged in Amsterdam, and that the yard would release his ship any minute.

"Call up your captain and give him your sailing orders," said the Norwegian manager. He listened with a smile. "Glad we could help you ... Oh, no bother at all."

He put down the receiver and said, "On Monday morning we'll get confirmation. Until then I'm not going to worry about it."

The young German bank manager—intent, correct, stiff—had listened, first with interest, then with wonderment, and finally with dismay. Now he seemed absolutely petrified.

"I could give you half a dozen reasons why I would be immediately dismissed from my bank if I had done what you did," he said to the Hambros man. "How can you be sure that you *really* talked to that shipowner in Norway? It's easy to imitate a voice over the phone. How do you know he's good for two hundred thousand pounds? Furthermore, you sent the order out over the telex, and there can easily be a misunderstanding. And worst of all, you didn't even check with your superiors! *Two hundred thousand pounds!*" He shook his head incredulously.

"If I had waited half an hour longer," the Hambros man

said quietly, "it would have been too late to arrange the credit in Amsterdam. Our client would have lost twenty thousand pounds over the weekend, and we might have lost a good client. He comes to us because we give him fast, personal service. I couldn't tell him, 'I'll call you back.' That's exactly what the big joint-stock [clearing or commercial] banks would have done. It would take them a week, processing his request through channels and committee meetings. If we acted like that, we would be out of business in a couple of years."

The German said, "Yes, but—"

"I've known the Norwegian shipowner for years," said the young Norwegian. "I trust him. I immediately translate his request into what it means to us here. A simple mathematical equation with one unknown quantity: will it work out? The banker's usual gamble. I make my decision and tell him either that we will do it or we won't. We have no large bureaucracy inside Hambros but a vast network outside. We know a lot about a lot of people. And we rely on the prestige of our name. People trust us. These things happen all the time. A freighter strikes a pier and causes damage. The port authorities want a promise of indemnity before releasing the ship. Or two ships collide. The regular procedure is to hold both ships until an inquiry has been made. That may take weeks or months. The shipowner asks us to issue a guarantee to the government that, if he's found to be liable, we'll pay the repairs. We know, of course, that he's insured with Lloyd's. So we make a couple of phone calls and issue the guarantee. The government authorities are satisfied. They might not trust the shipowner but they trust Hambros. We've dealt with them for many years. The repairs are made and the ships sail out again. No one worries. Hambros promised to pay no matter what happens. We've helped the movement and promoted international trade. That's the basic function of a merchant bank."

The German was not satisfied. He was a very thorough man.

"Why didn't the Norwegian shipowner call the Amsterdam bank directly? Surely he must be known there?"

"He may be known but they wouldn't accept his word over the phone as security for two hundred thousand pounds," the Norwegian said drily. "They will accept ours. Actually, the risk isn't as terrible as it seems to you. I know the company, I know the ship, I even know the cargo. It's my job to know all these things. Admittedly, one has to be careful. Other banks have burned their fingers in this business. One has to keep a lot of useful information in one's head. And—one has to know where to get the money at once."

Hambros has been doing business with Scandinavia for over a hundred and fifty years, and knows all about financing ships and shipping. To build a new vessel nowadays may cost five million pounds. The shipowner rarely puts up more than twenty-five per cent, and he borrows the rest. He couldn't find that kind of money in Scandinavia. He comes to London, as his father and grandfather did. Hambros will not put up all the money—such loans are for ten or twenty years and merchant banks don't handle much long-term credit—but they will arrange for a long-term loan elsewhere. In 1965, the Norwegian manager told us with pride, Hambros was requested by Scandinavian shipowners to arrange credit for new orders with British yards that may involve a total contract value of thirty million pounds.

Financing ships can be a risky business though. "During the Suez crisis a Liberty ship, built in America in 1944, would fetch a million pounds," said the Hambros man. "Two years later, the price had dropped to £60,000. Last year, when Canada and America began shipping wheat to Russia, the price went up to £120,000. If we had arranged an £800,000 loan on a Liberty ship before Suez, we would be lucky to get back £300,000 now." He smiled. "We didn't arrange it."

There is always a market for ships, said the Hambros man. Most people would rather give a mortgage on a plant than on a ship but a ship is safer, provided the company is good, the ship is good, and it's "the right ship at the right time." The Hambros man knows what the ship is going to be used for, when and where. Most of their shipping-business customers are Scandinavians and Hambros knows a lot about Scandinavia, where the name means as much as the name of Rothschild means in London.

"Norway's imports are paid for by shipping," said the Norwegian. "Norway's merchant fleet has over 2900 freighters in operation, more tonnage afloat than the United States has. Not bad for a country with a little over three and a half million people. They have tradition and know-how. Sweden, on the other hand, is a great shipbuilding country. The Swedes are outstanding engineers. So Hambros tries to bring together the good Norwegian shipowners with the good Swedish shipbuilders. I am always on the phone to New York, Hong Kong, Oslo, Brussels, Stockholm, Toronto. I sign letters written in five languages, but the bank corresponds in fifteen. We think internationally here."

THE QUEEN CAME TO LUNCH

Lunch is a quaint ritual with many individual touches in the old merchant banks. The guest is taken right back to the early nineteenth century, the *belle époque* of merchant banking, after 1815, when the Barings, the Rothschilds, the Schroders, the Hambros, the Lazards were the world's most powerful bankers. To be asked for lunch was like being received in audience by a king. The great merchant bankers didn't need the help of the kings but quite a few kings needed the help of the bankers. Back in 1797, the Court of Lisbon approached the Barings for a loan, pledging "diamonds from Brazil and the rich kingdom and island of Mozambique together with other islands north of the Cape of Good Hope." Barings was not impressed.

At Rothschilds, sherry is still served exactly at one o'clock and lunch a quarter of an hour later. At Hambros the ceremony begins at a quarter past, on the second floor. An important client or a friend of the house has been asked. All the partners who happen to be in town are present. Over drinks business may be discussed in a casual way. During lunch it was the rule until a few years ago never to talk about the sordid subject of money. The tenet is still in force in the old clubs—White's, Brooks's, Pratt's. But in most merchant banks one now may, and does, discuss business at the table.

Hambros' dining room is on the fifth floor, looking out over the roofs of the City and the cupola of St. Paul's. The walls are covered with old prints of Paris, the historical buildings along the Seine. Lunch is simple—the way an expensive Dior dress is simple. Fine smoked salmon from Scotland, grouse, old Stilton, good hocks and clarets, all properly served. On the wall hangs a painting by Edward I. Halliday called

"Lunch at 41, Bishopsgate." It shows five Hambros around the table, which is covered with beautiful goblets and old silver cups. They look somewhat distant, as though the whole thing were pleasant but not too important.

Some people will never learn the elusive technique of conversation during lunch in an old merchant bank. One talks about everything except the matters one really would like to talk about—such as getting a million-pound credit. The conversation is about farming, roses, horses, politics, families. The chairman grows roses and the deputy chairman breeds race horses. The guest unfamiliar with the City's strange customs doesn't know that all the time he is being carefully scrutinized—his manners, his clothes, his speech, his sense (or lack) of humor, his attitude and personality. The general impression will eventually decide whether he's going to be backed by a million pounds and whether any security will be demanded. This is the merchant banker's assessment—a mixture of experience and flair, analysis and instinct, inherited from generations of shrewdly assessing ancestors. At Hambros they like to say that merchant banking is not a concrete science but an abstract art, and during lunch the practitioners of this art seem to work at their best. By the time the butler has served the traditional fruit cake and a fine old port, there is usually unanimity in the minds of the partners about the risk—and about the client.

An aura of trust and tradition pervades the second floor of Hambros Bank Limited where the partners' room, the boardroom and the executive suites are located. Dark colors, deep rugs, mahogany paneling, ancestral paintings, archaic grandfather clocks abound here—the partners' desk lamps were converted from kerosene.

The visitor immediately gets the idea: merchant banking with a custom-tailored touch of dignity. The voices sound subdued. Everything is designed—artfully designed—to convey the impression: "This is big money but keep calm, don't get excited."

The atmosphere is different from an American bank where everything is open for inspection, or from a Swiss bank with its hidden cubicles for coupon-clippers and discreet offices with padded doors. Here the accent is on history. The old clockmaker who comes every week to attend and wind the

Windmill & Whiteman grandfather clocks is a fifth-generation clockmaker, which puts him nearly on a par with the present Hambros, sixth-generation merchant bankers. The old clocks make you think of elaborate props in a carefully designed stage setting; merchant bankers seem conscious of the paraphernalia of their past. But the spirit is real—the pioneering spirit of the merchant adventurers and Viking entrepreneurs.

Above the entrance to the second floor a model of an old sailing ship hangs from the ceiling. The founder of the dynasty, *Hofraad* (Court Councilor) Joachim Hambro, an eighteenth-century silk merchant from Copenhagen, made his fortune with the help of sailing ships. By contrast, there is also a glass chest next to the entrance with a model of one of the world's biggest motor tankers—*Berge Bergesen*, 91,875 tons. Larger than the *Queen Elizabeth*, and financed, naturally, by Hambros. The late *Hofraad* would be very pleased.

An impeccable butler, the right mixture of dignity and hauteur, morning coat and striped pants, takes the visitor's Burberry, cautiously, as though it were lined with sable. In the entrance hall a teleprinter is painstakingly camouflaged in a polished mahogany cabinet. Teletype messages, newspapers, financial volumes line the wall. Through Venetian blinds light filters in discreetly. There is the bust of a celebrated Hambro ancestor who lived through dire crises and came out richer than before.

The butler asks for one's appointment. He carries himself with the assurance that comes after forty years of faithful service. He belongs here with the grandfather clocks. After the visitor has been here a few times and been given the partners' invisible seal of approval, the butler may permit himself the luxury of a reminiscence. He remembers dark days when panic raged in the City—but never up here on the executive floor. During the general strike of 1926 when nearly everything came to a standstill in the City, Hambros' staff met at the Russell Hotel and quietly did their work there.

At the beginning of the Second World War the bank's ledgers and files were evacuated to "Mr. Jack's" estate in Bedfordshire. Along with the ledgers and files went a few older employees. Every night two messengers carrying dispatch cases would meet at the Cockfoster Underground station: one came from the bank in Bishopsgate, the other from Bedfordshire. Many terrible things happened in London in those terrible days and nights, but the two messengers never missed one another at the Cockfoster station, exchanging their dispatch cases. Business, what little there was of it, went on as usual.

The butler abruptly stops talking—perhaps he feels that he has already said too much. The cult of secretiveness has been developed to perfection on the executive floor of Hambros Bank. When the King of Sweden came to lunch a few years ago, even the bank's own public-relations advisers didn't know about it.

Two years ago Queen Elizabeth came to lunch. Only the partners and half a dozen trusted people were in on the secret. There had been some talk in the partners' room over what they could arrange by way of a little surprise for Her Majesty. Banks are rather dull institutions, full of ledgers and checks and balance sheets. Doubtless there is real drama in a bank but it is rarely visible or audible. You couldn't very well show the Queen a parcel of accepted bills of exchange, which is Hambros' most important business. Or a sketch of the (then unfinished) Pan-Am Building in Manhattan which Hambros helped to finance in one of the century's most "elegant financial operations."

Then somebody had a simple, brilliant idea: why not build a pile of gold, silver and platinum that would be worth exactly one million pounds? Chances were that Her Majesty had never seen what a million pounds looked like. So they built the pile in great secrecy, down in the vault. It was three feet high, weighed 5322 pounds, and consisted of 400-ounce and 32-ounce gold bars, sovereigns, Dutch guilders and Persian rials; silver minted in Peking, Broken Hill, Australia, Peru, San Francisco and Bunker Hill; and a few Bank of England pound notes, placed on top.

The Queen loved it and graciously accepted a tiny, three-ounce gold bar as a souvenir. It's called a "smuggler's bar." It can be carried in the vestpocket and furtively passed from palm to palm, and it is worth about forty-five pounds.

Hambros' bright young men exude confidence. People there have been fired for incompetence but never for making an occasional mistake.

"When something goes wrong, and the matter comes up in the eleven o'clock meeting, it's often decided to cut one's loss," one bright young man says. "We are always encouraged to make fast decisions though it may be the wrong decision once in a while. This is competitive, aggressive business. Very exciting. There is no routine. Every day is different, and you learn as you go along. The challenge and the confidence placed in us are real working benefits. I could make more money in industry but it wouldn't be half as interesting."

Most of the young managers are immigrants who know their homelands well and understand the workings of the City. The manager of the Swedish and Finnish department is a young lawyer from Sweden. He went to university there, came to London, worked at Lloyd's, started again at Hambros. He knows many young bankers and industrialists in Sweden who went to school with him and are now his customers. He talks to them in their language, often goes to Sweden. He says, "It would be difficult for a Swedish customer to put something over on me." Looking at his homeland from the outside, he often sees more than the people who live there, and comes up with ideas that wouldn't occur to his Swedish customers.

"I look at their problems the way an American in Europe looks at the business problems of the Europeans. A merchant banker lives on his information and I try to get all the available information on my territory. Much comes from the customers; a man gives himself away by talking about himself. Often my decision depends on some intangibles: can I trust the customer?"

In the course of a recent and rather typical day, Hambros' experts decided to back a chain of shopping centers on the Continent; to finance greenhouses in Denmark, an English furniture maker, and a Swiss film producer who was guaranteed by another bank; to back a food-mix business in Holland and a manufacturer of appliances in Scotland; advised a client on the changing eating habits of the French and recommended the setup of a new chain of snack bars in the country of Brillat-Savarin; planned the construction of parking lots in Germany; investigated a project of supermarkets in Western Europe; advised two big companies on big merger deals; and in addition covered all customary banking operations, gave acceptance credits, acted as an issuing house for companies who go to the public for capital, as a trust company and investment advisers, developed new real estate, operated in the City's commodities markets, financed the diamond trade, dealt in bullion (gold) and foreign exchange.

Hambros' Scandinavian Service offers special package deals to exporters and businessmen in Scandinavia—everything from preliminary reports to plane tickets, even introducing customers, negotiating credits and arranging loans, and generally "taking the risks out of the deals."

There is no set pattern. "Hambros is consciously unorthodox," says Chairman J. O. Hambro. "Anything that concerns money we attempt to cater for." The risks may be routine or spectacular—developing Iceland or backing hydroelectric power in Norway. As a result of such unorthodox thinking the bank's assets have tripled in the past ten years. Last year's (1965) balance sheet exceeded £214,000,000.

Hambros even profited from de Gaulle's exclusion of Great Britain from the Common Market. Suddenly there were new problems for Britain's industry, and Hambros prospers on problems. The bank acts as a bridge between the EFTA countries, the Common Market and the world-at-large. It takes more than de Gaulle to discourage a London merchant banker.

WILD SCHEMES IN THE FAR WEST

The obsession with secrecy and the Dickensian trappings of many merchant banks occasionally convey the impression that the "Princes" are getting senescent, but they are still adventurers at heart. Adventure was in the minds of the partners of Hambros at the end of the last war. Britain was nearly broke and Lord Keynes had spoken gloomily about the country's "economic Dunkirk." The newspapers exhorted the City "to stave off disaster." The Governor of the Bank of England, whose father-and-headmaster image is omniscient in the City, approached the leaders of the financial community to go out and "earn dollars" for Britain.

Wild schemes and strange risks were discussed in the mahogany-paneled partners' room of Hambros under the stern glances of the painted ancestors. The trouble was that the partners knew little about the United States, which was not considered "Hambros country."

One of the painted ancestors, Carl Joachim Hambro, had gone to America as a commercial apprentice in the 1830's. Carl Joachim had been fascinated by American inventiveness and returned with a new method of milling flour by the use of steam which he promptly turned into money in Copenhagen. At one time he had dreams of becoming a banker in London and New York. But that had been long, long ago.

As a rule, the younger members of the family were sent to New York to serve time in Wall Street as part of their international bankers' training but they didn't attempt to find out much about the country, and had no special knowledge of American business methods. Hambros did all the business it needed in Scandinavia, Greece, Italy, France, Germany, Spain, Portugal, Holland and Canada. It knew nothing about the Far East, The Middle East, South America. Why take the risks that one couldn't properly assess?

Among the many schemes "to earn dollars" one had been proposed to Hambros by Owen Slater, a British businessman with some connections in America. He suggested sending British goods to the States through the Gulf ports, directly to "the wide-open, rich Western market." Neither Slater nor Hambros had the slightest idea what sort of goods should be sent there but the magic vision of the untapped, "wide-open, rich Western market" seemed to take hold of everybody's imagination in the conservative, dim partners' room.

J. O. Hambro, whose father was then chairman, began to discuss the project with Slater. Jocelyn is a tall, slim, relaxed man who speaks softly, in a detached manner, as though he were only mildly interested in the world around him, but this does not fool his friends who know that he is *very* interested. Merchant banking is said to be an occupation for English gentlemen, perhaps because nearly all merchant bankers came from elsewhere, and Jocelyn is very much the type. He was born in London in 1919, educated on the playing fields of Eton, the Hambros' favorite public school, and at Trinity College, Cambridge, the Hambros' (and the Barings' and the Rothschilds') favorite college. During the Second World War he served in action with the Coldstream Guards, the Hambros' favorite regiment, attained the rank of Major, lost one leg and was awarded the Military Cross. He loves racing, is a member of the Jockey Club, and runs a first-class dairy farm. He is also the present Chairman of Hambros.

Famous surgeons who write their memoirs dwell lovingly on their success but rarely mention operations that end with the patient's death. Perhaps it is just as human that bankers rarely talk about their losses. They like to convey the impression that losses are natural disasters which happen only to other people. But when I met Jocelyn Hambro (who, according to the bright young men around him, is said to be "more than ninety per cent right") he said right away, "We are often wrong—we lose money as frequently as everybody else." I asked him where he'd learned merchant banking, and he said, with a shrug, "I guess in the Coldstream Guards."

There is some truth in this. Merchant banking is not taught at a school. A knowledge of finance, banking, economics is taken for granted. The Harvard Business School is said to be a fitting way of preparing oneself for the calling. While it is agreed that it is no longer true that, as they used to say, "the important thing is not what you know but *whom* you know," Eton and the Guards are good places to get to know some people. Modern merchant banking is a tough, complex business, dealing with all aspects of present-day finance. The merchant banker no longer can afford to sit in the partners' room waiting for the clients to come to him. He must go out after business. He must know the various techniques of issuing, investing, merging, or he won't stand up against the competition.

"We grew up with finance," Jocelyn remembers. "In our home finance was often the subject at the dinner table." As Bagehot wrote, "The banker's calling is hereditary: the credit of the bank descends from father to son; this inherited wealth brings inherited refinement."

When Hambros decided to go out and "earn dollars" at the end of the war, the assignment was given to Jocelyn. He was twenty-eight, a "hereditary" banker. His father, the formidable Olaf, then the chairman of Hambros, represented the City's Old Guard. Jocelyn was different. A merchant banker in the 1950's cannot afford to think like his ancestors in the 1890's.

Looking for British exports that were available and which "Hambros liked to handle," the partners agreed on the eccentric combination of 125-c.c. two-stroke motorcycles (a "revolutionary" product) and British pottery (a "traditional" one). The Hambro Trading Company of America, Inc., was set up in the state of Louisiana. The idea was to buy the motorcycles and sell them on credit to the American importers. Not exactly an orthodox merchant banking operation: normally Hambros would leave the trading to the experts and provide only the financing. Still, it would help British trade overseas, and the Bank of England, which must be told of everything, gave its blessing and allocated some dollars from its precious reserve.

The hopeful opinion in Hambros' partners' room was that the younger American generation, momentarily unable to buy jalopies as a traditional means of transportation and self-expression, would buy British motorcycles instead. But when Slater tried to recruit people in the States who were willing to sell motorcycles he discovered that few citizens had ever seen one. At last he found some prospective salesmen among radio dealers, people with soft-drink franchises, and men who owned liquor stores.

Strangely enough, over fifty thousand motorcycles were sold—a pleasant fact which no one at Hambros is able to explain. But when Detroit began to catch up with the growing postwar demand, and the secondhand car market became alive again, the younger American generation reverted joyfully to the jalopy. The motorcycle boom was over.

Jocelyn Hambro went to America to see what else could be sold. He and Slater decided that Americans were ready for small British cars, specifically M.G. sports cars, made by the British Motor Corporation, the country's largest automaker. Jocelyn returned to London and made his proposal to Nuffield Exports Ltd., which handled all exports for B.M.C. An unusual step: in the great, old days a Hambro wouldn't go after a customer; the customer would come to him, hat in hand. But Jocelyn didn't mind that things had changed; he isn't the melancholy-Dane type. He sold his idea and went to Dallas, Texas, with six M.G. sports cars. Why Dallas? No one at Hambros knows the answer. Maybe the partners liked the sound of the name.

The six M.G.'s were sold quickly, more cars followed, and it became necessary to build up a chain of agents. American automobile dealers were not allowed under the terms of their franchise to sell British cars. Jocelyn had to find and educate men who had never sold cars. In Dallas the distributor happened to be in the beer business. In another city in Texas a man took one look at the small M.G.—a *very* small car by Texas standards—and refused to bother with "a malted-milk machine on wheels." The former Coldstream Guards Major with his artificial leg traveled all over the country, looking for agents. He would step into the local bank and ask about a "nice chap" in the neighborhood. It might be a jukebox distributor or a refrigerator salesman.

Jocelyn reminisces about the episode in his detached manner but it must have been a frustrating experience for a sixth-generation Hambro. Texas was a long way from Bishopsgate; no one in the West had ever heard of Hambros Bank. One of the intramural stories told at 41, Bishopsgate concerns an unidentified ancestor who refused credit to a man because, as he said to his partners, "I didn't like the color of his socks." The story was later embroidered by the postscript that the man went broke two months afterwards. Obviously a bad credit risk.

Unfortunately, in the American West it seemed impossible to judge a man by the color of his socks. American socks had shockingly noisy, confusing patterns. Jocelyn began to learn, as so many visitors before and after him, that Americans look like Europeans and sometimes even speak like the English, but that they are very, very different.

Nearly everything went wrong. One distributor went bankrupt. Another said he'd been slandered; he sued and collected. A third sold quite a few cars but failed to pay up. It was a mess. And to make it worse, there was also the disastrous venture known as the Hambro House of Design in New York.

It had been set up in 1950, on Manhattan's Fifty-fourth Street, by the Hambro Trading Corporation. It would sell British and Scandinavian goods—beautiful Swedish glass, Danish silver, Irish linen, English furniture and foodstuffs. The Hambros hired able clerks and high-powered executives; they had much enthusiasm and good intentions. But the Hambros were no longer merchants. They were bankers, experienced in financing trade, but not in the physical risks of trading.

Again everything went terribly wrong. Goods arrived late,

glass was broken, specifications were wrong, furniture badly designed, and the quality was often below American standards. They had bad trouble with the foodstuffs. They brought over thousands of pounds of fine English honey and stored the pots in a Chicago warehouse. It was hot, fermentation set in, and the pots exploded. They imported Scottish kippers which were the wrong size for the American market and had to be hurriedly dumped in the North River. Hambros was losing a fortune and the Bank of England was frowning at this sort of "earning dollars."

In 1956 Hambros cut their losses and closed the House of Design, which was written off to experience. They had learned that a modern merchant banker should stick to banking. But then something happened that no one had expected: the small-car business began to boom. After an earlier agreement with the Nuffield people the Hambro Trading Company was selling Austins all over the United States. They took over the Austin showroom in New York's Sixty-seventh Street, set up spare depots in the Bronx and San Francisco—and prospered. By 1962, Hambros men had sold £40,000,000 worth of Austin cars and £75,000,000 worth of M.G. sports cars, and had earned a lot of dollars for the Bank of England. They had done it under difficult conditions in a country which they hardly knew. So they were, after all, merchants as well as bankers.

Hambros recently sold a half share in their automobile export business to the British Motor Corporation, which now manages the car business. It has been very successful. Last year they sold over 35,000 cars, worth thirty million dollars. The partners in Bishopsgate are quite pleased—and well they might be.

SOME VERY SPECIAL SITUATIONS

Merchant banks can be no better than the people working in them. The late Lord Brand of Lazards once said, "The joint-stock banks live on their deposits, we merchant bankers on our wits." When he was asked by Lord Radcliffe during the investigation if bankers had always been regarded with suspicion, he answered that they "always will be by people who cannot get credit."

Financially, the merchant banks cannot match England's "Big Five"—Barclays, Midland, Lloyd's, Westminster, National Provincial—which have thousands of branches. The merchant bankers dislike large counters and discourage check books for the small depositor.

Everybody would like to have a check book from Barings or Rothschilds or Hambros but very few are chosen. There is a rumor that Hambros is not interested in deposits below ten thousand pounds but friends, and *their* friends, are always welcome. The wife of a friend who used Hambros' elegant checks to pay for her laundry and grocery bills, after a few months was tactfully asked to open an account with the nearest branch of Barclays Bank, "where they have better facilities for that sort of thing."

The merchant banks are still wealthy but some of their clients are much wealthier. Money alone wouldn't attract these clients. The merchant bank offers tradition and prestige, the high credit rating of an old name, experience, expert advice and, above all, trust. The visitor in the City is impressed by the absolute confidence placed in the spoken word. A press photograph of the floor of the stock exchange was titled, "Where a nod is as good as a contract." A lot of business is done with very little paperwork. Every day countless verbal promises, involving millions of pounds, are made over the telephone. "However tired you get of hearing that an Englishman's word is his bond, London's custom of verbal contracts is one of the planks of its reputation," writes Paul Ferris. The merchant banker's business is based on this anatomy of trust.

A Hambros man just back from New York is amazed about the omniscience of lawyers in American business. "No one would talk to me without first consulting his lawyer," he says. "We have no lawyers at Hambros. An outside firm of solicitors draws up our contracts. We don't talk to a lawyer before making a verbal promise. Lawyers, by their very nature, tend to be distrustful. Merchant bankers are basically trustful optimists, otherwise they couldn't go on. It works. The City isn't big and you know who belongs here. Lawyers like to complicate matters. We like to simplify them."

Individual flair and old-fashioned instinct are still needed in merchant banking, but they are now coupled with aggressiveness and dynamic "forward thinking." The merchant bank's most important assets—the experience of the experts inside the bank and its outside contacts—don't show up on the balance sheet.

"Thinking internationally" is not a mere figure of speech at Hambros. The other morning one of the bright young men who works as general troubleshooter reviewed the picture of the moment. "Scandinavia is a chronic borrower, Germany a chronic debtor, France is booming, Switzerland until recently offered lower interest rates than the other European countries, Spain surprises us with new, interesting situations, Italy is in real trouble with a backlog of debt problems to solve, Austria is rather limited to straight banking, Belgium has a small trade volume but is busy in diamonds and investments, Holland has a sophisticated banking community but needs trade financing . . . There it is, in a nutshell, and the important thing is to remain flexible."

Hambros' flexible system may appear downright amateurish to conservative bankers but the Hambros don't take foolish risks. The client who was just granted a million-pound credit is well known in the bank, or his brother or uncle is well known, and the general belief is that "he's going to be all right." Naturally they know that he was elsewhere before he came to Hambros but that doesn't worry them.

"We have ways of finding out more about him than the big banks," says a partner. "We've looked at his business, his customers, his special transactions, the monthly statements. We keep track of him. The joint-stock banks won't do it. They don't have the accumulated experience."

But Hambros has turned down tempting offers that don't seem to "belong" to them. "If somebody comes in with a promising scheme for Brazil we tell him to go elsewhere," Jocelyn says. "We don't know enough about Brazil. We don't want to expand too fast. It's a question of finding the right people. If one gets too big, one loses one's flexibility."

At Hambros they like to say, "We could advise a whole economy." They have experts in production, finance, marketing, management, credit, accounting, investing, commodities, bullion, foreign exchange, and a network of five hundred correspondents all over the world. Some people come for advice and some come for money. Most come for both. The Hambros men talk about "moneys" as grocers talk about canned goods.

"We try to have as our stock-in-trade as many different kinds of money as we think people in industry or commerce could conceivably need," says Jocelyn Hambro. The merchant bank is a general store dealing in all kinds of credit. Strangely, many customers don't really know how much money they need. Most ask twice as much as necessary. Or they ask for expensive long-term credit and are surprised when the experts tell them that they could reach their objective with cheaper short-term credit.

Jocelyn's grandfather would have been shocked if somebody had asked him to back a chain of hamburger stands on "the Continent of Europe," but Europeans have become enthusiastic hamburger eaters. The venture became a sound success for Hambros. They also backed, with Schroders, Intershop A.G., a company set up by several Continental banks to finance retail shops in shopping centers. And when Meyers Bros. Parking System decided to build Europark garages in major cities of Western Europe, Hambros took a hard look, liked what it saw and backed the operation in Germany, Holland, Belgium.

Small industrialists are often suspicious of the *mystique* of a great merchant bank, thinking of finance as a sinister, dangerous force (which it often is). Why should these chaps in the bank know more about his company than he does? But experience proves that the company owner is often in the dark while Hambros' experts, after a few days on the spot, know the solution to his problems. They stay with the company for a while and make their recommendations.

"Often the company is sound but doesn't project its image effectively," says a Hambros braintruster. "Or it needs expansion and we suggest how this should be financed. Or we tell the man to sell his factory and lease it back. We tell him to get the right amount of money at the right price in the right place at the right time. Sounds easy but takes a lot of experience. We tell him about the purchase of raw materials and how to protect himself against loss due to foreign-exchange fluctuations. The efficient import of raw materials is as important as an efficient sales organization but many manufacturers don't know that the skillful use of 'forward purchasing' will save them trouble and money. The other day a cheese manufacturer asked us whether he should buy out a competitor who made imitation Camembert. I told him we are no cheesemakers. He must know whether the imitation Camembert is any good and what he could do with the business. But if he should decide to buy it, we can tell him how he should do it and how much he should pay. The business of buying a business demands a very special technique and even prominent industrialists don't know it. They don't realize that issuing stocks means printing one's money and they usually pay far too much for the business they're buying. All this has to be done tactfully. Prominent industrialists don't like to be told there is something they don't know."

After investigating the Camembert deal they advised the client that instead of buying the company he should expand his own business and run the imitation Camembert maker into the ground. This would be cheaper and looked like good business, and they decided to back him. It worked out very well for Hambros.

The bank's "special situations" department likes to nurse promising ideas from birth to a moderate success as a private company and finally to a big success as a public company. They are doing again what the nineteenth-century merchant bankers did when they began to finance the industrialization of Britain. Then it was done with money; now it's done with money and advice, and the advice is often more valuable than the money. They remember a man who came in after the war with a good manufacturing idea and one thousand pounds borrowed from his father. Hambros backed him over the years; he's now worth half a million pounds, plans to expand on the Continent with the help of Hambros.

"A Swedish company told us they want to expand in Holland," said the Hambros man. "We happen to know that a British company had been looking for just such a setup in Holland. We became marriage brokers, arranging another amalgamation. A process of economic cross-fertilization. Incidentally, we may take a minority interest, but never control. We believe the management should be left to the managers. We want to keep sensible influence—after all, we're involved with our money—but we don't want to run hundreds of companies. We charge an annual retainer fee for our services and are always at the disposal of the board."

At the end of the last war Britain's coal mines were in bad shape, needing new pitprops that had been imported from

Finland. They approached the big commercial banks who in turn asked Hambros' advice. Hambros knew exactly where one could get the pitprops, and the big banks provided syndicate credit on the basis of Hambros' recommendation and management.

Once in a while a "mad inventor" comes to Hambros. A man who claimed "spiritual guidance" showed them his invention for stopping lung cancer—a plastic container filled with cotton that could be stuck into a sash window and would keep out dirt, dampness and germs.

"He knew exactly how much money he needed," says the Hambros man. "In that respect he wasn't mad at all. He'd figured there were about fifteen million sash windows in Britain. Other people are less honest. They want us to back nonexisting firms of which they show us the balance sheets. We try to see everybody. You never know whether the next fellow hasn't got a great idea. Years ago a man showed us a machine that bent steel frames and cut holes in them, making shelves with slotted angles. It seemed like a big Meccano toy, but it's a real success and will be a big business. We try anything that generates the making of money, and in the process we sometimes lose money."

Sometimes losses are caused by events beyond the control of the most cautious banker. Hambros bought an interest in a promising textile factory. A week after the contract was signed, the factory was inundated by the first flood in a hundred and fifty years, which spoiled the investment. Once they backed a young manufacturer who made an excellent start and suddenly died, whereupon the one-man business collapsed. A good product may be ruled out by new specifications, laws may be changed, and there are always the incalculable whims of fashion and changing public taste. But the merchant banks face big and small losses with resourcefulness and go after other business. Merging tradition with progress, old-time connections with modern know-how, they are in better shape than ever before.

BLACK CREPE AND CREDIT

Hambros' recorded history begins with Joachim Hambro, a silk merchant who died in Copenhagen in 1806. (His birthday is not known.) There are no Hambros in Denmark today but a distinguished branch of the family—scholars and statesmen—exists in Norway. The legend in the bank is that Joachim made his way from rags to riches but there are also stories of earlier Hambros, smart Viking adventurers who did well for themselves. A Hambro sea captain with his own intelligence sources on the Continent got word that the Queen of Denmark had just died in Paris, whereupon he cornered the black crepe market in Copenhagen and made a small fortune.

Merchant bankers love to reminisce about the colorful coups of their ancestors. Almost every house has a supply of fascinating stories. Samuel Montagu made his first money in the foreign-exchange business with the seamen in his native Liverpool. The Browns of Brown Shipley, founded in 1810, held the Blue Riband for the fastest crossing from New Orleans to Liverpool in 1827—twenty-six days. As a result of such lore, more is known about the early history of some houses than about their current activities. The great Hong Kong firm of Jardine, Matheson proudly advertises "the early pioneering days" when two tough Scotsmen, William Jardine and James Matheson, formed a successful partnership in 1828—as opium smugglers.

Long before Hambros Bank was founded in London in 1838, the Hambros had been bankers to the kings of Denmark, Sweden, and Norway. A blue-leather book with the "Pedigree of Hambro" is sometimes shown to friends at the bank. The entries are made in old-fashioned copperplate script. The first Hambro mentioned is Joseph, the son of Joachim. ("Joseph Hambro of Copenhagen in the Kingdom of Denmark and of Upper Portland Place, co. Middlesex. Sometime Councellor to the King of Denmark. Born 2 Nov 1780 at Copenhagen. Died 3 Oct 1848, buried in Whitechapel co. Middlesex.")

Exactly when old Joachim turned from trading in silk to banking is not known. He kept his silk business after he'd added banking and so did Joseph. (It's no accident that the earliest Hambro merchant banker was in the silk business. Buyers of luxury goods were granted long-term credit and a resourceful silk merchant had to be sure about his credit risks.) Joseph switched from silk to food, provisioning the sailing ships. An anonymous chronicle about sea travel in earlier times says, "a wise pilgrim would never set out on a trip without a larder full of ham, salted meat, hard cheese, pickled food that could be kept in good condition for a long time."

Not much had changed since then. In 1807 Robert Fulton was still experimenting with his steamboat. Wise travelers would buy ham, salted meat, hard cheese and pickled food from Joseph Hambro in Copenhagen. He began to export flour and bacon, bred pigs, built a salting house, a bakery, a flour mill. At the same time he carried on his banking business at Kongens Nytorv, in the center of the city. He prospered, was honored and became court banker to the King of Denmark at the age of forty.

The country was in bad shape. In 1807 neutral Denmark had rejected an alliance offered by England. The English bombarded Copenhagen and forced the capitulation of the Danish Navy. As a result King Frederick VI joined the French—a fateful mistake. The Napoleonic Wars were disastrous for Denmark, which lost Norway to Sweden in 1814, and Heligoland to Britain. The country's trade was hit, inflation was mounting, all real estate was subject to a six per cent tax.

Joseph Hambro did well though, enlarging his food business. In 1827 his holdings were worth £67,000. Five years later he owned £100,000. His bank had over four hundred different accounts, among them the leading merchants and merchant bankers. Meyer Amschel Rothschild of Frankfurt and his son Nathan Meyer Rothschild of London were customers. So was Count A. W. Moltke, a liberal Danish aristocrat who later played an important part in Danish history.

Joseph's only son, Carl Joachim, was born in Copenhagen in 1808. After going to school in Copenhagen, he studied in Bremen and Le Havre, and went to America for a kind of postgraduate course, to observe what one of the world's most expanding economies was like. When he returned, he had many new ideas, and already sensed that ideas are a merchant banker's lifeblood. He became American Honorary Consul in Copenhagen and a junior partner in his father's bank, with a share of eight thousand pounds. The bank financed the first Danish railroad, from Copenhagen to Roskilde, and the first steambath in Copenhagen. For many decades Hambros Steambaths were a local attraction.

After the loss of Norway, Denmark had become a small country. Carl Joachim began to think of moving elsewhere. His father cared only about his food business (his descendants who tried to sell food in America one hundred and twenty-five years later and failed could have learned something from their cautious great-grandfather) although he had to give some time to his banking business. Count Moltke, now Prime Minister, approached his friend Hambro when the Danish government decided to negotiate a loan abroad. "Your ... honest will, your experience, and your skill in adapting yourself to difficult conditions is to me the best promise that you will obtain the best results," Moltke wrote, unwittingly outlining the requirements of a nineteenth-century merchant banker. And he recommended that Hambro get in touch with the Rothschilds.

The Rothschilds liked Joseph Hambro ("an experienced financier") but made it clear right away that he was not in their class. Denmark, a very minor power, might need the Rothschilds, but the Rothschilds, a major power, certainly didn't need Denmark. The negotiations for the loan dragged on and the Rothschilds became impatient with "this unpleasant business" and patronizing toward Joseph Hambro. Once they complained indignantly that they were surprised to be misunderstood by Hambro, "a businessman to whom one should only have to indicate the main points without further clarification."

Old Joseph Hambro didn't mind but his son got very angry about the Rothschilds' arrogant attitude. A hundred years later one would have diagnosed his inferiority complex toward the Rothschilds. It can be traced through his whole life and made him take some spectacular risks. In the light of subsequent history the Hambros owe a lot to the Rothschilds.

Carl Joachim had been impressed in America by the proud spirit of free men. He admired the Rothschilds for their wealth and power but that didn't give them the right to treat his father like a clerk. The situation didn't improve when the Danish government decided it didn't need the money and Joseph Hambro had to settle the matter with the Rothschilds. He himself waived his own commission. He was a businessman, but he also was a patriot.

In 1837 Carl Joachim went to England on a business trip, to trade foodstuffs and timber in Liverpool. He liked the English and the way they did business, and he heard alluring stories about how the "London bankers" lived.

"The name London banker has especially a charmed value," writes Bagehot. "There has probably very rarely ever been so happy a position as that of a London banker and never perhaps a happier one." Bagehot gets carried away somewhat; he must have known that the *nouveau-riche* London bankers were not accepted socially, were often maligned and ridiculed. A proper Victorian would snub a City man (though he might secretly watch him with fascination and envy). Admittedly the fellow gave splendid parties and went shooting grouse in Scotland—shooting grouse was the big status symbol of the nineteenth-century banker—but it was too bad that he had to make a living in the City.

Carl Joachim Hambro knew that from 1815 to 1830 at least three bankers had failed every year. But he was encouraged to see so many newcomers establish merchant banks in the City. The Barings, Rothschilds, Schroders, Brandts were already there. Antony Gibbs had come in 1808, Brown Shipley in 1810, Kleinwort in 1830, Marcus Samuel in 1831, Arbuthnot Latham in 1833, Guinness, Mahon in 1836. (All of them are still around.) And so, in 1839, Carl Joachim Hambro moved to London and founded the firm of C. J. Hambro at 70, Old Broad Street, with a capital of fifty thousand pounds.

It was not a good moment for a young banker. Two years before, three of the seven leading "American houses" in London hadn't met their obligations. The depression reached its nadir in the early 1840's, when Maryland and Pennsylvania defaulted in their interest payments and no one in the City wanted to touch American securities. Carl Joachim seems to have got into some trouble, for in 1840 his father had to come to London to straighten out the difficulties.

"I have been told," writes one Louis Bramsen, a former clerk at the bank, "that Carl was almost deranged, and in any case found the situation too much for his spiritual strength." But Bramsen admittedly did not like Carl Joachim. A better writer, Hans Christian Andersen, who came to England to visit his friend Carl Joachim Hambro describes him in his autobiography as a man with a good sense of humor. When they went out together, Andersen, quiet and withdrawn, was often thought to be the banker, and Hambro, outgoing and joking, the writer.

In 1848 Father Joseph died, leaving his son £295,515; and there were no death duties. Carl Joachim now had the position of a London banker, "never perhaps a happier one." Having noticed that London society had no use for "the money people?" he kept away from them. He could afford it, being forty years old, rich and independent. In 1843 the English Parliament had passed a bill making him a British citizen. The following year he had been appointed court banker by King Charles XIV John of Sweden, the former Marshal Bernadotte, in recognition of his bank's success.

Carl Joachim Hambro was thinking of retirement. But things didn't quite happen that way. Retirement was not yet in his stars.

THE DANISH LOAN

In 1848 war had broken out between Denmark and Prussia after the Prussians attempted to recapture the Duchy of Schleswig-Holstein. Great Britain and Sweden failed to mediate an armistice. In February, 1849, the Danes resumed the war against Prussia.

Wars were a costly business even then. Prime Minister Moltke considered an income tax but rejected the idea as being "extremely inquisitorial." There would have to be informers, the government would inquire into the private lives of the citizens, people's privacy might be invaded. Once you started that dangerous trend, you never knew where it might end. Moltke, a man of noble principles, didn't like the idea of an enforced internal loan either.

The best solution seemed a foreign loan. Moltke sounded out bankers in St. Petersburg and Amsterdam, and was turned down cold. In London the situation was not much better. Denmark was known to be in a precarious position. Foreign loans had often ended with losses for British investors. The Napoleonic Wars had been a severe financial burden for England. In 1813 England had been forced to levy an income tax to pay for the interest on various loans.

Moltke approached Hambro, who was more optimistic than most people in the City. Hambro thought a loan might be possible, provided the terms would attract "serious investors." That was his whole philosophy in life. He always told his clerks that a merchant banker needed "experience and knowledge, common sense and calm."

Both Barings and Rothschilds refused the Danish loan. Then Moltke's emissary, Count Treschow, a brilliant lawyer, came to see Hambro. Treschow knew how Hambro felt about the Rothschilds. Here was the great opportunity of launching a coup against the offenders! A few days later Hambro suggested a bond issue of £800,000 of which he himself would take half at 84. He asked Treschow to publish the terms in Denmark. People in his homeland must not think that "he had done well out of the war."

After raising £250,000 Hambro needed another £150,-000. He went to Barings, which was willing to take the bonds—but at 77½, which would have killed it. Hambro didn't even bother to see Lionel Rothschild. Instead he decided to offer interim bonds in the market as a private venture.

For a man who always preached "experience and knowledge, common sense and calm," this was quite a risk. Hambro offered the bonds at 86. They were six times oversubscribed.

Treschow congratulated Hambro. "I should think that Rothschilds and Barings were gnawing their fingers."

A few days later the bonds were traded at 100. Hambro had made a fortune but the Danish Finance Minister reported to King Frederick VII, "Hambro's glory is in no way lessened because the swing of the market has turned into an unexpectedly large profit for him."

By Royal Patent of October 6, 1851, Carl Joachim Hambro was made a Danish Baron. The title was to be inherited by the head of the family. Baron Hambro obtained permission from the Royal College of Arms in London to use the Danish crest in somewhat modified form in Great Britain. It hangs above the fireplace in the boardroom of Hambros Bank.

Hambro was a rich man now. He purchased the estate of Milton Abbey for a quarter of a million pounds. He collected paintings and looked after his estate.

He had reached his ambition. He was rich and respected in his new country and had been honored by the country of his birth. He would have been very surprised if someone had predicted that the climax of his life was yet to come.

FINANCING THE RESURRECTION

When Count Camillo Benso di Cavour became Finance Minister of the Kingdom of Sardinia in 1851, no one in the City of London paid any attention to the appointment. The Apennine peninsula was a jumble of divided, opposed states. Modern Italy hadn't emerged yet. Among the men who fought for their country's freedom, Mazzini and Garibaldi, the colorful revolutionaries, were well known. But in the end it was Cavour, the statesman, who unified his country. He started out with a tiny kingdom named after an obscure island in the Mediterranean, and located at the foothills of the Alps and in the plains of the Po.

Cavour, forty-one when he became Finance Minister, was the second son of a noble, impoverished family, and traditionally bound to go into the army. But he was not made to be a soldier; he loved mathematics and finance. He was a liberal monarchist, a pious Catholic, but he also opposed the absolutist power of the Church. He had a quick temper, was a gambler and nonconformist. His enemies feared his sarcasm and razor-sharp mind but they admired his patriotism and sense of loyalty. For a short time he had been an army engineer officer, then his family sent him to the country to manage the run-down family estate; they hoped he would keep out of trouble there. Cavour became interested in agriculture, and went to France and England to see how the big estates were managed. He liked England—the country, the people, the political climate. He met English aristocrats who were liberal monarchists and gamblers, like himself. He told his friends that if he were not a Piedmontese, he would have liked to be an Englishman. Many people, before and after Cavour, have had a similar wish.

In 1847, Cavour founded with Balbo and Count Santa-Rosa the newspaper *Il Risorgimento* (The Resurrection). It later gave its name to the movement for the unification of modern Italy. When the anti-Habsburg revolt broke out in Milan, Cavour was in favor of war against Austria.

War was declared. Cavour was elected to the Parliament of Piedmont. (He always called his country "Piedmont.") Even after the Piedmontese defeat at Novara, Cavour didn't abandon his great dream. Defeatism didn't exist in his vocabulary. After a short tenure as Minister of Agriculture he became Minister of Finance. It was the hardest job in Piedmont, which was bankrupt. The budgetary deficit was three million pounds.

To make Piedmont prosperous again, Cavour pleaded for public education, new industries, new railroads. The railroad from Turin to Alessandria was almost completed; two more, from Lago Maggiore to Alessandria and from there to Genoa, were planned. Cavour planned new port installations. But Piedmont had to pay off a large indemnity to Austria. A big loan was needed.

On the merchant bankers' map of the world Piedmont was known as "Rothschild country." The Rothschilds had handled former Piedmontese loans. Trying to break the Rothschilds' financial monopoly over Piedmont, Cavour approached the Barings, who turned down the proposal. Cavour wrote to the Marquis d'Azeglio, his ambassador in London, "These gentlemen are hardly prepared to enter into a struggle with the House of Rothschild."

Cavour's friend, the Genoese banker Emile de la Rue, then approached Hambro. Hambro recommended a very modern means of raising capital. He suggested that there should be a mortgage on the Piedmontese railroads and that the bondholders should later have an option of exchanging their bonds against shares in the railroads. Hambro made it clear that the loan should not finance a political movement but the construction of the Piedmontese railroads. Investors wanted profits, not political slogans. Four million pounds, at five per cent.

Cavour liked Hambro's ideas and through Count Revel, an intermediary, asked him to handle the loan. Hambro was honored but worried. It had been one thing to launch the successful Danish loan; he knew Denmark, and the City, where trust is an important if intangible element, had trusted him. But he knew nothing about Piedmont; would the City trust him again? Unless he took a large part of the loan for his own account, he wouldn't convince the British investors that he believed in the future of Piedmont.

Hambro hesitated. Then Count Revel used the same argument that Count Treschow had used prior to the Danish loan: here was another chance to break up the hegemony of the House of Rothschild.

Hambro decided to take £400,000 on his own account. This was more money than he owned. It was no longer a question of "experience and knowledge, common sense and calm." It was an outright gamble. Hambro speculated with his fortune, his prestige, his credit.

Sir Henry Drummond Wolff, the brilliant Jewish-Scottish financier, once said, "The mortgage represents caution, the speculation boldness, and the financier a mixture of both qualities." There was more boldness than caution in financier Hambro's gamble. If the loan went wrong, he would be finished in the City.

There were delays: Cavour had trouble in the Piedmontese Parliament where the opposition was against the projected loan. Hambro almost lost heart, and Cavour had a terrible rage and wanted to break off negotiations. At last Hambro put through the Anglo-Sardinians, as he called them, at a price of 85.

Things didn't go well. The initial subscription was only £2,194,000. The first installment of the loan had to be made by the bond buyers, and Hambro was informed of "cowardly, underhand conspiracies." In Paris, James de Rothschild said, "L'emprunt était ouvert, mais pas couvert." A witty bon mot but it didn't help the loan. Hambro was now convinced that the Rothschilds were out for his neck. Rumors spread in the City that there might be a ten per cent discount, don't buy now.

Hambro had to act quickly to avert disaster. He teamed up with one Lewis Haslewood, "an energetic speculator," who purchased £400,000 worth of Anglo-Sardinians. Haslewood's brother Edward went to Piedmont to investigate. He reported that the Sardinian railways had a sound future and wrote he would recommend them "as an investment for the window or orphan . . ." In October, 1851, the Anglo-Sardinians were quoted in Berlin and Hamburg, but not in Amsterdam and Antwerp where, according to Hambro, "Rothschilds kept them off the market." In London, the bonds fell to 79½. These were dark days for Carl Joachim Hambro.

Possibly to forget his worries, Hambro began to write letters to Cavour, advising him on the future of Piedmont. A merchant banker's job is to advise his client but in this case the client happened to be an "insufferably domineering Finance Minister" (as Cavour's own Prime Minister called him) who resented unsolicited advice, and probably knew more about his country than his London banker did.

Cavour must have felt Hambro's deep concern, however, for he listened to him. Hambro suggested "caution" and "prudence"—qualities which he hadn't exactly shown himself when he launched the big loan. He asked Cavour to impose heavier taxes and reminded him that £1,400,000 worth of bonds was still unsold. He emphatically rejected Cavour's suggestion to offer the bonds at a discount. That would finish Piedmont's credit in London, and "this credit must be as dear to you as your own honor as an individual." Strong words from a London merchant banker to a hot-tempered Piedmontese aristocrat. By late November, Anglo-Sardinians had gone up to 82½.

Cavour was winning new friends in England, where Lord John Russell had coined the slogan, "Italy for the Italians." Most people were on the side of the Italian freedom fighters. Cavour obviously was the great unifying force. He had style and wit, spoke well, avoided shallow oratory, imitating the urbane manner of the great English statesmen whom he admired. The English newspapers liked him. Anglo-Sardinians were going up to 87, but Hambro still wasn't satisfied.

"If people knew you as you deserve," he wrote to Cavour, "your funds would be quite at a different price . . . I am united heart and soul and fortune with Piedmont because I believe that country is destined to be yeast for the regular progress of humanity, and that neither despots nor anarchists can stop it."

Cavour took Hambro's advice, reorganized the government bookkeeping system, introduced heavier direct taxes, instigated measures to stimulate free trade. (Early in 1852 Anglo-Sardinians rose to 90.) He favored the sort of two-party system that Britain had and began to merge his own party with Rattazzi's left-of-center group.

The maneuver is remembered as *connubio* (marriage) in the history of *Il Risorgimento*. It was a play for power but also an effort to stop Cavour's enemies who threatened freedom of the press. A new alliance was formed, Rattazzi became President of the Chamber, and a new cabinet was formed—without Cavour. That was his masterstroke. He wanted to prove that he was indispensable. Sooner or later they would call him back—as Prime Minister.

For a while Cavour traveled in France and England. In Paris he managed to interest Napoleon III in his vision of a unified Italy. In London he met, at long last, his banker, and they became friends. A few months later Cavour was asked to return and form a new government in Piedmont. As Prime Minister (also keeping the portfolios for finance, agriculture and trade) he signed new trade agreements, built new roads, and led Piedmont toward prosperity.

In February, 1853, Mazzini made his unsuccessful revolt against the Austrians in Milan, after an earlier attempt in Mantua. Cavour calmed Hambro; the revolt wouldn't damage Piedmont's credit in the City. But many investors sold the Piedmontese bonds and Hambro unhappily wrote to Cavour that Anglo-Sardinians "had gone to the devil."

Cavour had other troubles too: his country's vineyards were destroyed by *Phylloxera*, the dreaded pest that later cost France twice as much as its war with Prussia. He remained optimistic, however, and wrote to Hambro, "I hope that whatever may happen you will continue to remain interested in us and lend us aid and support."

The two men had only one serious quarrel. In 1854, Cavour asked his friend whether Hambro could no longer accept bills for the Piedmontese government without securities in hand. This letter, addressed personally to Hambro, was answered by a form letter from C. J. Hambro & Son, informing the Prime Minister "that such guarantees were in fact necessary." It nearly wrecked their friendship but later they made up again.

Cavour was emerging as an important figure on the world's political stage. In February, 1855, he shrewdly signed a treaty for Piedmont to send fifteen thousand troops to the Crimean war. He knew that Piedmont's participation in the war would later give his country the right to speak up at the peace table. Palmerston was pleased. Queen Victoria said, "It must be our object and interest to see Sardinia independent and strong," and called Victor Emmanuel *"eine ganz besonders abenteuerliche Erscheinung."*

In the spring of 1856 a Convention was signed between Britain, France and Sardinia. Britain would provide Piedmont with a loan of a million pounds at four per cent. Cavour no longer needed a merchant banker. In the British Parliament, Disraeli criticized the principle of the British government's granting a foreign loan. Loans should remain the domain of the merchant bankers.

Twenty-five years later Disraeli went to the Rothschilds for the most celebrated short-term loan in history, asking Lionel de Rothschild for four million pounds "for a few days," to buy the Khedive's share of 43¾ per cent of the common stock of the French Suez Canal Company. Rothschild let Disraeli have the money at the patriotic rate of three per cent, with "the word of the Prime Minister" as the only security, and Disraeli wrote to the Queen, "It is just settled: you have it, Madam." The £4,000,000 investment gave England control of the Canal and prior to the Second World War was worth around £90,000,000.

While Disraeli had doubts about the wisdom of the government's acting as a banker, he had no doubts about Sardinia. Gladstone agreed. "Sardinia has succeeded, amidst difficulties almost unprecedented, in establishing for herself the blessings of a free government."

It was sweet music for Hambro. He had long known that Cavour would create an island of liberty and constitutionalism in an ocean of dark absolutism. C. J. Hambro & Son promptly provided the funds under the terms of the Convention, and later acted as Cavour's agent in America. In Piedmont, the railroads were running. And in Paris, Charles Laffitte promoted the Vittorio Emmanuele Company which connected the railroad systems of France and Italy. When war was declared on Austria in 1859, the French troops were able to reach quickly the plains of the Po. After the battles of Magenta and Solferino, Lombardy became part of Italy.

The unification of Italy was under way. After a plebiscite in 1860, Parma, Modena, Romagna and Tuscany joined, then came Sicily and Naples, the Marches and Umbria. On March 17, 1861, the first Italian Parliament declared Victor Emmanuel King of Italy.

A few weeks later, Cavour wrote his last letter to Hambro, asking his friend's advice about unification of Italy's debts. He died unexpectedly on June 19, 1861. He was only fifty-one but had achieved his mission in history. "Free church in a free state" were his last words. Five years after his death, Mantua and Venetia joined Italy, and the remaining Papal States were taken over by the Italian troops in 1870.

Italy was unified, and a Danish-born merchant banker from London had financed the initial operation. Hambros Bank Ltd. is still fiscal agent to the Italian government.

THE KING-MAKERS

Two years after having helped to make Victor Emmanuel King of Italy, Carl Joachim Hambro became a kingmaker again. After the 1862 revolution in Greece that had deposed King Otto, the son of King Ludwig of Bavaria, the Greek nation by almost unanimous vote elected Prince Alfred, the second son of Queen Victoria, as their new king. But Great Britain, France and Russia, the "protective powers," had previously agreed to exclude any member of their own ruling houses from the Greek throne, and the wish of the Greek nation had to be ignored.

A compromise candidate had to be produced in a hurry. While the Greek emissaries were in London to discuss the delicate situation, a Danish naval boat with Prince Wilhelm of Denmark on board happened to arrive. Prince Wilhelm was accompanied by Count Sponneck, a Danish nobleman and close friend of Carl Joachim Hambro.

The following Sunday the Prince attended the service in London's Danish church. Perhaps not quite by accident, the Greek emissaries happened to be there to take a discreet look at the Prince. Count Sponneck and (Baron) Hambro were also there, needless to say.

The Greek emissaries must have taken home a good impression. In March, 1863, the eighteen-year-old Danish Prince was nominated to the Greek throne, and later became King George I. Hambros issued its first Greek loan in 1881.

During the second half of the nineteenth century the wars on "the Continent of Europe" were followed by banking panics in various capitals. The City saw great crises in 1856, 1867, and 1890. Some private banks failed; others were absorbed by larger houses. C. J. Hambro & Sons survived because the dynasty was lucky enough to produce able bankers during the critical third and fourth generations.

(When Kurt Forberg, senior partner in the German banking firm of C. G. Trinkaus, was asked how the firm had managed to stay in business for a hundred and seventy-five years, he said, "The right successors were always there at the right time.")

Of Carl Joachim's three sons, Everard had chosen to become a City banker. He studied at Eton and Cambridge, joined the bank in 1864, and after Carl Joachim's death in 1877 was left over half a million pounds, and became sole owner of the bank.

Everard, a commanding Viking type, six feet five inches tall, practiced banking, in accordance with Bagehot's definition, as "a watchful, but not a laborious trade." There exists a drawing made in 1888 by a famous caricaturist, "Lib," showing Sir Everard Hambro with the first Lord Rothschild and the first Lord Revelstoke of Barings. The Hambros had arrived in the innermost circle of "the Princes of the City."

Everard was a close friend of John Pierpont Morgan. A contemporary chronicler called him "a keen observer of the stars in the monetary firmament." He was made a director of the Bank of England, and was knighted; it is said that he refused a peerage. He spent little time in England and lived in a beautiful villa in Biarritz, where he became the friend of the Prince of Wales, later King Edward VII, with whom he played cards. Every day Everard received a report from his London bank in copperplate script. It took several days to get there and his answer reached London a week later but there was no hurry.

This was the era of great foreign loans, which had been considered somewhat dubious transactions in the earlier decades of the century when so many governments defaulted. Now they became prestigious affairs. Foreign governments preferred to deal with the great merchant bankers in London who were free from all political pressure and operated independently. Cities and nations came to London to finance their utilities and communications. Hambros arranged loans for Rome, Copenhagen, Christiania, Gothenberg. A Danish loan was launched in 1863, and another one three years later, after the Danish defeat by the Prussians.

With the help of the great merchant bankers some countries were put on the gold standard. In 1881 Hambros and Barings raised £14,000,000 for Italy, and shipped most of it in gold, without so much as disturbing the London gold market. The shipments formed the nucleus of a gold reserve for Italy's currency (which Carl Joachim had suggested to Cavour twenty-six years earlier.) In 1888 and 1890, Hambros and Barings issued Russian loans, and the following year they helped the Imperial Russian Government to put the currency on the gold standard by successfully issuing a three per cent gold loan of £19,775,000. But it was only in 1897 that a gold basis for Russian currency was established.

Throughout these years the bank didn't change its traditional appearance. Kings, statesmen, prime ministers and ambassadors came for sherry and lunch. Every effort was made to preserve the unhurried pace of the past and the atmosphere of quiet dignity. The risks became larger but the merchant bankers took them in their stride. In 1922, C. J. Hambro & Son amalgamated with the British Bank of Northern Commerce, and has since been known as Hambros Bank Limited. The British Bank of Northern Commerce had financed Finland after the country gained its independence from Russia in 1917, and later again after the civil war. Finland is now considered "Hambros country."

In 1926 the bank moved from Broad Street to larger quarters at 41, Bishopsgate, a dignified building in late-seventeenth-century style, with a small-brick façade. The old interiors were carefully restored so there would be no visible break between past and present, tradition and progress.

Sir Everard was succeeded by two sons, Eric and Olaf. Old Hambros hands reminisce about Olaf with awe and nostalgia. Born in 1886, Olaf went to Eton and Cambridge, like his father, and served in the Coldstream Guards during the First World War. Becoming chairman in 1932, he led the bank through three critical decades in the classical tradition—proud and dominating, deeply aware of his prerogatives, but also of his responsibilities.

During the Second World War, when the pound sterling was often under attack from "the Gnomes of Zurich" and other speculators in Switzerland, Olaf would take the phone and launch private, long-distance counterattacks against the Swiss.

"The Swiss know nothing about banking!" he would shout from his desk in the chairman's room.

Many other merchant bankers in London are inclined to

agree. They say the Swiss see everything in terms of black and white, are too concerned about short-term gains, rarely take the all-important, detached "forward look."

ALL QUIET IN THE PARTNERS' ROOM

Until the beginning of the First World War, Hambros had always been run by one or two members of the family, the "senior partners," who would consult their senior managers but made all executive decisions themselves. Important clients always liked to talk to "a Hambro" which gave them a sense of getting personal attention on the top level. The merchant bank was an ideal combination—efficient and unbureaucratic.

After the First War the pattern of policy-making began to change. The golden era of merchant banking that had begun after the Congress of Vienna, in 1815, had ended ninety-nine years later in Sarajevo. The City of London lost its power to Wall Street which became the center of credit. The pound was under pressure and no longer a freely convertible currency, severe restrictions went into effect, and the foreign-loan business, once a staple of the shelves of the merchant banks, dwindled down to almost nothing. The merchant bankers were badly hit by the Nazi expansion on the Continent, the breakup of the British empire, the loss of the China trade, the Labor government. The Second World War, when all international trade came to a standstill, drove them into hibernation.

Taxation brought big changes. In the good, old low-income-tax days (now called "the ice age era" by fiery critics of the City) the merchant-banking dynasties had one or two members "working in the bank" while the rest of them could afford the pleasures of English country life. Now everybody must work, and more jobs than before are needed for the members of the family.

Taxation also brought an end to old-fashioned partnerships. Partners cannot average their earnings in good and bad years, while directors of a public company may do so. With the sole exception of N. M. Rothschild & Sons, all merchant banks have become public companies. But most merchant banks remain family-controlled. Anybody may buy shares of

Hambros Bank Limited at the stock exchange but he has little chance of wresting control from the Hambro family.

In 1962, Olaf Hambro was succeeded by his nephew Charles J. Hambro, an able financier who was also a director of the Bank of England. He died the following year.

The last chairman, J. H. ("Jack") Hambro, was not a Hollywood casting director's idea of the formal City banker. Casual and charming, a cheerful optimist with the slightly ruffled appearance of the born-and-bred country squire, he often laughed but there was a thoughtful expression in his eyes. During the last war this relaxed-looking Englishman helped to run an economic cloak-and-dagger outfit known as the United Kingdom Corporation. Operating in the Balkans and in Turkey they systematically weakened the German war machine by preemptive buying, setting up and feeding black markets in the German-occupied countries, dumping certain goods and making others disappear. It was the right job for the descendant of the shrewd Viking sea captain who had cornered Copenhagen's black-crepe market a few centuries earlier.

Jack considered it significant that Hambros had managed to retain the family flavor and the atmosphere of partnership in spite of the bank's growing structure. The "fundamental traditions" are something one can feel at Hambros. The ablest man takes over as chairman. "No problem," said Jack. "It just happens."

The ablest man, after the sudden death of Jack Hambro at the end of 1965, was Jocelyn Hambro, Olaf's son. Jocelyn is the present chairman. Another Hambro now serving on the board is a son of Sir Charles. C. E. A. Hambro is always spoken of as "Young Charlie." Jocelyn Hambro calls the system of succession "enlightened nepotism." The family selects those best suited for what is now often a "laborious" trade. If a Hambro is as good as the outside chap, he gets the job. Many clients still prefer to talk to "a Hambro." One expects it in a family bank; one's father and grandfather were clients and they would talk only to "a Hambro." Still, if a Hambro is not as good as the outsider, he won't get the job. Some members of the family had their chance but didn't quite make the grade. One later went into charity work; another joined a merchant banker just around the corner where he is now a managing director, doing very well. Everybody at Hambros was pleased.

No one outside the family knows how the truly important decisions are made: The Hambros won't say. Why let in "daylight upon magic"?

The complexities of modern banking make it impossible for any man to know everything. Jocelyn Hambro doesn't believe in flair and instinct as sufficient qualities for a merchant banker.

"Common sense and dedication are more important. One can always find competent technicians, but technicians with plain common sense and dedication are rare. Our young men are carefully trained and observed before they are given authority. Some people cannot carry the burden of responsibility and drop out. Others worry so much that they have to give up. They will be able clerks but won't rise to the top. The few who stand up in the line of fire are worth their weight in bullion."

Seven managing directors are now on the board, five of them non-Hambros. One is related by marriage to the family: a former East India merchant with experience "on the other side of the desk," as a borrower. One managing director was partner in a firm of solicitors. Three began as bright young men in the bank and reached the top through their ability. The merchant bankers still consider themselves "Princes of the City." But worthy outsiders are no longer barred from the ranks of financial nobility. (The energetic young Norwegian who was manager of Hambros' Norwegian department and so impressed the young German when he arranged for a £200,-000 credit in Amsterdam within a few minutes late one Friday afternoon, has since been promoted to the board of directors.)

The partners' room (in some old banks it is still called "the parlor") is a large chamber facing Bishopsgate, with crystal chandeliers, coal fireplaces, dignified ancestors in gilded frames. There are seven desks, one behind the other. The chairman's desk stands in a small chamber. After the death of Sir Charles it was reverently left vacant for over a year. The chairman worked with the rest of the directors in the partner's room.

The atmosphere is informal, casual, but extremely efficient. Many top executives would find it hard to work in a room with half a dozen other men. At Hambros the theory is that a man who sits alone in his office is bound to make more mistakes than a man who is constantly surrounded by his partners. In one merchant bank all letters are opened in the morning and shown to all partners. There are a few papers, no files, no rate books. "We carry most information in our heads," they say. Risks are assessed, opinions exchanged, solutions found in quiet conversation, not after long speeches in committee meetings. There is no chain of command; no matters are cleared "through channels." A very civilized way of doing business.

"If I want to talk to one of my partners I don't have my secretary call up his secretary before we talk on the phone like the directors in those superbureaucracies," a partner says. "Most likely he sits in front of or behind me and I can turn around and talk to him. In an emergency, if I am the only one in the partners' room, I make the decision myself."

The risks are bigger than ever in scope though less spectacular than in the old days. "When we decided to back the modernization of Iceland, we took a bit of a risk," says Jocelyn. "After all, what have you got? An island in the North Atlantic with no great resources other than cod. But we investigated, and we decided that the people were absolutely honest. There is some Communist influence but we think that neither the United States nor England could afford to let Iceland become a Communist outpost. It worked out quite well. We're building up more trade and commerce there, though it's not very exciting. And for excitement there are take-over bids."

"LE CITY, C'EST MOI"?

Take-over bids became the most sensational operations in the early 1950's. (The City makes a careful distinction between the take-over bid, which usually degenerates into a battle, and the peaceful merger when both parties agree to the transaction.) Basically, take-over bids were a symptom of free enterprise and economic progress. After the financial restrictions imposed by the war and the postwar years the balance-sheet value of the shares of certain companies was much higher than their stock exchange quotation. A smart bidder might exploit this margin by making an offer above the current price to the shareholders. If he succeeded, he might buy the company as a bargain and either reorganize it or sell it later at great profit.

Some take-over bids were just smart coups, brought off by financial wizards. Others had solid economic reasons. By integrating managerial supervision and the combined resources of two different companies better results could be achieved than if the companies had worked separately. Competitive power was increased by reduced overhead and improved production. Directors of companies with undervalued shares began to be more careful; they modernized their plants, became more generous in their dividend policy.

The structure of Britain's industry still points to a continued merging of interested companies, and the merchant bankers with their flair for new opportunities have quickly grasped the details of the intricate technique of the take-over bid and become advisers to the fighting companies. Most of them did not know anything about the subject fifteen years earlier, but merchant bankers have always learned fast.

It is a risky business since the board of the company relies completely on the merchant banker's advice. If the shareholders later disagree with the advice they may fire the board. Unfortunately it is impossible to predict the reaction of shareholders, particularly when the shares are spread among hundreds of thousands of people.

The utmost secrecy is essential in these involved negotiations in order to keep out greedy speculators. Advance tips could be *very* valuable; a merger may double or triple the value of the shares. Theoretically, a merchant banker could secretly buy up shares of the merging companies through "nominees" but this would gravely violate the unwritten ethics of the profession.

While tension mounts around the bankers they must sit tight, advising the board, waiting to see whether their advice will be followed by the shareholders' vote. The merchant bankers have learned to move with the skill of seasoned Intelligence operators. They furtively meet their clients as though they were spies. All papers are put away as if they were top-secret official documents. Secretaries are sworn to secrecy. The tension often becomes unbearable.

"No one can accurately predict the shareholders' reaction,"

a banker says. "It would be easier to predict next month's weather."

This was dramatically demonstrated during the great Aluminium War of 1958-1959, the most sensational take-over battle in the annals of the City of London. In Hambros' partners' room it is unhappily remembered as "the merchant bankers' war." No one likes to talk about it. It was a war between two powerful factions of the fraternity, created a schism between the "Princes of the City," tested American versus English methods, the "shareholders' democracy" against "authoritarian finance." Its foxholes were the partners' rooms of some of the greatest merchant banks; eventually the entire City became the battlefield. Its generals were "old men drunk with power." The Aluminium War appalled the conservative City and delighted the newspapers and the public. It broke up old friendships and shattered once and for all the carefully built glass-house of the merchant bankers' secretiveness and the legend of City harmony.

The war was fought between two American aluminum giants—the Reynolds Metals Company of Virginia and Alcoa (the Aluminum Company of America)—for control of the British Aluminium Company, Britain's largest producer. Lazards and Hambros, representing the merchant bankers' Old Guard, acted as joint advisers for British Aluminium and Alcoa. S. G. Warburg and W. Lionel Fraser of Helbert Wagg jointly advised Reynolds.

Lazards and Hambros were the losers in the Aluminium War (which is described blow-by-blow in the chapter on Siegmund G. Warburg, the winner). Lord Kindersley, the chairman of Lazards, and Olaf Hambro, the chairman of Hambros, had declared in a letter to British Aluminium's shareholders that the Reynolds offer must be "resisted in the national interest." Thus the war moved out of the City's black-and-white financial battlefield into the wide-screen, Technicolor arena of touchy international relations.

Lazards and Hambros represented a formidable consortium of fourteen powerful financial institutions but they were soundly beaten. The Reynolds group came out of the Aluminium War with eighty per cent of British Aluminium's shares.

Old Olaf Hambro went back to his desk in the small chairman's room at Hambros and somberly surveyed his Waterloo. Smoke was still hanging over the battlefield. Olaf

Hambro read the reports of the financial war correspondents and became very angry. He took his pen and wrote a letter to the *Times* which was published the following day, and in which he said, "It is very unclear why the majority of the City editors of the Press seemed to be against City opinion and openly in favor of the take-over bid."

The press didn't react very kindly. Was old Olaf trying to say, in effect, *"Le City, c'est moi"?* Certainly Olaf had shown none of the "prudence and caution" which his grandfather Carl Joachim had often preached to Cavour. Anthony Crosland, a Labor Parliamentarian, wrote to the *Times* of a consortium, "whose outlook appears as contemporary as the architectural style in which the City is now being rebuilt—both make one shudder."

It was also noted that three great merchant banks—Barings, Rothschilds, Philip Hill—had prudently and cautiously kept out of the war.

Eighteen months later, Alcoa joined forces with Imperial Chemical Industries to form Imperial Aluminium. Alcan, the Aluminium Company of Canada, and Kaiser Aluminum later acquired their own British outlets.

In Hambros' partners' room they realized that the invasion of the American "aluminium forces" was a fact, and that "the national interest" had not suffered. Reacting with characteristic flexibility, Hambros quietly surveyed the debris of the Aluminium War and its effect on the firm's public image. The partners quickly decided that something would have to be done about it. Without fanfare they appointed the public-relations firm of Patrick Dolan to see that they would not be caught short in the future. When the news filtered out, it was noted that Patrick Dolan was an American.

AN "ELEGANT" DEAL

Hambros scored a triumph of financial flexibility when it helped to build the financial foundation on which later the world's biggest office building, Manhattan's Pan Am Building, was erected. Many New York entrepreneurs had dreamed of putting up a tall building on top of Grand Central Station, just as entrepreneurs in Paris and London dream of a tunnel under the Channel. In both cases the entrepreneurs were discouraged by the enormous cost of the projects.

In the late 1950's, two entrepreneurs with vision, Erwin Wolfson in New York and Jack Cotton in London, agreed on the general strategy for the big project in Manhattan. Both men had been very successful in high finance. First: they would have to convince the railroads owning the site that they meant business. Second: having the consent of the railroads they might raise long-term money on a mortgage. Third: with work starting *and* a mortgage they might get a main tenant for the building.

The strategy was clear but the beginning wasn't easy. Cotton would have to provide $25,000,000 as "starting money." He could easily raise $5,000,000 by issuing common stock. But he needed $20,000,000 more, and this money would have to be subordinate in security to the mortgage. Who would take that risk? The $20,000,000 became the key to the whole project.

Cotton talked to the Helbert Wagg merchant bank of London and Wagg talked to Hambros. The two merchant banks decided to take the chance and raise the money by a letter of credit. It was the old story again: without adequate security Cotton might have been unable to borrow $20,000,-000 in New York, but when Wagg and Hambros guaranteed, it was easy. The London merchant banks are not unknown in Wall Street. (In New York Hambros is now represented by Laidlaw & Co., which was founded by two young Americans, David Heron and James Lee, who began as "commission merchants" at the time when Carl Joachim Hambro founded his bank in London. They employed Henry Bell Laidlaw, a young man from Edinburgh, whose descendants later took over the firm and gave it its present name. In the tradition of the European merchant bankers the firm gradually switched from trading to banking.)

Wagg and Hambros had stipulated that their guarantee could be called only when a mortgage of at least $40,000,-000 had been raised. Merchant bankers take spectacular risks but usually they know what they are doing. Cotton and Wolfson found Pan-American as main tenant who would take twenty-five per cent of the space and give the building its name. With the lease in his pocket Wolfson raised $66,000,-000, which has been called the largest mortgage in history.

The two entrepreneurs now had $66,000,000 in long-term money, and $20,000,000 guaranteed by Wagg and Hambros. Later they got a second mortgage and the largest office building in the world was completed. All in all Cotton had put up $5,000,000 of his own money, and Wolfson $2,000,000. Hambros was pleased with what students of high finance have called an "elegant" merchant banking deal.

THE BILL ON LONDON

Despite such spectacular achievements Hambros' primary business is still the traditional financing of "the movement of goods in international trade."

"English trade is essentially a trade on borrowed capital," wrote Bagehot in 1873. "It is only by refinement that we are able to do the sort of trade we do."

The ebb and flow of international trade is reflected in Hambros' acceptance figures during the last hundred and twenty-five years. The differences are startling in the past four decades. From £7,000,000 in 1922 acceptances rose to £14,000,000 in 1937 and suddenly fell to £700,000 in 1941. By 1951 they had gone up again to £19,000,000 and last year they reached an all-time high of nearly £45,250,000. The bank met the new demand for credit by issuing new shares in 1947 and 1951.

The acceptance business is based on the "bill on London," which is still proof of the City's "economical delicacy." It is an ingenious invention of London's money market, and its most important contribution to financing international trade.

There are two ways of doing this: by straight loan, on which the customer pays interest, or by the more sophisticated method of having the bill of exchange "accepted" by a merchant banker. Suppose a Scandinavian exporter of timber promises to deliver to a British buyer one million pounds' worth of timber in six months' time. The seller wants his money as soon as possible. The buyer doesn't want to pay before he receives the timber. The buyer goes to Hambros where the gap between felling the trees and shipping them to England is bridged by the bill of exchange.

The Greeks used such bills in the fifth century B.C. Herodotus mentions them, and so does Cicero, later on. They were

used in Florence, Siena, Hamburg and Venice in the twelfth
century. In 1697 "inland bills" were legal in England, and
the rules were codified in the Bill of Exchange Act in 1882.

The City's immense precision mechanism turns out fine
credit the way a Swiss precision-watch factory turns out fine
timepieces. Both City credit and the Swiss watch are based
on the passage of time. Both have existed for centuries and
are constantly being improved. In the age of the supersonic
plane the bill on London is, in principle, the same as it was in
the sailing vessel days; an order addressed by one party (the
shipper or buyer, called the "drawer" of the bill) to a second
party (the "drawee," in this case the merchant banker), to pay
a third party (the "payee" in Scandinavia) a certain sum of
money on a certain date. Most bills are payable "90 days
after sight," a habit going back to the long, long journeys of
earlier centuries.

Acceptance credit may finance home trade, international
trade, even trade between foreign countries, with the goods
never reaching the shores of England. To be effective, the bill
of exchange must be "accepted" by the drawee. When
Hambros signs its name and writes "accepted" on the face of
the bill, it becomes an "acceptance." For lending its name
and taking a risk Hambros gets a commission from one to two
per cent (per annum).

It all seems very simple but the "sensitive mechanism" of
the "bill on London" presumes an elaborate network of
agents, great experience, exact knowledge of the standing of
both buyer and seller, of the different commodities, of the
ways of transport, of all possible economic and political
upsets that might affect the transaction. Obviously Hambros
will not guarantee payment of a shipment of Scandinavian
timber to England three months from now if there is the
slightest danger of losing a million pounds.

Hambros must also satisfy the Bank of England that the
bill of exchange is a first-class security—in case anyone wants
to deposit it at the Bank as security against a loan. Such a
first-class bill is called "eligible paper" or "a fine bank bill"
in City jargon.

For the seller and the buyer the transaction is finished, but
the accepted bill is still there. You can almost hear it tick, like
the watchwork of a Swiss precision watch. It is practically
alive and is lovingly treated like a baby, a baby with financial

appeal. Hambros may nurse it and earn interest on it. If they prefer to have the money, they may sell the bill to a member of the City discount market who buys it at the lowest rate of discount, currently 4½ per cent. (The rate has been as low as 3¾ and as high as 6½ per cent.) The discount rate is formed by supply and demand. It is always a little over the Treasury Bill rate. The difference is minute, but the values of the bills are large and discount brokers make a good profit. A considerable part of British imports and of exported British tweeds, whiskies, pottery, automobiles, television sets, chemicals, and machines are financed by London's merchant bankers.

The discount market (also called "Lombard Street," where most discount houses have their old-fashioned, deceivingly shabby offices) is another unique City invention. Only in London is there a shortest-term money market, and seven-day money a normal thing. The discount brokers ("bill brokers") are intermediaries between the big commercial banks, that keep most of the money, and the Bank of England. They borrow large sums of money from the big banks and lend it, through Treasury Bills, to the government. When "money is scarce" they are seen running around like busy ants. In this intricate machinery of profit where everybody makes a little money for performing some small but necessary service, the discount brokers, who wear top hats, striped trousers and nonchalant faces seem slightly archaic cogs. They are said to have uncanny powers of detection, are able to "smell" a bad bill (for which they pay less) and express their hunches in infinitesimal differences, such as one sixty-fourth of one per cent. They may keep the accepted bill and earn interest on it, or take it to a joint-stock bank and borrow money on it, or sell it to the bank, which keeps it for the remainder of the ninety days.

Somehow somebody is going to make money on the baby. If money is scarce, they may take the acceptances to the Bank of England "at half past two on any trading day" and either sell them or ask for a loan on them. No matter what happens, the baby will be taken care of. "You have devised and sustained a most marvelous system of credit," Disraeli said in the House of Commons in 1866.

One of the unwritten rules of thumb says that a bank's acceptances must never be higher than three and a half times the bank's resources. But in the City there are many exceptions for every unwritten rule. On Hambros' balance sheet there is an item "Current, Deposit and Other Accounts, Provision for Taxation based on profits to date, *and Inner Reserves.*" (The italics are mine.) A very useful item. Banks may transfer unspecified amounts in hidden (inner) reserves. You may not want to show huge profits in a good year, and small profits in a bad one.

The unwritten code of the London money market tells exactly who may get acceptance credit. "In principle," says Hambros' leading expert, "the acceptance credit should finance trade. It must be a self-liquidating, short-term, commercial transaction. A British exporter shipping machinery abroad falls under the rule but not a ten-year building program. There are, of course, certain exceptions. We may finance British exports up to eighteen months, or the working progress of a British company overseas. Installment-buying companies are entitled to acceptance credit. Strange, isn't it? Or a seed company storing seeds in warehouses abroad, since the stocks are continuously changed over. Well—and if a man has been an old customer and friend we'll do *any*thing for him. Even when money is tight, we won't take advantage of him. We are very jealous of our name."

No wonder. It's the name of the merchant banker that builds a magic bridge between buyer and seller. They may not trust one another but both trust Hambros. A while ago a French manufacturer who wanted to export to England lost valuable weeks negotiating with his bank, trying to get reliable information on the British buyer. At last, the query landed on a desk in Hambros Bank, a few phone calls were made, and half an hour later the French bank was informed that the British buyer was all right.

"We promised to pay cash to the Frenchman upon receipt of the documents," said a Hambros man. "That did it. You know how suspicious a Frenchman can be."

Until 1914 the large merchant bankers were able to finance almost any deal they liked. Nowadays some deals are too big for any one house. Oil shipments between the Middle East and Great Britain run into millions of pounds. They are a legitimate field for acceptance credit, bridging over the period of shipping the oil, with fuel stores in Great Britain as a security.

The banker investigates the financial management and the position of the oil company. This examination is never a mere formality though it may deal with a world-famous company. Then he investigates the proposed transaction.

"We want to be sure that this is the sort of deal we want to get involved in," says a Hambros man. "If it's too big for us, we invite other merchant bankers to join us in a syndicate credit."

DIAMONDS ALMOST FOREVER

Hambros demonstrated the merchant banker's flair and flexibility when it set up its diamond business. It all started as an improvisation. In 1941 the German invasion of Belgium and Holland destroyed the historic diamond centers of Antwerp and Amsterdam where the elusive trade had for centuries been in the hands of Jewish dealers. Many of them were killed, many were deported. The lucky ones got away to the nearest diamond-trading center of London. A few very lucky ones managed to get away with their diamonds. Precious stones are easy to carry. A man may transport a large fortune in his vestpocket.

London's Board of Trade encouraged the refugees to set up shop again on the City's western boundary, in Hatton Garden, the traditional center of London's diamond and pearl trade. It's an unpretentious street with shabby offices and broken windows. (It would have been a perfect Raymond Chandler background for mayhem and murder if Chandler hadn't preferred the sunlit alleys of Southern California.) The shabbiness seems almost contrived, possibly to camouflage the fact that enormous values are handled in these run-down offices. Behind the peeling façade and the unwashed second-floor window a man examines a parcel of diamonds worth a cool million dollars. Provided it is a clear day. The color and brilliance of the stones can be judged only under perfect northern or eastern light. A typical London fog makes even the whitest stone look yellowish.

It is a picturesque, quaint district. In a side alley stands the diamond dealers' favorite pub, Ye Olde Mitre Tavern, founded in 1546, the only pub in London with a cherry tree on the licensed premises.

The refugees felt at home in this anonymous neighborhood and were eager to start dealing again but most of them were short of cash. Otto Oppenheimer, of the Diamond Trading Company, a De Beers subsidiary, approached Hambros. Would they be interested in financing the diamond dealers? It wasn't exactly an orthodox transaction for an old merchant bank but it did mean financing international trade, so why not take a look at it?

Hambros took a look and liked the setup. In fact, it felt a warm affinity for the diamond people, with whom it seemed to have much in common. Diamond dealers, like merchant bankers, are an exclusive clique. Outsiders are not welcome. Trust and integrity is their motto, imagination and experience their asset. Diamond dealers are fierce individualists, each working for himself; only a few have one or two trusted employees. Many don't even have an office and carry their goods—small, white, folded paper packets containing the stones—in their pockets when they go to lunch to the Diamond Club or the Diamond Bourse where they will show them to potential buyers.

It's a clannish business, like merchant banking, where people trust each other absolutely. Men walk around Hatton Garden with a hundred thousand pounds' worth of diamonds that were handed over to them on trust. In a dingy office a man shows another man a number of stones that cost him a fortune, and then goes away while the buyer inspects them carefully.

No contracts are made. Nothing is written down. All deals are settled verbally. The standards of business ethics among the diamond aristocrats of Hatton Garden are as high as among the "Princes of the City." Any dealer committing an irregularity would immediately be posted in every Diamond Club on earth. He would never get another diamond as long as he lived.

Hambros knew nothing about the diamond trade. As always in such a case it got the best available advice, and learned that seventy-nine per cent of all diamonds come from Africa, most of them from South Africa and the Congo, which gives the diamond mining industry a formidable monopoly. But no one seems to mind very much, and the Diamond Corporation, which buys up under contract the diamonds of producers outside the Union of South Africa, is supported by the South African government.

People remember what happened in the late 1920's after the discovery of the rich Namaqualand deposit when a price break threatened. There is no danger in the near future of an oversupply of diamonds. Mining diamonds is a tough, slow, difficult business. In order to produce a single-carat diamond, workers must blast, crush and sort over two hundred fifty tons of "blue-ground" rocks.

Hambros Bank set up a special branch at the top of Charterhouse Street, a few steps from Hatton Garden, across from the white, new building of the Diamond Trading Company, where all diamonds arrive from South Africa. Once a month a "sight" is held for the lucky people on the "buyers' list." Some dealers wait for years to get on the list. The demand for diamonds always exceeds the supply, and the Diamond Trading Co. is in the enviable position of choosing the dealers and allocating the available supplies.

There is no haggling about prices or bidding among the dealers. A dealer must take a parcel at the price fixed by the Company, or leave it. He cannot split the lot in the parcel. If he wants a certain fine diamond, he must take the small stones that go with the fine one. Yet the dealers accept these conditions. The fine stone will be worth the sacrifice. The dealer knows that three quarters of all diamonds are only good for industrial uses, that a large part of them are only fit to be crushed into an abrasive powder. But the remaining quarter of "gem" diamonds accounts for eighty per cent of the entire annual turnover of a hundred million pounds. The dealer doesn't even mind paying cash first. Only then does he get his parcel.

Hambros learned fast. Visitors at the Charterhouse Street branch are scrutinized and escorted to a small room near the entrance. Everybody is security-minded. Dealers bring in their diamonds, which are examined on the premises by a diamond comptroller, a member of the Board of Trade, before they are expertly packed and mailed by staff members. Diamond dealers are always specialists. Some deal in rough stones and others in polished ones; some are experts in small and others in large diamonds. Bargaining is out but there is an active market among the dealers who want to get rid of the smaller stones which they had to take along with the one fine diamond that they really wanted.

A dealer's profit comes from his skill in having the stone cut so expertly that flaws are removed with the smallest possible loss of the stone's weight. At this point the dealers need help from the bank. Hambros financed the dealers' workshops, imported modern machinery and tools. It took care of the formalities connected with the import and export of diamonds. Customs controls are very strict and all stones have to be checked for value both as they arrive in England and when they leave the country. Dealers also need financing to export industrial diamonds to the United States. And there are always losses and claims to be made.

Hambros took care of everything. Satisfied clients began to send their friends there. The profit margin is very small but the values are very large, and Hambros says it is "doing nicely" in the diamond business.

During recent years London has lost some of its diamond trade. Some dealers went back to Antwerp and Amsterdam and others emigrated to Israel and New York. Hambros accepts all this with its usual philosophical calm. No one gets excited about minor crises. One morning two diamond parcels arrived from Ghana. One contained diamonds; the other had been opened, and contained only shavings. A few phone calls were made, somebody at Lloyd's took over; a matter of routine.

Diamonds, like merchant banking, is a business for gentlemen. There was consternation a while ago when a couple of international crooks managed to approach a well-known dealer. He has a reputation of being careful but he wasn't careful enough that day. The custom in the trade is to let the potential buyer inspect the stones. If the buyer is interested, the diamonds are packed, taped and sealed in small parcels, which are left with the seller. The buyer has forty-eight hours' time to decide whether he wants them. When the two "buyers" didn't come back, the dealer opened the parcels. One of them contained pebbles.

"The dealer is insured but it's a bad thing just the same," said the Hambros man. "Those stones didn't belong to him. In the trade a man is expected to defend himself—against violence and against cunning. There have been cases of violence in some diamond centers and lately even in Hatton

Garden. These days a diamond dealer won't let a man into his office unless he knows him. It's all very, very sad—the end of a great tradition."

GOLD RUSH

Foreign exchange is a traditional staple of a big merchant bank. Hambros has always dealt in foreign exchange, but there was little speculation in currencies until the First World War. Currencies were stable, backed by gold reserves, there were no exchange controls, and foreign-exchange deals were unspectacular. Between the two wars international crises, devaluations, revolutions and strict currency controls made the foreign-exchange business very important. People on the Continent tried to get their money into a safe country, often at a terrible loss.

Not surprisingly, many foreign-exchange dealers in the City came from the Continent. There they had lived through the astronomical inflation in Germany and Austria after the First World War, when no one in London understood this strange, bewildering phenomenon. These men have the minds of computers, are experts in monetary crises, are able to talk on the phone to three people in three different cities on the Continent at the same time, making lightning-like arbitrage calculations in "forward Swiss" (Swiss francs that will be bought or sold at a later point) and seem to thrive in an atmosphere of well-organized bedlam. They speculate in tiny margins of "long-term sterling," "forward dollars," and "Eurodollars" (regular American dollars owned by someone outside the United States), trying to anticipate pressures, attacks and crises, wondering whether the Germans will change the value of their money, whether the Americans will devaluate the dollar. ("The dollar will never be destroyed by pressure from abroad. Only the Americans could destroy the dollar.")

Hambros' bullion expert, E. E. ("Jock") Mocatta, sits in the foreign-exchange department, comfortably surrounded by telephones, teleprinters, calculating machines. Foreign exchange crises, reflecting the loss of confidence in a certain currency, are often followed by gold shipments between nations. Contrarily, gold sales generate large amounts of dollars, and the bullion expert must know all about foreign exchange.

Mocatta is the senior partner of the firm of Mocatta & Goldsmid, Limited, which a few years ago became a subsidiary of Hambros. Mocatta & Goldsmid was founded in 1684—ten years prior to the Bank of England, and the firm's name is uttered with reverence in the City. Next to Mocatta & Goldsmid even the Barings and Rothschilds are upstarts. It is one of the three firms of bullion brokers (with Samuel Montagu & Co. and Sharpe, Pixley & Co.) and two refiners (Rothschilds and Johnson Matthey) that meet every morning at half past ten in the offices of Messrs. Rothschilds to "fix" the price of gold. In an archaic ritual the official gold price is established.

Few people understand the intricate mysteries of the bullion market ("I know nothing about bullion," says Jocelyn Hambro) but few fail to be fascinated by the *mystique* of gold. It is a monetary metal, not a commodity; its value is not backed by the needs of modern industry; no one really uses gold except goldsmiths and dentists. But since time immemorial it has been the one basic international currency all over the world. Everybody respects and wants it. The Communists have no use for capitalism but they value gold, the very symbol of capitalism. The world has changed; mining technologies have been improved; dictators, economists and certain bankers (such as Dr. Hjalmar Schacht) have demonstrated that one can manage, for a while at least, without gold, but people always return to it as the essence of permanence.

Goethe's words from *Faust*, "*Nach Golde drängt/ Am Golde hängt/ Doch Alles*" (Everything crowds after gold, is devoted to gold) are as timely as ever. The suspicious French peasant trusts no one, least of all his own family and his own government. He is convinced that all bankers are crooks and all tax collectors are out to get him. He only trusts the tiny gold bars which he hoards, and the coins with the picture of Napoleon. Paradoxically, the gold's industrial uselessness makes it independent from the law of supply and demand. It represents stability. The French peasant is right.

The City of London has always been the world's principal market for gold since, until recently, three quarters of the world's gold came from South Africa, Ghana, and Southern

Rhodesia and was sold through London; thus South African gold is always a little cheaper in London than in Switzerland. The rest comes from the Soviet Union which last year sent almost two hundred million pounds' worth of gold to London.

No one seems to mind. The United States Federal Reserve Bank and the European central banks have formed a consortium and buy up the Soviet gold in an orderly manner. The Soviets alleviated the drain from the American gold reserve which has been replenished from the London gold pool. Russia's current annual output is, of course, a top state secret; bullion experts in the City think it's close to a billion dollars. Some people claim that the Soviet Union already produces as much gold as South Africa.

The golden age of gold was the terrible thirties when currency flights and "hot money," sudden laws and Nazi confiscations made people rush their money across the Atlantic. At the beginning of the war, when the pound was subject to tight exchange controls, the London gold market closed. It reopened again on March 22, 1954. Nonsterling area residents may now buy gold in London, but an Englishman may not.

In times of crisis everybody wants gold, and the price goes up. Mocatta was a harassed man in the fall of 1960, on the eve of the Presidential election in America, when there was a scare about the dollar and the price of gold went up to $40 an ounce. (The official gold price is $35 per ounce, at which price the United States Federal Reserve Bank will buy gold tendered to it.) These days the gold price fluctuates from $35.07 to $35.12. During the Cuba crisis the price went up to $35.30.

Most gold dealings are between the central banks of the nations that settle their payment differences by way of gold, but there is much traffic with politically insecure countries where people hoard gold as the only symbol of monetary security and financial permanence. The English don't hoard gold; they were never a gold-minded nation. Neither do the Scandinavians who were not often enough invaded to become "gold-minded." France is the biggest hoarder of gold in Western Europe. The Swiss are big buyers, and so are the Germans (who have a tax on gold). The Belgians and the Dutch also buy a lot, which is not surprising since they have been invaded often enough.

Enormous amounts of gold are shipped to Beirut where well-known merchants cut the gold bars into smaller sizes and put on their own stamp, which is as respected in these regions as that of the Bank of England. Much of Beirut's gold reaches India by devious ways. Citizens of India are severely forbidden to bring in gold, but the fathers of India's marriageable daughters must provide the dowry in gold—even if it's only a tiny bracelet. As long as India's girls get married, there will be a nationwide, illegal thirst for gold. Much of the gold is brought into India by Arab smugglers who make colossal profits, and suffer colossal losses when they are caught. According to the Radcliffe Report, "Millions and millions and millions of pounds a year, nobody knows quite how much," are getting to India.

Mocatta, a tense, dark-haired man, speakes in staccato sentences in a highly technical jargon, assuming that everybody knows as much about gold as he does. Actually, bullion experts are as rare as great wine experts or violin experts. Mocatta's transactions include buying and selling gold at the right moment in the right place, and also the physical shipment of gold, by air or ship. Some of his shipments don't come through London, for instance when he buys gold in Russia and sells it in Spain.

The values he handles are enormous but the profit margin is tiny. On a 400-ounce bar, worth about £5000, his profit may be as small as 3s.6d. He deals in tons of gold—one ton is worth $1,150,000—and a tiny fluctuation of the price may make a considerable difference. Deliveries are made forty-eight hours after the deal is set, and he has to get the gold which he promised even if the price has gone up. The London market deals only in "fine" gold, which means bars at least 995 one-thousandths pure, weighing between 350 and 430 ounces.

The finest gold comes from the Soviet Union. The Siberian mines refine by way of electrolysis, producing gold 999/1000 pure. South Africa uses the chlorine process and produces bars 996 fine. This doesn't mean that Russian gold is better: payment is for the content, not the total weight of gold. Russian gold is handled through the Moscow Narodny Bank in London's Finsbury Circus, the only Soviet bank in Britain.

Mocatta is always haunted by the nightmare of being short

of gold on delivery day. The nightmare almost came true one afternoon when he suddenly discovered, after an especially hectic day of telephoning with Beirut, Zurich, Madrid, Hong Kong, New York, Frankfurt and Brussels, that he was three tons short. It was almost five o'clock. There was only one place where he could get it—if it wasn't too late. A friend who happened to be in Mocatta's office remembers a memorable call Mocatta made to the Bank of England.

"Sorry," Mocatta said when he'd reached his party. "Did I just catch you? ... Hope you won't miss your train ... I say, the three tons we were talking about this morning. ... Yes. ... Have you still got them? ... At the same price?"

The friend says that Mocatta covered the receiver with his hand and gave an audible sigh of relief, and then he said, quite casually, "Yes. ... I'll take them. ... Thank you very much. Good-bye."

"And then," the friend says, "he wiped his forehead, exhaled, took his bowler, and, after a day of percentage, margins, calculations, buying and selling twenty million dollars' worth of gold, he went out to play bridge."

Mocatta keeps his private gold reserve in the historic building of Mocatta & Goldsmid, in nearby Throckmorton Avenue. The entrance is anonymous, the decor shabby. The treasure is kept in a dungeon that might have appealed to the late Count of Monte Cristo but to no one else.

When I arrived there, I was greeted by a gray-haired, stoical clerk who said, "We take very few strangers down there." He descended a staircase and I followed him. We arrived at a door with a sign STRICTLY PRIVATE. Through an outer grid of bars we stepped into a small room that looked like a workshop: various tools on the wall, newspaper clippings and pinup girls.

It was tea time in the dungeon. Two sturdy men were drinking their tea, reading a paper. In a glass case I saw a balance made by De Grace Short & Co., London, which registers one thousandth of an ounce and is so sensitive it will react under a ray of sun. Gold is weighed down to a quarter of an ounce. Platinum, which is much more valuable—one ounce is worth about fifty pounds—is weighed down to one thousandth of an ounce. The clerk put a postage stamp on the left side of the balance and locked the glass case. After a few seconds the balance slowly tilted to the left.

I was asked to step on a square in the wooden floor which became a trap door, as on a stage. The clerk and I silently moved down along a well-oiled track into the cellar—two damp, dark rooms, with an old-fashioned safe in one corner.

The clerk turned the combination and opened the safe. It was filled with gold bars and with flat pieces of a colorless metal. They were about the size of a Swiss chocolate bar, and were wrapped carelessly in an old newspaper. This was platinum, with the imprint of English Platinum Sheffield Smelting, 999.7. Each bar weighed about 160 ounces and was worth over eight thousand pounds.

Through a trellised gate we stepped into a smaller room which was lit by two bright bulbs. There was the smell of wet stone. In one corner was a pile of brick-shaped gold bars. It wasn't a very large pile, about five feet high. I asked the clerk how much it was worth.

"Oh, about two million quid," he said, with a shrug. "One is never quite sure. People always get excited by the sight of that pile. Fact is, I've been here over forty years, and one gets used to it. But I never permitted my wife to come down here. Better not. These bars are mostly made in England. A few come from Russia."

He bent down and showed me a bar with the sign USSR in Cyrillic letters, and the hammer and sickle. The bars were disappointing. They had no luster, were badly scratched, looked orange rather than gold.

The clerk said, "I read somewhere that the entire gold reserves of the world would be only a pile fifteen yards on each side. To think how much violence has been committed for that pile of gold." He shrugged again; he didn't like the gold.

There were bags filled with small "smuggler's bars," and with coins—sovereigns, napoleons, Swiss vrenelis, American eagles. The clerk said that in the Middle East old sovereigns fetched a higher price than the new ones with the Queen's head on them, because the customers out there didn't want coins with a woman's head. "Same gold content, but they pay less for it. It's all very strange, isn't it?"

In another corner was a big pile made of larger, grimy-looking bricks. That was silver. Each brick weighed seventy-eight pounds. Unlike gold, which is a monetary metal, silver is a commodity, and so much in demand now that the world's free stocks were exhausted about a year ago. Speculators moved in and within a few months the price of silver went up almost thirty per cent. The price of platinum (which is used in transistors and electrical appliances, among other things) has been steadier. The market is limited. Only three countries—South Africa, Canada, the Soviet Union—produce platinum.

The men in the dungeon in Throckmorton Avenue always know when "something is up" somewhere on earth. Suddenly the flow of gold increases, and the sturdy men in the workshop do overtime packing and unpacking gold bars.

The clerk and I again stepped on the movable trap door which took us up to the workshop. It was a quiet afternoon. There was no major crisis anywhere in the world. Just a routine shipment to Zurich, Switzerland. The men put several gold bars into dark-brown fiber boxes, always two bars into each box. They said they were much more practical than the wooden crates that had been used before. They sprinkled sawdust over the gold bars, closed the box, placed a metal strip around both sides, and put the box on the scale. 48/15. The figure was written on the box with black ink. A red seal was applied. The men put the box on a small wagon. In a while the gold would be picked up by a lorry with unbreakable glass and radio control, and taken to London Airport. They hoped the lorry would come soon, so they could go home.

ELEVEN A.M. AT THE GAMBLING CASINO

Of Hambros' six hundred employees, about thirty are empowered to make decisions that are binding on the bank. A good many of the decision-makers meet every morning at eleven to share information on what each has been doing and to agree on what shall be done about any major undertakings that are pending. The meeting, which lasts from twenty minutes to an hour, takes place in the boardroom, just a few steps from the partners' room, on the second floor. Everybody sits at a large rectangular table, the managing directors with their backs to the windows, and department managers and specialists—they are known as "senior persons" at Hambros —opposite them, facing the light. (Some years ago, one of the directors of Hambros, sensing an atmosphere of distrust as he accompanied a client into the boardroom of a large firm, is said to have asked, "Would you like me to sit facing the light?") A slightly musty smell hangs in the air of the boardroom. There are deep carpets, red damask chairs, old mirrors, and a grandfather clock; the baronial coat of arms of the House of Hambro hangs over the fireplace. Yet around the rectangular table in this room more money has been risked than in the *cercle privé* of any gambling casino.

I was escorted to one of the eleven-o'clock meetings by Otto Norland. "When I first began to attend these gatherings, I was bewildered," he told me. "I heard clipped sentences, brief allusions, mere hints. I had no idea what everybody was talking about. Then gradually I got the feel of the meeting, and now I understand the code. People come in with blocks of business—the raw material, so to speak. By the end of the meeting, the blocks have been shaped into deals, loans, expansion plans, mergers, new stock issues. It's fascinating. You begin to understand why the Hambros always say that merchant banking is not a science but an art."

In the boardroom that morning, where nearly everybody was got up rather strictly in the City uniform of white shirt and dark suit with waistcoat, Jocelyn Hambro was wearing a light-blue shirt and a blue pinstripe suit without waistcoat. As he guided the discussion, he spoke in a soft, halting, remote-sounding voice; quite obviously, he was confident that the men assembled there would need only a word or two to catch his drift. A few matters had already been decided in the partners' room, and as Jocelyn Hambro reported on them the senior persons nodded, clearly making mental notes. There were very few papers on the table. Jocelyn Hambro did have some documents in front of him, but he rarely looked at them, and used his pencil only for doodling. The bank secretary, a tall man who sat at the extreme right of the partners, made brief notes as the meeting went on. One man after another, clockwise around the table, described what had been happening in his department and told of any problems that had arisen in the past twenty-four hours. The discussion was often interrupted by jokes, totally obscure to me, that made everybody laugh. Jocelyn Hambro once told me that the eleven-o'clock meetings he had attended between the wars were quite different. "Most of the people around the table were old and solemn," he said. "They gave you the impression that they were holding the weight of the world in their hands." Now about half the people around the table were in their thirties, and no one looked solemn.

Norland read two sentences of a letter from Norway—an application to renew a credit. He stated the facts in precise bankers' language, not wasting a word, as though he were sending off a cable. Jocelyn Hambro, doodling, asked a couple of technical questions. The foreign-exchange manager, a bald-headed man with what I recognized as a Swiss-German accent, answered the questions. The chairman nodded almost imperceptibly, and that was that. Hambros Bank had just committed itself to a guarantee of three hundred thousand pounds. Norland gave me an amused glance.

After another man had made a suggestion, there was a sudden silence. No one said anything, and I noticed that Jocelyn Hambro and the other directors looked slightly bored, like the figures in that picture of "Lunch at 41, Bishopsgate." The bank secretary, I learned later, recorded a negative decision, though the word "No" had not been spoken.

A complicated financing deal that involved the export of tobacco from the Philippines to the Soviet Union was discussed. Some figures were mentioned that caused eyebrows to be raised around the table. Jocelyn Hambro again asked a few concise questions as he doodled, and then he said in an offhand manner, "Let's do that." The other directors nodded, and it was settled.

One of the young managers inadvertently provided some excitement when he brought up what sounded to me like a routine matter. A shipowner wanted to refinance a loan of three hundred and fifty thousand pounds for some ships that would be chartered to a large oil firm for three years. "I had the feeling that it was quite all right," said the manager.

"That's what *you* thought," said Jocelyn Hambro, and everybody laughed heartily. The foreign-exchange manager spoke up, in a gloomy voice, to explain some complicated currency-exchange rules that would oblige the Bank of England to forbid the loan. No one glanced at the unhappy manager who had left out the Bank of England.

Then there was some technical talk about "a little over a million dollars for six equal half-year installments" and about the possibility that part of the sum could be "laid off." Jocelyn Hambro said, "Suppose we do two thirds at five and a half and the other fellows take two installments to be paid at five and three quarters?" I was left to guess who the other fellows were. The foreign-exchange manager suggested that three years was too long but that the bank might do it for two. There was a pause. Finally, the chairman said, "Then we'll do the lot for the first two years and see how it develops." He glanced around the table as if he were counting an invisible show of hands. The secretary made a note. Hambros was committed.

There were a number of other matters. A client's firm would be floated as a public company. Hambros joined in the underwriting of two big bond issues. A project developed by some unnamed people who, according to Jocelyn Hambro, had been "well on their way with it but couldn't get their teeth into it" was dropped, at a loss to the bank. Hambros' share of a large syndicate credit was granted to an oil company. One of the directors described some difficulties that had come up in what I gathered was a secret take-over bid, and everybody looked grave. Then Jocelyn Hambro picked up the documents before him in both hands, glanced once more around the table, and rose. The meeting had lasted less than half an hour, and Norland told me that he was now completely informed about what was going on in all departments of the bank.

"Sorry it wasn't more interesting," Jocelyn Hambro said to me as everybody walked out of the boardroom. I asked him how much credit the bank had extended so far that morning, and he said, "Oh, something like two million pounds." When I remarked that the responsibility must be quite worrying, he shrugged. "In this business, one can't avoid being wrong once in a while," he said. "The great thing is not to be wrong too often."

3

Barings: The Sixth Great Power

*"There are six great powers in Europe: England,
France, Russia, Austria, Prussia, and the Baring Brothers."*
Richelieu

THE rusty sign next to the entrance is hardly legible, a
reluctant concession to an old law obliging a public company in England to display its name on the outside of its
building. The red-brick façade in Queen Anne style, with
sash windows and glazing bars, was redone the last time in
1882 by R. N. Shaw, the architect of Scotland Yard. A
wrought-iron lantern hangs above the gate. Inside the entrance stands a trough that was used to water the horses
which were kept in the garden courtyard. The courtyard
is now the central banking hall of Baring Brothers & Co.,
Limited, the oldest merchant bank in the City of London.

Characteristically, the firm's letterhead shows the address—8, Bishopsgate, London E.C. 2—and the telephone
number but not the name of the bank. Anonymity
and self-confidence, pride and restraint. The Barings can well
afford such timeless luxuries. They have been merchant
bankers for two hundred and two years. They always kept
the bank in the family. They have been compared to the
Medicis, the Fuggers, the Rothschilds, the Morgans.

"The merchant bankers," writes Walter Bagehot, "go back
to generations of merchant princes in Venice and Genoa who
inherited wealth, power and culture, and combined the tastes
of aristocracy with the insight and verve of businessmen."

He must have been thinking of the Barings. Today one of
the partners (as the managing directors are called around the

house) is the Hon. John Francis Harcourt Baring, a seventh-generation Baring.

The Barings were *the* great bankers of Europe long before the Rothschilds appeared on the stage of international *haute finance*. Paradoxically, their finest hour came at the time of their worst trial—in 1890, when they were facing disaster. In 1903, thirteen years after "the Baring crisis," the worst predicament in the annals of merchant banking, a German diplomat reported to the Foreign Office in Berlin, "Anybody who wants to place a loan in London on a grand scale must apply to the Barings."

No other bank in London has sent as many directors to the Bank of England since Alexander Baring was appointed to the Court of the Bank in 1805. After him came Humphrey St. John Mildmay; Thomas Baring; Edward Charles Baring, first Baron Revelstoke; John Baring, second Baron Revelstoke; Sir Edward Peacock. The present Governor of the Bank of England is George Rowland Stanley Baring, third Earl of Cromer, who resigned as a director of Baring Brothers after being appointed in 1961.

The Barings now have five separate peerages—Ashburton, Northbrook, Revelstoke, Cromer and Howick. They have been a power both in the City and in Whitehall for centuries. Sir Francis Baring, the founder of the firm, was financial adviser to Lord Shelburne and later to William Pitt, the Prime Minister. Barings have signed state treaties, held high diplomatic posts, were among the early leaders of England's "Establishment." The oldest British banking dynasty, they convey the typical image of the great merchant bankers, of powers-behind-thrones—fantastic deals with the King of Spain and Prince Metternich, financing the Napoleonic Wars, getting through the Continental blockade with the blessing of the British government, shipping gold and arms to Britain's allies right through the enemy lines. Sinister intrigue and daring decisions—and always honesty and integrity. As Viscount d'Abernon writes in *Portraits and Appreciations:*

Nothing is more like itself, nothing less like anything else than a Baring ... The family is one of the few that produce a similar type with regularity—a regularity only accentuated by the rare occurrence of a freak. Strong, sensible, self-reliant men, with a profound belief

in themselves, in their family, and in their country . . .
not subtle or mentally agile, but endowed with that
curious combination of character which lends authority
even to doubtful decisions.

The early history of the Barings reflects accurately the
history of merchant banking in general. From 1763 up to
1828 the Barings financed European trade and helped to
make England a great mercantile power. Emperors and kings,
prime ministers and ambassadors anxiously waited for their
decisions, that might make or break a throne. In 1834 they
acquired the *Alexander Baring* and the *Falcon*, their first two
ships in the China tea trade that had until then been a
monopoly in the hands of the East India Company. Later,
they became interested in the United States and Canada.
Until the Civil War Barings was known in London as the
biggest "American house." There was always an American
partner on the board of the firm. Barings were intermediaries
between British investors and American entrepreneurs. From
1860 to 1890 the Barings raised £500,000,000 and £40,-
000,000 for various United States and Canadian government
loans. America was truly "Baring territory."

Times have changed. Today the United States is nobody's
territory, except the Americans'. But the Barings are still in
business and they are doing very well indeed.

The earliest known member of the family was one Peter
Baring of Groningen, West Friesland, who lived from 1483 to
1536. His son Franz later moved to Bremen where the name
Baring—pronounced *"Bar-ing,"* as in "bar"—remains well
known. In England there are so many members of
the various branches of the family that they have long given
up the hope of knowing each other. The founder of the
English Barings was Johann, who came from Bremen in 1717
to Exeter, a lively serge manufacturing and marketing center.

Johann Baring became an apprentice to Edmund Cock, a
local merchant, and liked life in Exeter so much that he
decided to stay. Naturalized in 1723, he changed his first
name to John, and married Miss Elizabeth Vowler, the
daughter of a wealthy local grocer. Ever since it has been a
Baring family tradition to marry rich women. Within a few
years the former apprentice had become a successful merchant. "Mr. Baring, the Bishop and the Recorder were the

only persons in Exeter who kept carriages," reports a contemporary chronicler.

John Baring died in 1748, leaving four sons. On January 1, 1763, a great day in the Baring annals, two firms were founded: John and Charles Baring & Company in Exeter; and John and Francis Baring & Company in London. The Exeter house was in the cloth business and owned a ship, the *Venus*. The London house, import and export, later became the great merchant bank.

John, the wealthiest brother, and a partner in both houses, was something of an eccentric—a trait that runs through the whole family and (secretly) pleases them very much. John Baring's son, also John, was called "Old Turkey Legs" by the people of Exeter, and described by Robert Dymond in his *History of St. Leonard, Exeter*, as "a tall, thin man with powdered hair and a sharp, penetrating look who seemed to measure with his gold-headed cane every step as he walked." His brother Francis, a Baronet from 1793, has been often compared to Nathan Meyer Rothschild, who founded N. M. Rothschild & Sons thirty-five years *after* Francis Baring had become cofounder of John and Francis Baring & Company, in London.

Both Baring and Rothschild began with modest resources and went far. Francis Baring owned only a few thousand pounds when he started in business but he had the genius of the born merchant adventurer. In a very short time he built up valuable connections with the Mediterranean countries, France, Holland, and the Baltic. He was well known from Cadiz to Hamburg and from Amsterdam to Philadelphia. His son Alexander once said that his father was "of all men the one who happily combined a capacity for distant and large views and for the detail of the business."

Francis Baring learned early in life the secret of the successful merchant banker: to find out a little more a little earlier than the next man. He had reliable intelligence sources in very high circles. His close friend Prime Minister William Pitt (the Younger) called him "the backbone and salvation of the country." Francis Baring advised the leaders of the government on such delicate issues as trade with Turkey, Gibraltar, and the American problem. He had a lot of business in America, most of which he lost in 1776. Providently, he had bought some stock in the East India

Company. Only about four thousand pounds' worth, but enough for him to become a director of the Company three years later.

Less than ten years after the American Revolution, trade between the United States and England was better than ever. The Americans had won their independence from Westminster, but not yet from the City: that came much later. The Barings had much to offer to American merchants but they used their influence wisely: they were the first to teach Americans "the mechanism of influence and control" that was later developed almost to perfection in the United States—not by private bankers, but by the government.

THE LOUISIANA PURCHASE

The Barings were the first merchant bankers who realized that beyond the Atlantic Ocean there was a land of unlimited possibilities. In 1783 Francis Baring opened a business in Philadelphia and became closely associated with the local business elite known as the Philadelphia Group: Robert Morris, Thomas Willing, William Bingham and Robert Gilmore. The firm was known for its integrity. Francis Baring said they were "ideal" partners who met all obligations "without collateral security." He would often tell his sons that all correspondents should be chosen on that basis.

The Group's leading member was William Bingham, said to be the richest man in America at that time. In 1793 he sent over an emissary who offered Sir Francis—who had been made a Baronet that year—one and a quarter million acres in Maine, then part of the state of Massachusetts, at two shillings an acre. Cautious as ever, Sir Francis sent his son Alexander to investigate, and gave him a letter of credit for £100,000.

Alexander arrived in Boston in November, 1795, and in Philadelphia in January, 1796, and late in February came to an agreement with Bingham for the purchase of the land for £106,875. According to Vincent Nolte who later acted as "special agent" for the Barings in America, Alexander had been warned by his father not to bring home an American wife. Two years later Alexander Baring married Bingham's oldest daughter, Anne Louise, but Sir Francis's disappointment was mollified by her dowry—nine hundred thousand dollars. Alexander furthermore brought back a lot of business from the United States. He speculated successfully in foreign exchange, and once imported from Jamaica to America 500,000 silver dollars in a few months "to great advantage." Only the real estate deal didn't turn out well and by 1835 the Barings had sold most of their land in Maine.

The Barings were now definitely in big business. In 1795, David Humphreys, the American minister in Lisbon who carried on the negotiations with the Barbary Powers of Algiers, Tangiers and Tripoli, was empowered to draw up to $800,000 at Barings. In London, Rufus King, the United States Ambassador at the Court of St. James's, supervised the operation. Later Barings advanced Humphreys another $200,000, at five per cent commission and five per cent interest. The Barings were on their way to becoming bankers to the United States government.

Three years later the Barings helped the United States in the undeclared war against France. They purchased 11,000 muskets from the British government and 330 cannon from the Woolwich Arsenal, at a modest commission of two and a half per cent, and shipped the arms to a consortium consisting of Stephen Higginson, Boston; James Watson, New York; Jeremiah Yellett, Baltimore; and T. Francis, Philadelphia.

In 1802, during the short time of peace following the Treaty of Amiens, President Jefferson decided to purchase from France the great tract of the Mississippi Basin that would at once double the size of the United States. Not surprisingly, the Jefferson administration called on the Barings to finance the deal. The total price was fifteen million dollars. Of this amount, $11,250,000 in bonds would be issued by the federal government and turned over to the French Treasury. The remainder of the price was to be expended in the United States in payment of claims of American citizens against France.

Before Sir Francis went to work on the deal he asked the British government for its consent. By that time England and France were again at war but neither country objected to the transaction. Whitehall realized that Napoleon would get a lot of cash out of the deal, which was not exactly in the interest of the British government. On the other hand, the transaction would make the United States instead of France the neighbor of the British possessions in North America. London gave its permission; obviously the advantages of the deal outweighed its drawbacks.

No French merchant banker wanted to act as intermediary. Once again Barings took the lead. Alexander Baring went to Paris, concluded the negotiations, returned to London, departed for America, waited until the Treaty was ratified, and sailed back to England on February 1, 1804. France and England were at each others' throats but a merchant banker always gets through.

THE GREATEST FINANCIAL ADVENTURE OF ALL

The most fantastic transaction in the whole history of merchant banking was the transfer of the Spanish-Mexican silver treasure. It is one of the great financial adventure stories, and surely the most unusual. Spanish payments were made to Napoleon with gold and silver removed from Mexico with the help of American merchants, under the direction of the great merchant bankers, and with special permission of the British government to break the Continental blockade. A lovely deal. Compared to this super-coup, most merchant-banking operations nowadays are dull routine.

Some very strange bedfellows were involved: the King of Spain, a formidable Frenchman named Gabriel-Julien Ouvrard, the Barings, the banking houses of Hope & Co. and David Parish, who made a fortune in America and shone briefly as a power in Austria after the Napoleonic wars, and two "special agents," Vincent Nolte and A. P. Lestapis. The combine's idea man was Ouvrard, a financial genius and perhaps the most controversial entrepreneur of his time. Ouvrard provisioned Napoleon's armies, negotiated enormous credits, thought up incredible deals and carried out bizarre transactions. His contemporaries could not agree on him. Richelieu, who knew a great deal about finance, considered Ouvrard his closest adviser. Thiers publicly called him a cheat. Several times Ouvrard was arrested; once he spent five years in jail.

Ouvrard went bankrupt, made another fortune, lost it again. He had more ideas than principles. He worked for all of them: the Directoire, Napoleon, the Consulate, the Revolution, Louis XVIII, the Empire, the Restoration. All needed his help and money, and he survived them all, a symbol of financial durability though not of personal integrity. Nothing has changed since Vespasian said of money, *"non olet."* A type of international financier still exists who is ready to work for anybody who needs his advice and pays well for his service.

The story of the Spanish-Mexican silver treasure begins in the early days of the nineteenth century, when Spain was forced to take sides against England in the Peninsular War. Under the Treaty of October 19, 1803, Spain was obligated to pay an annual subsidy of 72,000,000 francs to Napoleon. Why the treaty was ever signed, no one of sound mind could understand. It was common knowledge that Spain would never be able to raise such a sum. The Spaniards didn't even try, and informed Paris in 1804, *sans regrets,* that they did not have the money.

There was consternation in Paris until Ouvrard came up with his ingenious idea. Obviously, France would never be able to collect the money from Spain. But Spain owned gold and silver mines in its colonies, Mexico and Peru. Large amounts of silver were known to be stored in Vera Cruz. Ouvrard pointed out that all one had to do was to get the Mexican silver treasure out of Vera Cruz and bring it to Paris, through the British blockade, in the middle of the war. As easy as that.

Everybody said that Ouvrard was crazy but he went to Madrid and talked to King Charles IV. He promised to lend Spain some money if His Majesty would graciously consent to help him get the treasure out of Mexico. The treasure would be the collateral. His Majesty had little choice and signed a blank license permitting trade with the Spanish colonies. Ouvrard had won the first round.

The major obstacle now was the British blockade but Ouvrard was certain that the Barings could probably make a deal with the British government. Ouvrard explained his scheme to his old colleagues, Henry Hope and Labouchère, both partners in Hope & Co., the leading financial establishments in Amsterdam. (Still there, it is the oldest merchant bank in the world.) They first thought that he was "quite mad." But Ouvrard was a good salesman, he had some enticing figures to back up his mad ideas, and he had His

Majesty's blank license. Somehow he convinced Henry Hope that it could be done, and done very profitably for all concerned.

Next, Henry Hope went to see his friend Sir Francis Baring. No record of their conversation exists, but Sir Francis, in turn, went to see Henry Addington, the Prime Minister. Sir Francis, too, was a good salesman of great ideas. He convinced the Prime Minister that the operation would basically "stimulate British trade." Silver was scarce in England and would be valuable to the East India Company—of which Sir Francis happened to be a director.

The British government agreed, provided that "British as well as neutral vessels" would be included in the trade with the Latin American ports. Today people who are sometimes shocked by the British trading with anybody who is willing to trade with them ought to read up on their history. Four frigates were dispatched to bring back the treasure. The *Diana* had its cargo insured by Lloyd's of London for £656,800—the largest risk written by Lloyd's during the Napoleonic Wars.

There remained the American end of the operation. The Barings and Hopes sent David Parish to the United States in 1805, carrying the Spanish king's signed blank license and a letter of credit for one million dollars. In Philadelphia he enlisted the services of two "special agents," Nolte and Lestapis, who had "excellent connections" in Vera Cruz and New Orleans. The names "of certain American merchants" were filled in on the blank license. The merchants dispatched cargoes to Vera Cruz where "special agent" Lestapis sold the goods and turned the proceeds into silver and gold from the "treasure," which he put into the return cargo.

An interesting operation, well thought out, beautifully executed. It lasted three years; by 1808 almost all silver and gold had been removed from the Mexican Treasury. But payments to Napoleon had ceased long before. The Emperor did not understand the complicated financial transaction, was dissatisfied with the arrangements and became convinced that the whole thing was a swindle. Napoleon, a soldier, knew only two ways of raising money for the state: by conquest and by taxes. Credit and profit were inventions of these "devilish financiers."

After the final accounting, in 1811, total profits of £862,-

000 were divided among the Barings, Hope, Parish and the "special agents." Actually, the real profits were much higher because the transaction had really stimulated direct trade between Britain and Mexico, exactly as Sir Francis had predicted. This trade was financed by the merchant bankers. More profit.

Only Ouvrard who had thought up the grand scheme got not a penny out of it. Once again Napoleon quarreled with his brilliant banker, confiscated his property, and put Ouvrard into prison.

The partnership of John and Francis Baring & Company had been dissolved in 1800 after John's retirement, and for a few years the firm was called Sir Francis Baring & Company. In 1806 the name was changed to Baring Brothers & Company which it has remained to this day.

It must have given Sir Francis quiet satisfaction to look back at his life as he left the bank in the hands of his three sons and his son-in-law. The descendant of a poor German immigrant was now rich and respected. He served in Parliament until 1806, belonged to the moneyed aristocracy, had reached international prominence and furthered the development of British trade.

In 1802 Sir Francis purchased Stratton Park from the Duke of Bedford for £150,000. His annual income was £80,000. He commissioned Sir Joshua Reynolds to paint his three great political friends—Lord Shelbourne, Lord Ashburton, and Isaac Barré—and Sir Thomas Lawrence to paint himself with his brother John and his son-in-law Charles Wall. The painting, done in 1806, belonged to Lord Northbrook and now hangs in the partners' room of Barings. It shows Sir Francis with his hand cupped to his left ear; he suffered from incurable deafness.

After his retirement from the bank, Sir Francis remained a power in the City. He was active as underwriter at Lloyd's, Chairman of the Patriotic Fund, and devoted his Wednesdays and Fridays to the affairs of the East India Company. He remained a loyal friend of the United States; in 1808, at a dinner given at the London Tavern for the Spanish patriots, Sir Francis was booed when he proposed the health of the President of the United States.

He died in 1810, and was called by Lord Erskine "unquestionably the first merchant of Europe—first in knowledge and talent, and first in character and opulence." "A pillar of the City," wrote the *Times*. Shelburne called him "the Prince of Merchants."

ADVENTURE IN PORTUGAL

Alexander Baring, the most gifted of Sir Francis's sons, overcame the handicap of having to live up to the memory of his great father. He led the Barings to the zenith of their fame and made them *the* great bankers of Europe, until he clashed with the Rothschilds when they challenged the power of the Barings on the battlefield of international finance. Today the Barings and the Rothschilds are friends—but it wasn't always like that.

Historians of the epoch point out that Britain's strongest ally in its war against Napoleon was British finance—the merchant bankers. The British in the early nineteenth century were wiser than the Americans one hundred and thirty years later. They didn't lend money to their allies. They gave it to them outright in the form of subsidies—ammunition, clothing, equipment. It was a sound policy but created grave financial problems. In 1813, for instance, Britain—then a country of twenty million people—had to raise £ 176,346,-023 by taxes.

After Napoleon's return from Elba, Lord Castlereagh, Britain's Foreign Secretary in Lord Liverpool's cabinet, signed treaties for outright subsidies of almost £ 9,000,000 to Russia, Austria and Prussia. An issue of thirty million pounds in three per cent bonds was allocated by the British government to Barings and to Smith, Payne and Smith, at 77. The issue was simultaneously placed on sale in Vienna, Hamburg, Frankfurt, and St. Petersburg, and was a success in all countries. Only one million pounds, raised by British investors, was actually transferred from England; the rest of the money was raised by the people in the allied countries. With Barings' name behind the issue, investors on the Continent had complete assurance that all would be well. It was a massive vote of confidence for England and for the Barings.

The merchant bankers helped to solve Britain's problems, and in the process became powerful and prosperous. From

1792 to 1816 the Barings shared with other bankers the honor, and the profit, of remitting Britain's allies on the Continent various subsidies amounting to fifty-seven million pounds. Today only state banks and government agencies could carry out such enormous transactions. There was almost nothing a merchant banker could not do in those days. They had their fingers in every pie. They knew how to "remit" gold bars through the French lines to Britain's allies in Europe. (It wasn't called "smuggling"; after all, it was strictly patriotic business. In times of war the enemy "smuggles" and "spies" on you but when you do it, it's called "subsidy payments" and "collecting intelligence.") The merchant bankers had valuable contacts from prime ministers down to local chiefs of police. They always knew the right people in the right places at the right times. When Portugal had to send funds to France in 1802, the Barings pulled off another astonishing coup: they remitted £700,000 to Napoleon, for account of the Portuguese government, under British license!

Actually, the loans for Portugal had started earlier. One day in 1797 Sir Francis Baring received a letter from Messrs. William and John James Stevens in Lisbon who were writing "with the sanction of the Court in Lisbon," as they pointed out in a postscript marked "very secret." Could Sir Francis and Henry Hope arrange for a loan of £1,200,-000 for the Court of Lisbon? As security they offered uncut diamonds from Brazil "of greater value than the amount of the loan." If not acceptable, they offered "to pledge or sell the Islands of Timor, Solor & Bolea, all of which are subordinate to Goa." They hinted that the Court might be willing to pledge "the rich kingdom & Islands of Mozambique" together with other islands north of the Cape of Good Hope, and "to hypothecate a part of the revenue of the Snuff Contract for the payment of the Interest; this Contract renders net to the Crown £20,000 per month." They also expressed their confident belief that they would be able to obtain a rate of interest of seven per cent "or even a trifle more."

After consulting with the British Prime Minister, Sir Francis informed the Stevens brothers that owing to "the particular distressed situation of this Country at present" the Prime Minister had "declined distinctly the Sale or temporary Cession of any of the territorial possessions; and he could not in any degree encourage the expectation that the Government in this Country would become guarantee to the Money Lenders." Being therefore "reduced to the necessity of discussing the loan as a private operation," Sir Francis indicated it might prove very expensive. To raise £1,196,500 an outlay of £2,297,500 would be necessary—a discount of £1,101,-000. The present time was unfavorable in London where three government loans were on the point of being issued. Sir Francis advised postponement, and in a private postscript suggested £100,000 as a "realistic" figure at which to start. If the operation proved to be a success one might later on go up, perhaps to £600,000.

A little later Portugal's relations with Spain and France became critical and Lisbon appealed officially to the British government for help. This time Pitt suggested an outright subsidy of £200,000. In the summer of 1797 the first British troops arrived in Portugal.

Toward the end of 1801 another proposal for a loan to Portugal reached London. The situation had further deteriorated. Portugal had been overrun by a Spanish army that was supported by Napoleon, and had to pay a subsidy of twenty million *reis* which Napoleon had demanded as terms of surrender.

This time Sir Francis Baring and Hope & Co. were anxious to secure the loan and willing to take it entire if possible. They realized that the money would be raised in Britain to subsidize Britain's mortal enemy. But the ethics of a merchant banker were rather liberally interpreted at that time. Sir Francis indicated that a peace treaty would probably soon be signed which would be the right moment for a coup by the house of Hope in Europe—by way of a successful Portuguese loan. He had also another reason. He was sixty years old, and Henry Hope was sixty-five. Sir Francis, the dominant figure, had trained the successors—his son Alexander in London and his son-in-law Labouchère in Amsterdam. If he could merge Hope & Co. into his firm, Barings would become the world's biggest, most powerful merchant bankers.

Sir Francis did not accomplish his great ambition. In October, 1802, he wrote to his friend Lord Lansdowne:

. . . I am compelled to abandon the colossal plan, one

foot in England, the other in Holland; it is a sacrifice
such as no head of a family ever made before, but I
must confess there is enough left for consolation. . . .

In November of that year Labouchère went to France and
Spain to see what could be done by way of new business for
the Baring-Hope interests, and from there he went to Lisbon.
He was accompanied by twenty-year-old George Baring, Sir
Francis's youngest son, a trainee at the Amsterdam firm. Sir
Francis had issued strict regulations for Labouchère's guidance. He was prepared to lend £700,000 at five per cent,
with an additional charge of £50,000 for expenses. The
security was to be the income from the state tobacco contract, and Brazilian diamonds. A sinking fund would be
established to pay off the loan in fifteen years. Sir Francis
showed a fine flair for the political necessities, stating that the
commercial transaction—the shipment and delivery of the
diamonds—should be done in England, and the financial
side—the issue of the bonds and remittance to France—in
Holland. This might help to restore Hope & Co. to its former
eminence so that "foreign European courts should be induced
to look at you & as much as possible to you alone on similar
occasions." Sir Francis concluded his letter with a character
analysis of the men with whom Labouchère would deal in
Lisbon. Sir Francis was frankly doubtful about the ability of
the leaders of Portugal and highly skeptical about the whole
operation.

Labouchère and young George Baring went to Bayonne.
They couldn't get passage on a ship to Lisbon and engaged
the services of a muleteer to take them to Madrid. They
started from Bayonne on January 11, 1802, and reached
Madrid nine days later, three hundred and twenty miles over
the snow-covered passes of the Pyrénées and the Guadarra-
mas, in midwinter, and on muleback! The early merchant
bankers were robust men.

Negotiations in Lisbon lasted nearly a month and were
often frustrating. "The Minister and I were agreed upon
every point," Labouchère reported later to Sir Francis, "but
in putting the documents into Portuguese they constantly
alter the Text & I have to puzzle my brain to find out in a
language I do not understand the right from wrong. . . ."

But Labouchère also had surprising news for Sir Francis:

The means of this Country, the intentions of the Sovereign & of his present Ministers are such as ought to inspire the greatest Confidence, & the pledges are of such a solidity as nothing I know even in England can equal. Whatever doubt or hesitation remain in your minds can only be with regard to the political dangers. These I am not apt to underrate, & I have made it my particular study to enable myself to set a true value upon them. This Country like all others has its share of Jacobins & they are not wholly unemployed. . . .

Eventually Labouchère settled the terms with the Minister for a loan of thirteen million Dutch florins at five per cent to be issued at 90 in bonds of 1000 florins. On February 25, 1802, the first chest of diamonds, of weight 20,000 carats, was shipped on board the packet *Prince of Wales* for London. One month later the Treaty of Amiens was signed but the peace that followed was short-lived and "made everybody glad and nobody proud," as people said in England. Once again Sir Francis had assessed the future well and done the right thing.

After his arrival in Paris, Labouchère wrote to Sir Francis,

Our tour has been . . . little more than a trial of what our constitutions could stand for though I have avoided fatigue whenever it could be done by dint of money, yet in consulting the map you will perceive that we have hardly allowed ourselves the time to pay the post boys. Our friends here however say we look better than when we left Paris. Thank God I feel perfectly well. . . .

A STAR GOES DOWN

On Sunday, June 18, 1815, the Duke of Wellington defeated Napoleon at Waterloo. The merchant bankers who had financed Britain's wars—first against revolutionary France, than against Napoleon—quickly adjusted themselves to the new situation.

Financing the peace turned out to be a far more difficult task, but also a more profitable one. The Napoleonic Wars had proved beyond doubt that there was only one country in

Europe that was financially safe: England. The City of London became the great fortress of *haute finance*.

In Paris the situation was desperate. Napoleon had gone and the Bourbons had returned but they had learned nothing since 1789; *"Ils n'ont rien appris ni rien oublié,"* as Talleyrand is supposed to have said. Louis XVIII was more interested in getting cash for his personal expenses than in the future of his country. He didn't improve the country's financial climate by raising a compulsory loan of one hundred million francs. Wealthy people in France lost all hope in their country's future.

The Allies thought they were being lenient with their former enemies. They demanded that France should pay 700,000,000 francs as "indemnities for the past," in five annual installments, and an annual 150,000,000 francs as "guarantees for the future," that would support Wellington's Army of Occupation. France was unable to raise these sums. The country was rich and had vast hidden resources but at the moment no funds were available. The first installment on the "indemnity for the past" was paid in 1816, and then the French government was at the end of its resources.

It was a great chance for a merchant banker with vision, courage and connections. Once again it was the incomparable Ouvrard, temporarily out of jail, who came up with a masterful idea, his greatest ever. He told the dumbfounded French ministers that it was totally wrong to raise new taxes and make compulsory loans. Such methods were bound to kill what little economic life was left after the long war years. No—the solution was to borrow abroad in order to pay back one's debts abroad.

"Only in following the example of England and treading the path of credit will France be able to escape bankruptcy," Ouvrard said. He had learned that ruthless taxation destroys economic life while sensible loans may create new life. No one was able to raise money in France now, he explained. But it would be possible to raise a loan in England to settle the claims of the Allies. Only one house there could do it: the Barings.

Ouvrard's brilliant theory has long become a truism accepted by finance ministers all over the world. You mortgage the future in order to finance the present. Everybody does it nowadays and no one gives credit to the genius of the late

Ouvrard who thought it up first. A lot of people in Paris said, as before, that Ouvrard was quite mad. On the contrary, said Ouvrard. He was the only one who was absolutely sane. It was really quite simple, as are all great ideas: a foreign loan would be raised in London, payment would be made to the Allies, the Occupation in France would end, and with her honor restored, *la grande nation* would make a fast economic comeback.

Ouvrard shrewdly concluded that he had to sell his idea to the man who counted more than all French ministers together: the Duke of Wellington. Happily the Duke understood finance much better than did his former antagonist Napoleon; he agreed at once. Ouvrard sent word to London where those old hands at delicate transactions, the Barings and the Hopes, began to proceed "slowly and cautiously." In 1817, a five per cent bond issue of 350,000,000 francs was offered at 53, and subscribed in full. The credit of France was still good in the City of London. In a short time the loan rose to 55. A second loan was floated by Barings and Hope & Co., in conjunction with the Paris houses of Laffette & Co. and Delessert & Co. By July, 1817, French *Rentes*, as the bonds were called, were traded at 67¾ at the Paris Bourse. For the Barings-Hope-Ouvrard combine it was a phenomenal success. Profits have been estimated conservatively "between one and a half million to three million pounds." But it was a costly success because it started the historic clash between the Barings and the Rothschilds.

James Rothschild, who represented the family in Paris, had tried hard to get in on the deal. It was not so much a question of profit but a matter of prestige. Alexander Baring might have accepted the Rothschilds as partners. He had a soft spot in his heart for Nathan Meyer Rothschild whose career closely paralleled that of his ancestor Johann Baring. And he had watched with professional admiration as Nathan used his special advance information of the outcome of the Battle of Waterloo to make a killing in the market. Having received from a courier a Dutch newspaper with the first report of the English victory, Nathan (after dutifully informing the British government, which didn't believe his information) had gone to the stock exchange and started to sell, whereupon word spread that "Rothschild is selling," and prices broke. At that point Rothschild's agents began to secretly buy—very cheaply. A brilliant maneuver that had deeply impressed Alexander Baring. It would be hard to lick the Rothschilds; why not let them join?

But Ouvrard and Henry Hope were very much against it. They said the Rothschilds were not in the same class. They were successful "coin-changers," but coin-changers just the same. Meanwhile James Rothschild kept trying. He failed—but not for long.

Early in 1818 negotiations started for an additional issue of 270,000,000 francs' worth of *Rentes*. After the success of the earlier loans it was a foregone conclusion that the Baring-Hope-Ouvrard combine would again get the business. In Aix-la-Chapelle the loan that would completely liquidate the French war indemnity would be discussed at a conference of the victorious powers.

Alexander Baring was the star performer in Aix-la-Chapelle. He was often seen in the company of Lord Castlereagh, the British Foreign Secretary, and he was on the friendliest terms with Prince Metternich from Vienna and Prince Hardenberg, the Prussian delegate. No wonder; the *Rentes* had done well and the great statesmen had done a little speculation on their own account—on margin, to be sure. A splendid investment, really; you just sat back and watched your money grow. *Rentes* were going up all the time at the Paris Bourse. The statesmen agreed that Alexander Baring was a splendid fellow. They paid no attention to Salomon and Kalmann Rothschild who also happened to be in town, and were trying to get into the charmed circle. The statesmen wouldn't even talk to "the coin-changers from the Frankfurt ghetto."

Negotiations were concluded and the Baring-Hope-Ouvrard combine decided to take a large slice of the third French loan, at the "preferential" price of 70. Early in November, 1818, *Rentes* were traded in Paris at 74. Metternich was so delighted that he asked Alexander Baring to buy more *Rentes* for him. Suddenly, on November fifth, *Rentes* began to drop. As usual the experts had many explanations. There had been "too many issues in too short a time"; the market showed "not enough resilience"; the technical position was "vulnerable"; people needed money and sold large bundles of *Rentes*.

As usual, the experts' explanations completely ignored the truth: the Rothschilds had launched a massive bear attack against *Rentes*. Having been snubbed, the "coin-changers" went back to their offices and gave orders to secretly buy up *Rentes*, using huge amounts of untransferred indemnity funds in their treasuries. Ironically, France herself, through the Rothschilds, financed the big speculation in French *Rentes*, selling France short. Too late the combine learned the bitter truth that the Rothschilds had dumped their *Rentes* within a few days on the stock market. In a single week *Rentes* dropped from 74 to 68, well beyond the "preferential" price at which the combine had bought. Instead of large profits there were huge losses. And there was more trouble to come.

Alexander Baring was summoned by Prince Metternich. The expression on the statesman's face told Baring everything: he was through as the financial star performer. Well, what about the *Rentes*, Metternich demanded to know. A lot of people in high places might be ruined unless "new arrangements" were made at once. What did Mr. Baring have to suggest?

Alexander Baring made it very clear to Metternich and the other statesmen that margin dealings in *Rentes* were possible only on a rising market. None of the statesmen was able to pay up. There was an unpleasant scene. Metternich was furious but Baring didn't give in. It was well known that Metternich was not a man to ever forget what he considered an insult. That day the Barings lost their financial hegemony on the Continent. From now on the Rothschilds were "the financiers of legitimacy." The Barings might join—but by invitation only.

In 1823, Byron wrote in *Don Juan*:

> Who hold the balance of the world? Who reign
> O'er congress, whether royalist or liberal?
> Who rouse the shirtless patriots of Spain?
> (That makes old Europe's journals squeak and gibber all)
> Who keep the world, both old and new in pain
> Or pleasure? Who make politics run glibber all?
> The shade of Bonaparte's noble daring?
> Jew Rothschild and his fellow-Christian, Baring.

It was not only for the sake of the rhyme that Byron in his off-hour effort mentions Baring in second place. Much later, French *Rentes* recovered and went up to 80; by 1830 they stood at 110, while British consols rose only from 62 to 90. As so often before (and afterwards) the vanquished recovered more quickly than the victor.

Wellington and the Army of Occupation were recalled, and France made a swift economic comeback—exactly as Ouvrard had predicted. Incidentally, as had happened before, Ouvrard who had thought up the great deal was the only one who made nothing out of it. The Bourbons charged him with fraud and didn't even pay his commission. Even a merciless district attorney would feel some sympathy for the cheated cheat.

On the Continent the Barings had now lost their dominant position to the Rothschilds but in London they remained the leading Anglo-American house. "East of the Cape of Good Hope the name of Baring had been heard since 1770, and had become synonymous with friendship for merchants and mariners of the United States," writes Hidy.

Alexander Baring, later the first Baron Ashburton, was a man with vision, integrity and a shrewd sense of business who became one of the builders of Britain's credit structure and had modern ideas. In a letter to his "special agent" Girard in America he wrote:

People cannot transact business confidentially with 24 directors. A private banker will be found so great a convenience that I think you will have almost all the commercial houses for customers ... And then you must know that exchange operations require decisions and will not be managed by a board of directors. That this branch is susceptible of being profitably managed I am certain, for I myself made a good start in this way during my residence in America. ...

Alexander Baring became an authority on trade with Turkey, the Mediterranean and Baltic areas, and America. He had strong ideas about laissez-faire that often shocked his contemporaries. "Every regulation is a restriction, and as such contrary to that freedom which I have held to be the first principle of the well-being of commerce," he would say. He was born in 1774 and died in 1848; he was lucky not to have lived today. John Quincy Adams and Daniel Webster were among his close friends. "He was the greatest merchant banker England perhaps ever had," Disraeli said.

In 1823 Barings made a loan to the Bank of New York. The reception in the City of London was indifferent. Alexander Baring complained that "American institutions were not enough known." From then on the Barings never stopped doing business with America. In 1829 they financed the Planters' Association in Louisiana, the first loan placed in London for a North American state. Loans for Maryland and Massachusetts followed. Barings survived the crisis of 1836 which was caused by crop failures, grain imports, overblown credit and excessive speculation. Three of the seven "American houses" in London failed to meet their obligations. Barings had small losses but they remained liquid. They had been conservative and held only £150,000 in securities for American accounts.

The Bank of England tried to stem the crisis but its own situation deteriorated rapidly. Money was scarce in France and Belgium, and large funds were withdrawn from the Bank of England. Russia, preparing the introduction of the silver ruble, was buying silver which caused a further drain on the Bank's reserves. The Bank raised its discount rate to five, then to five and a half, and finally to six per cent but its reserves were shrinking. In 1839 its gold reserve was so low that the Bank of England was "on the verge of ruin." Historians call it the worst danger in the long history of Threadneedle Street. And in its most desperate hour the Bank of England was saved through the intervention of the Barings.

The Bank had tried in vain to procure foreign exchange and turned to the Barings for help. Humphrey St. John Mildmay, a son-in-law of Alexander Baring, was then a director of the Bank. Using their name, credit and prestige, Barings reached an agreement with fifteen French banks to accept Barings' plain finance bills, worth two million pounds (forty-eight million francs) which were discounted by the Banque de France. Other banks involved in the rescue operation were Salomon Heine in Hamburg, Arnstein and Eskeles in Vienna, and Barings' old friend, Hope & Co. in Amsterdam. The rescue action was not unlike the short-term bonds which the United States Treasury much later placed with Europe's central banks in order to replenish its gold reserves. In the 1840's the Barings had the power and credit status of today's state banks.

One hundred and twenty-five years after the crisis in Threadneedle Street another run on the pound sterling was averted only by the intervention of the central banks of eleven nations which lent the Bank three billion dollars, and the International Monetary Fund which contributed an additional billion. The crisis of 1964 was too big for *any* merchant bank. But in 1839 the Barings saved the Bank. The decline was halted; by April, 1841, all bills were paid. Fifty years later, the Bank of England repaid its moral debt to the Barings when it bailed them out of *their* worst crisis.

The Barings survived the lean years between 1839 and 1842 when Maryland and Pennsylvania defaulted on their interest payments. American credit was so low in the City that no one wanted to touch American securities. Criticism against the Barings spread in the City. The *Circular to Bankers* reprimanded them for "sacrificing patriotism to profit" by facilitating the export of British capital to the Continent and Canada. The newspapers attacked the British government for "abandoning the national interest to the concupiscence of contractors." Specifically, the papers named Alexander Baring and Nathan Meyer Rothschild "who own no country but the Bourse." The *Times* said that Anglo-American bankers were "a curse to both the United States and England by inducing the poor states to contract debts" and came out with the suggestion that an investigation be made into the conduct of mercantile banking firms which first introduced American bonds in England. Often, it was said, the prospectus of a loan painted a deceivingly optimistic picture of the American states. There was a widespread feeling that English creditors had suffered badly for the dishonesty and bad faith of the American debtors. Some newpapers demanded that sales of American securities should be discouraged by English bankers.

(About a hundred years later, after the banking investigation in the United States, the Johnson Act prohibited new loans to defaulting governments.)

Sensing that something would have to be done quickly to restore American credit in the City, the Barings started a long-range, public-relations campaign, explaining that distinctions should be made between American states that paid up and those that didn't. "One must not brand the whole United States as wanting in good faith," they said. The *Circular to Bankers* pointed out that of all the states of the Union "only nineteen" were in debt, and of these "only seven" were in trouble. At the same time the Barings also started a spirited campaign on the other side of the Atlantic to convince the American people that one simply has to pay one's debts though one may hate doing it.

The *Boston Daily Advertiser*, edited by Nathan Hale, became the key paper in the widespread press campaign against lack of morality in state finances. Articles began to appear everywhere. Even the clergy joined the campaign which had partial success in Pennsylvania, Maryland, Louisiana, Illinois and Indiana. By 1848 the federal government of the United States could again borrow in London.

Alexander Baring had retired in 1831, and for a while his second son, Francis (later third Lord Ashburton), managed the bank. His wife was the daughter of the Duke of Bassano, Napoleon's secretary of state. Francis Baring had lived in Mexico before 1825 when he bought the enormous Aguayo estate. He was unable to make his title good, however, owing to Mexican legislation preventing foreigners from holding land, and had to sell it, which is still regretted at Barings for this estate later was absorbed into Mexico City.

Francis Baring lived much in Paris and the dominant partners at Barings became Thomas Baring and an American, Joshua Bates, who had become a partner in 1828. He had a commission house in Boston which was very successful and later merged with Baring Brothers. Bates made fortunes in America and England which he spent on various philanthropies; he became a munificent benefactor of the Boston Public Library.

Thomas was another great Baring—a leading City figure, chairman of Lloyd's, a director of the Bank of England. Twice he refused the post of Chancellor of the Exchequer, preferring to work for Baring Brothers, to collect paintings and act as a trustee for the National Gallery. That he knew his business though is evident from many documents, among them two letters in the archives of Barings. In 1842 he wrote to Joshua Bates,

I had . . . anticipated that you would not want me and intend to pay a visit to Munich which I have never seen. The fact is that we have been lately over manned as to partners for the business which we are doing, which is almost as bad for a house as to be under manned, as the public sees partners who have nothing to do which has been my case for some time past. . . .

And in 1858 he wrote from Paris where he attended the meetings of the Committee of the Sino-Russian Railway,

I am very sorry that the absence of Francis and myself and our letters should prevent you from concluding what you think right about the Chile Loan. My absence was not voluntary but I always consider that the principle of our house is that the partners on the spot, especially when you are one of those, should decide all matters of business as they alone can be judge of time and circumstances. . . .

In the early 1840's, the Barings began to finance American railroads. Owing to their public-relations campaign on both sides of the Atlantic the tide had turned and once more the City showed much interest in the expansion of American business. But the Barings remained prudent. "Barings are not carried away by the excitement of the times," Joshua Bates wrote in 1855.

They were not carried away about the development of Canada either. Prior to the Federation in 1867, British North America consisted of the Maritime Provinces, and of the Provinces of Upper and Lower Canada. In 1835, Barings and T. Wilson & Co., joint financial agents of the Province, provided a loan for Upper Canada. During the following thirty years nearly all British capital to Canada was procured by the Barings.

In 1841, Lord Aberdeen, who was pro-American, replaced Palmerston, anti-American, at the Foreign Office in London. The following year, Lord Aberdeen chose Lord Ashburton to settle a serious dispute between the United States and Canada about the northeastern boundary. The territory in dispute covered some twelve thousand square miles. The

dispute, along with some other grievances, had brought the
two countries to a high point of exasperation.

Lord Ashburton and Daniel Webster, the American Secretary of State, were friends. Both were bankers and approached their problem as businessmen rather than as politicians. After short negotiations a settlement was reached and
the Webster-Ashburton Treaty was written. It was the cul-
mination of Lord Ashburton's career, and further enhanced
the prestige of the Barings.

The list of Barings' investments around the middle of the
nineteenth century raises interesting questions. Why did they
participate in the building of the Trans-Siberian Railroad but
refuse to get involved in the Suez Canal and turn down loans
proposed by Ferdinand de Lesseps? (The Suez Canal later
became one of England's greatest assets, owing to the vision
of Disraeli and the help of the Rothschilds.) The Barings
turned down Turkey and the Hungarian Railroads as "unsound risks" but invested in Pennsylvania and Virginia
bonds and the Panama Railroad. After 1853 they no longer
marketed American securities. The memory of the unfriendly
press campaign still rankled. From now on they sold only
securities in which they were willing to invest for their own
account. And they handled only new issues that could be
marketed at par or above. They were more cautious than ever
and turned down Chile, Norway and Russia.

Turning down Russia was difficult because after the Crimean War Thomas Baring had become financial adviser to
the Czar and Barings was financial agent to the Russian
government. But because it had good inside information and
knew the truth about Russian finances, Barings showed great
restraint in its dealings with the Czar. Prior to the First
World War it was said in London that the Barings knew
more about Russia than anybody else in the City. Sir Mac-
kenzie Wallace, the *Times* correspondent in St. Petersburg,
was very close to the Barings. Some people said the Barings
were "Russophile" when the second Lord Revelstoke was
sent as one of Britain's four delegates to the Allied Conference at Petrograd in 1917.

Safety First became the house rule though it might mean
less profit. The Barings evolved their own credit rating and
determined whose bills they would not accept. Firms that

had other accounts in the City were automatically blacklisted. American firms which issued their own acceptances in the United Kingdom were excluded. Barings' conservatism was their greatest achievement in these years. They made it clear to their American correspondents that they wanted America to grow, but not too fast, not too recklessly. Barings first introduced the mechanism of self-control that was later adopted by George Peabody in London and the Morgans in New York (and in 1933 taken over by the federal government.) The mechanism was based on caution and knowledge. The Barings had a widespread intelligence network; they knew some of the best-kept secrets. Their deals often seemed so audacious that everybody was astonished until it became apparent, much later, that they had acted on the basis of sound advance information and knew exactly what they were doing.

THE CRISIS

The Baring crisis, the firm's worst ordeal and the most dangerous predicament in the whole history of merchant banking, occurred in 1890. The seeds of trouble had been planted much earlier. In the 1820's Argentina suddenly became a glamorous attraction for the investors and speculators in the City of London. Three hundred and nine years after the country's discovery, in 1515, by the Spanish explorer Juan Diaz de Solis, and fourteen years after the proclamation of its independence, in 1810, the City took notice of Argentina. In Parliament Lord Russell had said, "When a people from good reasons take up arms against an oppressor it is but an act of justice and generosity to assist brave men in the defense of their liberties."

The City of London interpreted these idealistic words (which Lord Russell had borrowed from Emmerich von Vattel, the Swiss champion of the rights of men) in its own, materialistic way. To the financiers they meant that everybody with "good reasons" could get a loan—and nearly everybody did. Spain, Guatemala, Nicaragua and Greece failed to meet their interest payments when due. Colombia defaulted even the first payment of interest. People began to gamble in government loans and later they gambled in dubious gold mine stocks. Tempting, flowery circulars promised wealth from the Andes and Cordilleras. One prospectus pointed out that this was "no speculative undertaking, no problematic or visionary scheme." It was promised that "pearls can be found off the coast of Colombia," that there was so much silver in Peru "that all utensils of everyday use will be made of it." Skeptical people said that "a mine is a hole in the ground owned by a liar."

The first Argentine loan, a six per cent, one million pound Buenos Aires issue was offered, at 85, by the Barings in 1824. Four years later it went into default and was consolidated only in 1857. In spite of this unpromising initial experience both serious financiers and doubtful speculators considered Argentina a wonderful investment. Why, isn't clear. Instead of paying interest coupons due, the Argentinians offered promises of a better future for all. In the 1870's the country suffered a bad crisis and was saved only by the Barings, who had more power and larger resources than many governments.

All of a sudden the tide turned and Argentina became prosperous and booming, as though trying to fulfill the promises of a better future. In 1870, there were forty thousand immigrants; by 1889 two hundred and sixty thousand hopefuls had arrived. In 1878 Argentina began to export wheat and three years later the gold standard was introduced. It seemed as though the Barings had once again made a killing in the market. All over Europe, investors became fascinated by "the second America." Between 1881 and 1889, British banks took Argentine loans worth over £85,000,000. In most of these loans Barings was the leading house.

The steady inflow of money from London created a pleasant sense of euphoria in Argentina. People began to believe that this happy state of affairs was going to last forever. Confidence remained unshaken even when Argentina in 1885 suspended the gold standard, four years after it had been established. Faulty fiscal planning created inflation and political unrest caused trouble, but prosperity continued and gradually developed into uncontrolled boom. In 1888, Argentina received £36,102,766 in various loans from Europe. "No warning can save a people determined to grow suddenly rich," said the great British banker, Samuel Jones Lloyd (later Lord Overstone).

Euphoria became Argentina's national state of mind. Prices of land rose crazily; railways were built for traffic that didn't exist; banks were set up for customers who hadn't arrived yet. Everybody was rolling in somebody else's money; in due course the inevitable operators and cunning sharpshooters appeared on the scene. Gold rose to a premium of 320 per cent.

In London some cautious people began to get worried. The *Statist* wrote in its December, 1888, issue that too many foreign issues in London caused a dangerous outflow of gold which ought to provide the leaders in the issuing business "with food for thought." Just in case somebody didn't know what it was all about, the *Statist* reminded its readers that Barings had raised in the previous six years ninety-five million pounds for overseas borrowers. Argentina was on top of the borrowers' list, followed by Uruguay. Recently, a loan for Buenos Aires had proved impossible to place. "We are glad that Barings had no success in placing it among the public," wrote the *Statist*.

To curb the continuing drain of gold the Bank of England raised the Bank rate from three to four per cent in June, 1890, and a few weeks later to five per cent. By the end of October there was an uneasy feeling in Lombard Street, home of the City's discount houses, which soon spread all over the financial district. The name of "a certain house" which was said to have big commitments in Argentina was whispered. This house was rumored to have lately increased the amount of its acceptance in circulation.

On Friday, November 7, the Bank rate was raised to six per cent. It was not a black Friday but a pretty gray one. William Lidderdale, the Governor of the Bank, was trying to protect the Bank's dwindling gold reserve against continuing remittances to South America. A former immigrant from Russia, Lidderdale proved himself a man of great courage and steady nerves in the hour of danger, and ultimately its real hero. He, too, had heard the rumors about that "certain house." The rumors became more disturbing by the hour. Lidderdale braced himself for some bad news but even he was shocked to learn that Barings might not be able to go on.

Edward Charles Baring, a partner in the bank since 1856, was a typical Baring, "proud and self-reliant, with a profound

belief in himself." He had been a director of the Bank of
England since 1879, and was made Lord Revelstoke in 1885
when his friend Nathaniel Rothschild was also raised to the
peerage. Under his leadership Barings had placed in the
market nineteen million pounds' worth of Argentine loans in
the past seven years. Apparently, the philosophy of conservatism and the house rule of Safety First that the previous
generation had developed to such perfection were temporarily abandoned. Even among the firm's partners there was no
agreement about Lord Revelstoke's methods. Thomas
Charles Baring (whose father, Charles Baring, was Bishop of
Bristol) had resigned the previous year from the partnership
when he was certain that Lord Revelstoke was not going to
listen to his warnings. Characteristically, Thomas Charles
Baring later put his entire fortune at the firm's disposal when
he heard of its difficulties.

All members of the family acted that way. A favorite
family story is about the first Earl of Northbrook visiting the
fifth Baron Ashburton, who had no contact with the firm, and
was something of an unworldly eccentric, like so many
Barings.

"Did you hear?" Lord Northbrook said. "The house is in
trouble."

Lord Ashburton looked up. "What's the matter? Roof
leaking? Dry rot set in?"

Henry Mildmay, one of the partners, was so upset that he
kept his family awake all night while he paced back and
forth in his room. In the morning, after much soul-searching,
he had come to a heroic decision. He announced to the
assembled family that they would have to economize. As a
first step he dismissed all the footmen and hired footmen of
smaller stature, at somewhat lower salaries.

Viscount George Joachim Goschen, Chancellor of the
Exchequer, had written in his diary earlier in November:
"Went to the Bank. Things queer. Some of the first houses
talked about." There were rumors that Barings had secured a
considerable loan "from a great house," that they were selling
"large blocks of securities," that they had disposed of some
four million pounds before "a certain bank in Lombard
Street" advised them to go to the Bank of England.

People in the City have sensitive antennae. They depend

for their livelihood on very sharp hearing. Even those who usually paid no attention to rumors knew there must be something very wrong when Sir Everard Hambro, the head of the great merchant bank of Hambros and a director of the Bank of England, was seen in St. Swithin's Lane, presumably on his way to Rothschilds, at the unlikely hour of eight o'clock in the morning, on Saturday, the eighth of November. Definitely, something was up.

Some people who had heard it from somebody who knew or pretended to know said that Sir Everard had been talking to Lord Revelstoke, "the night before," and that after his talk at Rothschilds he had gone straight "and very quickly" to the Bank of England and talked to the Governor. What happened in Lidderdale's office is no hearsay but history for we have his notes for it. Sir Everard Hambro told Lidderdale that Barings was "much involved." Lord Revelstoke had said to him, "I shall be able to tell you on Monday whether we can go on or whether we have to stop." Baring Brothers had liabilities amounting to twenty-one million pounds and needed help at once—or they would have to suspend payments. The Argentine crisis had left them with large blocks of unsalable loans on their hands. Their mercantile business was as sound as ever but their assets were partially frozen.

Lidderdale's first thought was that the fall of Barings would drag down many other banks and engulf the whole City in the greatest panic in history. This must not happen under any circumstances. Lidderdale was convinced that the Barings' situation was not hopeless. They were basically sound; they just needed time. He said little but sent a note to the Chancellor of the Exchequer and asked him to come to the City on Monday.

Later that Saturday morning a top-secret meeting took place at Hambros. Lidderdale had come over, followed by two Baring partners, Lord Revelstoke and Francis Baring. They showed Lidderdale a statement that was, according to Lidderdale's notes, "black enough but neither clear nor decisive." They would have "exact figures" on Monday morning. Little else was said. Leaving Hambros, Lidderdale decided that he wasn't going to let Barings spoil his weekend. He went home and spent Sunday with his small boy in the Zoological Gardens.

In the meantime, Goschen had received Lidderdale's note

and found it "very alarming," according to his diary. *His* weekend was definitely spoiled. He guessed the trouble was either Barings or the drain on the Bank's gold. "And if it's going to be Barings, 1866 will be a trifle compared to it," he wrote in his diary.

(On May 10, 1866, the great London discount house of Overend, Gurney & Co. had stopped payments; its liabilities were almost nineteen million pounds. The following day, England's Black Friday, "terror reigned in the City, the banks were besieged, consols went down to 84," reports Sir John Clapham, historian of the Bank of England.)

When Goschen arrived on Monday morning in front of the Bank of England, he found there "two great City figures" (whom the Chancellor of the Exchequer discreetly fails to mention by name) "both quite demoralized." He was at once ushered into the Governor's office and found Lidderdale "much more of a man."

"You gave me an unhappy Sunday, Mr. Governor," Goschen said. Then he sat down and listened quietly while Lidderdale made his report. It was agreed that in no case could the Bank of England interfere in behalf of an insolvent house. But if Barings proved solvent, Goschen promised to give "all the support in his power."

"I said the great houses must get together and give the necessary guarantees," Goschen later wrote in his diary. Rather shaken, the Chancellor left the Bank to consult with the Prime Minister and with W. H. Smith, the First Lord of the Treasury.

Lidderdale meanwhile ascertained that the reserve of the Bank of England was £10,815,000—"entirely inadequate should there be serious doubt about Barings' solvency" — but he was quite certain in his own mind that the Bank "must be protected." He asked the Chancellor to influence Rothschilds to get several millions from the Banque de France, and to work on the Argentine government "about those discredited securities." He must have known that the second task would be difficult, probably impossible.

Goschen talked to Rothschilds, which intervened at the Banque de France in Paris. The Banque de France promised to lend the Bank of England three and a half million pounds in gold.

On Wednesday, November 12, Barings presented their

statement. Against liabilities amounting to twenty-one million pounds, of which sixteen million were on acceptances, there were assets worth twenty-four and three-quarter million pounds. However—and this was the crux of the matter— these assets included five and three-quarter million pounds of Argentine loans and two million of Uruguay loans which "at the moment" could not be realized. Still, if Barings was given time and help—at once, before the acute crisis erupted into an outright panic—all might end well.

Goschen notes in his diary how "very cleverly and energetically" Lidderdale had made arrangements with Rothschilds. An Argentine Committee was formed, with Lord Rothschild in the chair. By twelve o'clock noon, on Wednesday, three million pounds of gold arrived from Paris. An additional £1,150,000 was bought outright from Russia.

("Those behind the scenes," the *Economist* wrote later, on November 22, "although their tongues were sealed, knew quite well what dictated the purchase of gold from Russia and the loan from France.")

Secrecy was no empty word to the Victorians. "Those behind the scenes" really didn't talk. On Friday, the fourteenth, John Daniell, an important City figure, and a member of Mullens & Co., government brokers, came to Lidderdale and asked the Governor to make a statement. "They say something awful is up," said Daniell. "And they are talking of the highest names—the very highest."

Lidderdale made no statement. And Chancellor Goschen refused "absolutely" to help the Barings. He pointed out that an overt act by government would require an appeal to Parliament which would "put the fat in the fire."

It is not certain who first mentioned a collective guarantee. Nearly all *dramatis personae* speak of the idea in their respective notes and diaries. Lidderdale probably tells the truth when he writes, "The thought was present to all our minds at a very early date." W. H. Smith, First Lord of the Treasury, promised to send Lidderdale his own check for a hundred thousand pounds "to prove that Barings could be saved only by private guarantees." He had no connection whatsoever with Barings. "My motive in offering a guarantee was entirely a public one," he later wrote to Lidderdale. "I thought it would have been a national misfortune if Barings had gone down."

On Friday night Goschen left London to make a speech in Dundee that had been scheduled for some time. A smart move. If the Chancellor of the Exchequer had canceled his trip, the news might have precipitated the panic everybody was afraid of. As always the English leaders demonstrated their genius for sangfroid at the moment of danger. Lidderdale showed particular presence of mind on Friday. When Barings' bills began to pour in at the Bank of England, he slipped away through the bullion court and went by a devious route to pick up a hansom for Whitehall. He hoped no one had seen him. He now had all the facts about Barings. Their statement proved that they were solvent but they would need "eight or nine millions" to meet their immediately maturing liabilities. "This somber thought" went through Lidderdale's mind as his hansom approached Whitehall.

The Prime Minister received him at once. Lidderdale asked him to increase the government's balance at the Bank of England. The Prime Minister hesitated.

Lidderdale spoke up sharply.

"Barings' bills are coming in fast now. Unless the government will relieve us of some of the possible loss, I should have to return at once and throw out all further acceptances of the firm." Bold language, but it achieved its purpose. The Prime Minister agreed that the British government would bear "half of any loss that might result between two P.M. Friday and two P.M. Saturday."

That was all Lidderdale had hoped to hear, and he went back to the Bank of England. It was almost four o'clock, and he would have to work fast; there wasn't much time left. He had made up his mind: he was going to raise a private guarantee fund to make the government's guarantee superfluous. Still, it was good to have the Prime Minister's assurance.

By five-thirty P.M. Lidderdale had promises of £3,250,000. The Bank of England itself started the guarantee fund with one million pounds. (It thus handsomely repaid its moral debt to Barings, which had come to the rescue of the Bank fifty-one years before when the Old Lady of Threadneedle Street had been in serious danger and Baring Brothers had organized the rescue syndicate in Paris and elsewhere on the Continent.)

The list of contributors to the Barings' guarantee fund soon read like a Who's Who of the City's prominent. Glyn, Mills, Currie put up £500,000, and so did N. M. Rothschild & Sons; Raphael & Sons £250,000; Antony Gibbs and Brown Shipley contributed £200,000 each; and the firms of Smith, Payne and Smith; Barclays; Robarts; J. S. Morgan; Drexel Morgans; and Hambros each contributed £100,000.

Perhaps the most amazing fact is that the whole transaction was carried out in less than forty minutes. Much of the work was done by Bertram Currie of Glyn, Mills, Currie, a personal friend of the Barings. Currie made it quite clear to the other bankers that this was not simply a case of brotherly love. The City leaders would have to give a dramatic demonstration of unity. The alternative was quite obvious—and not very pleasant to consider.

Meanwhile Lidderdale had sent urgent invitations to the five big joint-stock (commercial) banks, asking their representatives to meet with him at the Bank of England on Saturday morning. When the gentlemen came, he told them the story. There was a long moment of deep shock. "All were concerned for Barings' acceptances were widespread," writes historian Clapham. "No paper had stood higher."

The joint-stock banks suggested that they would double the guarantee fund. Three of them offered to contribute £750,000 each, more than Rothschilds. Lidderdale admitted later that this meeting had been the crucial moment of the Baring crisis. One of the representatives indicated coolly that "maybe one should let events take their turn." There was not the same *esprit de corps* among the commercial banks as among the great merchant bankers.

Lidderdale answered sharply that in this case he would close the account of this bank with the Bank of England, and that the fact would be advertised in the papers. That threat brought the reluctant representative quickly back into line. By eleven o'clock on Saturday morning Lidderdale had a guarantee fund of £6,500,000, "enough to free the Treasury of its liability," which Lidderdale had extorted from the Prime Minister. He sent a ciphered telegram to Goschen in Scotland who opened it just before lunch and gave a sigh of relief. Thank Heaven, the worst was over.

By four o'clock in the afternoon other guarantees had raised the toal of the fund to fourteen million pounds. In the end the City, in a remarkable demonstration of unity, raised

seventeen and a half million pounds for Barings. Even
provincial banks, private banks and discount houses joined
the fun. No one wanted to be excluded; to guarantee Barings
had become something of a status symbol, giving honor
without risk. Barings had dramatically proven the difference
between a good name and a great name in banking: a good
name is good in normal times but a great name is good even
in a crisis. "Those behind the scenes" later admitted that they
had been haunted all the time by the fear the Russian
government might withdraw a deposit of £2,400,000 that
they had with Barings. This might have created serious
international consequences.

It was decided among all guarantors that they would help
Barings to discharge at maturity its liabilities existing on the
night of November 15, 1890, and to make good any loss that
might appear at the final liquidation. As security the Bank of
England took over from Barings "all the Bonds and Documents representing value."

There was no run on the banks. What might have become
the worst panic in the history of the City was averted. On
Sunday, November 19, all newspapers praised the City for its
fine display of unity. Barings was severely criticized. It was
pointed out that it had known more about South America
than anybody else in the City. It must have known that the
standards of probity among businessmen and statesmen were
not always very high in these countries. W. R. Lawson, in
Bankers' Magazine, in 1891, wrote of "Gaucho banking."
After all, Barings had often dealt with the National Banks of
Argentina and Uruguay, the Buenos Aires Railways, the
Buenos Aires Water Works and Draining Company. The
consensus of City opinion was later expressed by Sir John
Clapham, "A charge that might be brought with justice
against [Barings] was that in their eagerness to do business
they had not considered all these enterprises coolly and
wisely enough." The *Times* wrote on November 15 that the
Barings had gone "far beyond the bounds of prudence." The
editor of the *Economist* stated, "Had Messrs. Baring Brothers
been able to shift the burden of their South-American obligations upon the investing public, they would now have been
standing erect."

The last word was said by Queen Victoria who wrote in
her diary on November thirtieth that "Lord Revelstoke had

rashly and credulously put all he had into these Argentine mines or works, and had been cheated by the Argentine agents who had come to him." Obviously the First Lord of the Treasury had thought it advisable to explain to Her Majesty the Baring crisis in a rather nontechnical way.

At Christmastime the Committee of the Stock Exchange said that owing to Lidderdale's "masterful ability" a panic of unparalleled dimension was averted. A deputation from the City expressed to the Governor of the Bank of England "their high appreciation of the admirable and effective manner in which the crisis was met." By January 29, 1891, the Bank rate was down to a normal three per cent. And at the end of his term, Lidderdale was elected to a second term as Governor, an unprecedented honor, and well deserved.

Baring Brothers was reconstructed as a limited company with a capital of one million pounds, and was henceforth known as Baring Brothers & Co., Ltd. The maximum figure advanced to the firm by the guarantee fund was £17,326,-000. It proved impossible to wind up everything within three years—the time for which the guarantors had undertaken their guarantee—but it became apparent that within another year all commitments would be met and the guarantors unanimously decided to carry on for another twelve months. By 1894 Barings had paid off all obligations.

There is, not unnaturally, a certain reticence even today around 8, Bishopsgate when "1890" is mentioned. It was not exactly a year of glory. But the fact is that no guarantor lost a penny, that not a single bill failed to be paid and that the directors were able to retain the firm's commercial credit business. In October, 1894, the Bank of England issued a circular to all guarantors notifying them officially of the happy ending of the affair.

Only Lord Revelstoke never recovered from the blow. He had retired in 1891 and died six years later. The Baring crisis literally broke his heart. Three years later, the *Times* predicted that the second Lord Revelstoke would soon "belong to the inner cabinet of the City." In 1898, one year after his father's death, he became a director of the Bank of England, and remained on the board until his death in 1929. The City values character. The Barings came out of the great crisis with their personal prestige unimpaired.

THE HUMAN TOUCH

In the 1890's the building of Baring Brothers was flanked on either side by old pubs. No sooner were the doors of the pubs opened than half the employees in the banking hall would disappear. One day one of the partners asked the manager, "Why does everybody go out for a drink?"

The manager shrugged. "What do you expect? They can't get a drink in here." Owing to the vicinity of the pubs the first Lord Revelstoke heard many customers complain about inefficient clerks. Lord Revelstoke's answer was, "But we don't have clerks here—we are just assisted by a few friends."

Such stories are now cherished at Barings because they prove that merchant banking has not quite lost the human touch. Barings' partners like to remember the favorite axiom of Alfred Mildmay, "When in doubt, do nothing." And there was the partner who "always asked the right people the wrong questions or the wrong people the right questions." They fondly talk of the Baring ancestor who, as do so many doting fathers, tried to protect his pretty daughters from falling in love with the wrong men. The ancestor solved the problem (he thought) by permitting them to talk only to the right men, the local parson and the local schoolmaster. Inevitably, one married the parson and the other the schoolmaster.

The human touch remains strong at Barings, a very patriarchal house. Barings was one of the first firms in the City that employed women, as early as 1873. Once a woman came to the first Lord Revelstoke and said she was going to quit because she didn't get enough money. Lord Revelstoke said, "One doesn't leave Barings because one isn't paid well enough," and gave her a raise. Today all Barings' employees get free lunch at the bank and many other fringe benefits which make them the envy of people in other merchant banks. They retire at the age of sixty with two thirds of their last salary. Naturally they have a strong *esprit de maison* and sense of belonging.

"Once you are here, you are here for life," a man says who has been with Barings for over forty years.

It is quite easy to get lost at Barings. In the past hundred and sixty years so many extra floors, rooms, cubicles, stairways, partitions, small elevators and other *ad hoc* constructions have been added to the old building, and to neighboring properties later acquired, that the bank has become a labyrinth where strangers are not safe without a guide.

Headquarters and command post of Baring Brothers is the beautiful, old-fashioned partners' room which was last redone in 1853 by Lewis Cubitt, the architect who also built Belgravia and King's Cross Railway Station. Fine paintings, old panels, genuine Victorian charm pervade here. Unfortunately the partners' room is located just off the central banking hall, overlooking the drafty entrance. From the banking hall the room looks like the First Class waiting room in a provincial British railroad station. A few passengers are sitting around as though waiting for a train which will never come. They are the "partners," as the directors are called around the house, though the partnership was dissolved after the Baring crisis.

Owing to the building's confusing architecture people whose offices are located behind the partners' room have to make long detours to get there. When they are in a hurry they tiptoe right through the partners' room, hoping they won't be noticed. I walked through many times on my way to the archivist's room, which is located way beyond, one flight of stairs up. Otherwise I would have had to turn left in the inner entrance, walk through a couple of musty-smelling departments where elderly people were busily clipping coupons, then step into a rattling elevator, arrive on the second floor, proceed through several corridors past empty rooms and piles of stationery (a proper setting for a surrealist film) until I would get down again by a winding, wooden stairway, pass the partners' dining room and private kitchen, and arrive at long last at the archivist's room, a small chamber with many old ledgers, two telephones and no daylight coming in. Characteristically, Barings has an archivist (who doubles as house historian) but it has no public-relations man, as most other merchant banks today.

History is something tangible at 8, Bishopsgate. One of the partners who joined the firm as a clerk in 1928 remembers that all incoming letters were placed in a wire basket that was held on a rope from a pulley above the floor of the central banking hall. On the second floor a man with a fixed hook would reach out, trying to ensure that the basket on its swinging rope caught on to the hook. "The skill required was rather that of casting for trout," the partner remembers. Downstairs bets were laid whether the man would make it the first try. This certainly couldn't happen today in the new transparent American bank palaces that are built of glass and steel and reveal their innermost secrets.

"We loved the sporty interlude and were dismayed when workmen appeared one day and put in the present contraption," says the partner. Today the basket is pulled up over a wheel. It isn't the very latest technological advance but as do so many things in this strange world of merchant banking "it works."

In the beautiful boardroom there are dignified paintings, old blue china vases, a framed letter from Daniel Webster, and a check dated November 23, 1907, "Pray pay to His Excellency, the Japanese Ambassador in London . . . four million eight hundred sixty thousand 440 pounds...." All this must not convey the impression that Barings is not in step with these changing times. Tucked away in a tiny cubicle there is a small Friden computer.

TOUCH AND GO IN THE PARTNERS' ROOM

Barings has no daily partners' meetings as do most other houses. The partners meet every Tuesday morning for an informal discussion of the week's agenda, and there is also a weekly investment meeting. In recent years Barings' deceivingly old-fashioned partners' room has been the scene of some highly successful strategic operations on the dangerous battlefield of modern finance. Barings is widely admired in the City for its skill in complicated merger transactions. It has demonstrated imagination, ingenuity and sangfroid in dramatic take-over battles, and is now much in demand by boards of undervalued companies in danger of being swallowed up.

England is by tradition a country of small, individual businesses. Some people in the City consider the present trend towards bigness and concentration "alarming and unBritish." They forget that amalgamations occurred early, after the turn of the century, when several giant companies, among them Imperial Tobacco and Calico Printers, were formed. A second wave of concentration, during the Depression, created Imperial Chemical Industries, Unilever, and Associated Electrical Industries. The trend continues. In many fields—chemicals, automobiles, textiles, printing, stores, entertainment—small firms have been swallowed up by big ones under pressure of rising costs, changes of popular taste, foreign interests. Even the secure, old beer industry has been caught up in a maelstrom of mergers.

The City makes a sharp distinction between peaceful mergers and warlike take-overs. Small companies sometimes don't mind being taken over provided the offer is fair. But ten years ago many people in the City took a dim view of the master raiders—Isaac Wolfson, Charles Clore, Cecil King, Roy Thomson et al.—who had discovered the true value of certain companies a little earlier than other people did. Not all take-overs are economically indefensible. Some have created greater concentration and more efficiency, higher profits and better products. Others are thinly camouflaged examples of raid and plunder.

Even some big companies which once fiercely resisted the trend are now following it. Early in 1962, the City was shocked when giant Imperial Chemical Industries attempted to take over another giant, Courtaulds. "The bid . . . revealed that in an extreme crisis, like men in love or war, the conventional trappings, the opaque annual reports, the secrecy, the smugness, become suddenly ridiculous and are thrown overboard in a desperate need for help," Anthony Sampson writes in *Anatomy of Britain*.

Until Imperial Chemical Industries (ICI) came along with its take-over bid, Courtaulds had been a conservative, typically British company. They were advised by the conservative, typically British Barings. In January, 1962, ICI dropped its "take-over bombshell," as it was described by the financial press when ICI announced its bid in the newspapers. The shock waves briefly disrupted the serene atmosphere in Barings' partners' room where it was realized that such a brazen announcement could mean only one thing: ICI must be very sure of victory. A company in its sane mind declares its intention publicly only when it is virtually certain of the majority of the shares of the company which it wants to take over.

In the venerable partners' room at Barings (that has seen bigger crises) calm prevailed. The consensus was that the price offered by ICI was just not enough. ICI went up with its bid. Barings said it was still not enough. For Barings it was a grave, calculated risk. The whole City was watching. If they made a mistake in judgment and lost, it would be a severe blow to their prestige.

Today the partners admit that they reached their decision after an agonizing reappraisal of balance sheets and other data, but mostly by following their intuition—that intangible element that distinguishes a great merchant banker from one who is only a good one. Much as they wanted to avoid a battle with its sensational headlines and bad publicity, Barings had to advise the Courtauld management that they would have to fight the ICI bid.

The battle that followed literally divided the City. Barings will not disclose any details but it is no secret that they advised Courtaulds to change its corporate image as quickly as possible. Conservative Courtaulds suddenly surprised everybody with modern advertising campaigns, revealed its own expansion program, spoke optimistically of future profits and at the same time accused ICI of a poor research record. "The conventional trappings" were hastily thrown overboard. The aim of the campaign was to convince Courtaulds' shareholders that they were much better off with Courtaulds than they might be with ICI. During these tense weeks the shares of Courtaulds went up from 30 to 50 shillings.

In the partners' room at Barings the strain began to show. They had to give day-to-day advice and moral support to the Courtauld management that was "in desperate need of help." Barings was talking like a surgeon who tries to convince his patient that he's going to be all right although the surgeon himself is not so sure that the operation will be a success.

"There are imponderables that no one can correctly assess," a partner remembers. "We had become convinced that Courtauld's assets were much higher than they themselves had realized. The question was, would enough Courtaulds' shareholders become convinced of it?"

An offer sent out to shareholders in Britain must be kept open for three weeks. No one at Barings likes to remember these weeks. No one made any predictions. At Barings they knew that shareholders are human and that humans are unfathomable. "There comes a moment when you can do nothing but sit back, cross your fingers and pray," the partner says.

It was touch and go until March 12 when news reached the partners' room that ICI had got only thirty-eight per cent of Courtaulds' shares. Privately, at least two Baring partners now admit that they had expected ICI to get "up to eighty per cent."

"It was a real victory," a partner says with feeling. "It was a good reason to celebrate—and sometimes we do celebrate things at Barings."

Two years after fighting off ICI's take-over bid, Courtaulds surprised the City when *it* announced the biggest take-over bid in the history of British textiles. Courtaulds, this time the attacker, was still advised by Barings. But this time there was no tension in the partners' room. Barings had smoothly engineered the transaction under the cover of total secrecy, and they did a beautiful job. Courtaulds' bid was £36,000,000 for two of the best and biggest Lancashire spinning groups, Lancashire Cotton, and Fine Spinners and Doublers. The new group assets would be worth over £370,000,000.

The big secret had been kept so well that when the announcement came at the stock exchange, Lancashire Cotton jumped within an hour from 44 to 54 shillings, and Fine Spinners from 33 to 49 shillings. It was a triumph for Courtaulds which had almost been swallowed two years before and now had done some swallowing itself, emerging as "the most powerful force in the textile industry," according to the *Times*, which added, "both bids are considered fair." Sweet words for the men in Barings' partners' room.

Absolute secrecy is vital in such negotiations and at Barings security is tighter than in many government offices. During a tense period preceding the merger of two big corporations, some Barings partners knew so many secrets that "one was afraid of talking in one's sleep," as a partner says. All negotiations were carried on *sub rosa* in secluded country mansions. The partners made it a point never to be seen in public with the directors of the company whom they advised. Nevertheless, on the day the merger was to be announced, something went very wrong. While the boards of the companies concerned were meeting in secret at Barings, the directors of a third company that had no part in the merger but was in the same line of business were inadvertently ushered into the room.

It was an awkward moment, to say the least. The intruders undoubtedly recognized some of the people present before they were hastily ushered out again. But there was no breach of security until announcement of the merger was made that evening.

No merchant banker likes to get involved in City battles and to see his name in the papers. Barings is no exception.

"It's always a dangerous thing to advise people," a partner says. "You are trying to come up with a proposal that is acceptable to the other side and suddenly you get into these situations when you are up against a fight. We advise the board of a company, and the board is responsible to its shareholders. If the board does not recommend to the shareholders to accept another company's offer for a merger, the board must prove to its shareholders that they will be better off alone—which is not as easy as it seems. The worst thing is a war between the shareholders of a company. That's poison for the corporate image. In these take-over situations one never knows exactly what may happen next. Sometimes terrific pressure builds up in a few hours and one has to keep a cool head. All around you headlines erupt in the papers like mortar shells. Headlines are always bad, and if you do the wrong thing, the headlines go from bad to worse. We merchant bankers are supposed to be objective outsiders, to know more than the board of directors. Nowadays most boards are conscious of their duty to keep their shareholders informed but it hasn't always been thus. Today the shareholders know how much they ought to earn. Inflation has made them profit-conscious. But many boards don't know the real value of their own properties. They don't realize, for instance, that a building outlet may be more valuable than a trading outlet.

"Among our clients is one of the biggest brewing companies in this country. Their directors are primarily interested in making and selling a lot of beer; that's what they get paid for. They sit inside and have no time to look out. We at Barings are outside looking in; we can see the whole operation in financial terms though we know nothing about the making of beer. We looked at their balance sheets and discovered that some of their assets were still listed at the prices they had been bought for, thirty years ago. The directors didn't realize that their assets are now worth many millions more.

"Other companies have no real assets but everybody knows they are worth a great deal of money. How much? Ah, that's the big question. You talk to the people who run the company, you get all available information, and then you try to make up your mind. Bids are made in cash or in shares but this is not an exact science. How much are the shares *really* worth? Is it a good business that is going to do even better? Is it going to go down? Here you get into the dangerous twilight zone of speculation. Sooner or later you will have to make a guess. We discuss the problem among our partners in an informal discussion that may go on for weeks. In the end it's a matter of experience and instinct. One has made many decisions, most of which turned out right, and one hopes that one will be right again once more. People value our advice and our name because we've made so many right decisions. Barings have not been defeated yet in an important case."

A PARTNER NAMED BARING

One morning recently, one of the younger partners of Barings arrived at the partners' room a few minutes before ten o'clock. Most Barings, including this one, now live in Hampshire. This partner had a few years ago demolished Stratton Park, the house bought by Sir Francis Baring from the Duke of Bedford in 1802 for £150,000. On the beautiful site he built himself a small, modern, functional house where he lives with his wife and children. They have a Spanish couple, as caretakers; more exactly, they still have them as this is written. The young Baring does not envy his grandfather who had fifteen gardeners—not to mention the rest of the household personnel.

The partner read his mail, was reminded by his secretary of things-to-do, attended a series of informal meetings in the partners' room. At eleven-thirty the chairman of a property company came to see him. They wanted to raise three million pounds. Barings arranged to discuss the matter with one of the institutions—the big insurance companies and pension funds that now have most of the big money.

Why didn't the chairman of the property company go there directly?

"He doesn't know the institutions as well as we do. We may get him a better deal. He feels protected when he does it through us."

After lunch in the Victorian, oak-paneled partners' dining room, surrounded by the portraits of eminent ancestors, the partner met with two directors of a large brewing company. They planned to build a brewery abroad and had come to discuss the remittance of the money, for which the consent of the Bank of England was needed.

"In these days of strict exchange controls when a company has to buy the foreign exchange it needs it may have to pay a premium in the free market. If we can help them to make a good case to the Bank of England for permission to buy money at the official rate, we may have materially lowered the cost of the whole project."

It was a fairly typical day in the life of the partner whose life has been fairly typical—for a Baring. He had been to Eton and Oxford, and had come to "the bank" one day in 1950. For a while he had worked in various departments as a clerk. "It was pretty dull work but if a man cannot get through the dullness he won't get places. It is a sort of negative test. I had a hunch it would be interesting once I got through the apprenticeship."

He was right. In 1953 he was sent to the United States and Canada. Two years later, after his return, he was made a managing director (the official term for "partner") at the age of twenty-seven. It was implied that he would be a "very junior partner," not allowed to do much. That suited him well. He was still uncertain in his own mind as to what the business was really about. And he was still inexperienced. The partners in the room talked in half-sentences as men will do who assume that everybody else knows what it is all about. Important decisions were made, apparently quite casually, based often on precedent and parallel which were unknown to the very junior partner. A great deal that was done was entirely different from anything he had ever learned or seen in the routine of the office. His hunch had been right. There had been much dull routine on the lower level but there was never any routine at the top.

The partner thinks he came in at the right time. "Practically ever since the last war, there has been a boom. One touches wood all the time. There have been very few big crashes—people are getting more affluent and business has been profitable. But one can always lose money in this game. We have, for example, a branch in Liverpool whose business is based on the cotton trade. Suppose one of our clients suddenly makes a mistake and gets over-extended. He may have been let down by a supplier, he may just have over-traded, he may have been deliberately gambling. In any case, he probably has no large resources, and one can wind up losing the money one has lent him all too easily. In the City everybody knows everybody else which is a great advantage in doing business quickly, and also a disadvantage—it is easy to become too conservative. There are no written rules for doing good business. In the old days, when a client came to see his banker, the skill of the merchant banker was based on good information and good judgment. Today, the merchant banker more often goes out to see his client; and with the diversity and speed of modern communications there are no longer many exclusive sources of information. Judgment, therefore, becomes more important all the time. You must be a judge of people—if you make a mistake about a man, you lose. And when you lose, you can lose heavily."

BANKER'S BANKER

The image of Barings is clearly reflected by the firm's senior partner and managing director. Sir Edward James Reid, second Baronet and a godson of King Edward VII, is a merchant banker by inheritance *and* vocation. "If I were asked to decide what I should rather have done in my life, I don't really believe I should change it in any way," he said recently. His friends call him "a banker's banker." He was elected chairman of the Accepting Houses Committee (which is the inner circle of the City's merchant banks), President of the Institute of Bankers, and Commissioner of Income Tax for the City of London.

Sir Edward Reid's mother was a daughter of the first Lord Revelstoke ("You can do all the business in the world if you do it for nothing"). He joined Barings in 1922, worked in Hamburg, New York and in Barings' Liverpool branch. It was the era of big commercial credits when the merchant bankers financed international trade. Barings' business concerned a large share of American imports, the imports of wool from Australia, rubber from Ceylon, tinned salmon from Japan. The firm still has many friendly connections in America and on the Continent. It has never had a branch in the United States but has preferred to work there with well-established local firms.

Things have changed a lot in Sir Edward's time. Americans no longer borrow in London. American coffee imports from Brazil are now financed by dollar credits, not sterling.

"Our friends abroad used to trust us more than their own governments," Sir Edward says wistfully. "But when exchange controls were set up, faceless bureaucrats appeared between our customers and us. In some places, like Kenya and Tanganyika, the joint-stock banks now provide the finance. In India, British industry increased its investment by setting up branch factories."

In the early 1920's, Barings was approached for a loan by the Czechoslovak government. No one in the City wanted to take a chance with the young countries that had grown out of chaos and confusion in Central Europe. Barings decided, in conjunction with Rothschilds and Schroders, "to help bring back Central Europe." There is a sense of idealism in almost every great merchant banker. Sometimes idealism proves to be good investment advice.

Few people in London were able to pronounce the name of the infant state, "Československá Republika," and hardly anyone knew Dr. Eduard Beneš, Czechoslovakia's Prime (and Foreign) Minister. When the Hon. Arthur Villiers drove up with Dr. Beneš in front of the Bank of England, where parking was forbidden even in those days, a policeman materialized out of thin air and asked them to move the car. Knowing that special concessions in this respect were allowed to V.I.P.'s visiting the Governor of the Bank, Sir Arthur explained that this was the official car of the Prime Minister of Czechoslovakia.

"The policeman laughed—must have thought that this was something out of Gilbert and Sullivan," Sir Edward remembers.

Of the £ 10,000,000 Czechoslovak State Loan of 1922, £ 4,650,000 was issued in London, £ 800,000 in Amsterdam, and $23,250,000 in New York. The London *tranche*, at eight per cent ("expensive," admits Sir Edward) was offered for 96½. Czechoslovakia, grateful to Barings for its help in the country's early, hard days, kept up the payments until 1959. Then the Communist government defaulted on interest payments for the loan, of which £240,000 was still outstanding.

Barings sent a letter, and another one. No answer. It sent telegrams which remained unanswered too. Individuals sometimes act that way but it is hard to believe that governments may behave like ill-mannered children. At last, Sir Edward Reid took a plane to Prague. There he stepped out into a strange, Kafka-esque world. He couldn't find anybody in the bureaucratic labyrinths on both banks of the Vltava River who knew or admitted to know anything about the 1922 State Loan. The Loan didn't seem to exist. Maybe it had never existed.

Sir Edward had several interviews with officials of both the Ministry of Finance and the State Bank but they were "entirely unsatisfactory." An official admitted finally that the Czechoslovak government still owed £240,000 in respect of the unpaid bonds still remaining in the hands of the public. He told Sir Edward they had plenty of money available to pay these bonds but said that they were not going to pay their debts to "the capitalists in the City of London." To the official the loan was not a matter of business but rather of dialectical materialism.

Sir Edward Reid still shakes his head in bewilderment when he recalls the strange conversation. Really! That the government of a once proud nation would risk the loss of its financial reputation for a paltry two hundred thousand pounds is, of course, inconceivable to the godson of King Edward VII. Sir Edward Reid just wasn't on the same wavelength with the people in Prague. He might as well have been on a distant planet. He was relieved to arrive at London Airport where most people still believe in paying their debts.

Through the help of the British government, Barings finally got seventy-five per cent of the Czechoslovak debt. The Communists took an impish delight in withholding twenty-five per cent from those British capitalists. It is highly improbable that they will ever get a loan from Barings, or from any other merchant banker in the City.

Sir Edward finds it more pleasant to reminisce about the Hong Kong Bank story. Barings has old connections with this bank. Sir Edward is chairman of the British and Chinese Corporation, and a member of the London Committee of the Hong Kong and Shanghai Banking Corporation, which issues its own notes in Hong Kong. When the Japanese occupied Hong Kong in 1941, they found that the Chinese would not accept the occupation currency that the Japanese had printed. Then they found almost ten million pounds' worth of unsigned notes in the bank's safe. The Japanese seized these notes and forced the British managers to sign them.

After the war, these notes were outstanding, as well as those which had been genuinely issued. The Chinese knew the numbers of the so-called "duress" notes which were traded at lower prices than the others. Eventually the question came up of what to do about these "duress" notes. It was a delicate, complicated matter involving the Colonial Office and the bank, and long discussions took place. Sir Edward Reid took part in these discussions and his view was very definite.

"We must honor these notes," he said. "They are genuine notes although they have been illegally issued."

"But won't that mean that the speculators will make a profit?" asked a British government official.

"If they speculated on the Hong Kong Bank fulfilling its obligations they deserve to make a profit," was Sir Edward's answer. Exactly what a London merchant banker would have said, according to Walter Bagehot, and it settled the matter.

Sir Edward Reid is an old hand at international financial complications. In 1934 the Germans defaulted on the foreign long-term debt. Later agreements were reached between the British and German governments over the servicing of the debt. Sir Edward was asked by the London paying agents of German loans, the Council of Foreign Bondholders and the Bank of England, to go to Berlin to negotiate arrangements. Great patience was needed to come to an arrangement. Mutual confidence was established on "a technical level"; there were two texts, English and German, and the experts had to agree on an exact translation. This was a technical problem which appealed to the thoroughgoing German mind. And it improved Sir Edward's knowledge of the German language considerably. After the war, Sir Edward was Chairman of the British Banking Committee for German Affairs and represented the London bankers at the difficult negotiations regarding Germany's prewar debts. The negotiations came to a successful conclusion. The German debts were being repaid in full.

In the Baring archives there is a thick folder with the prospectuses of all the foreign loans which Barings underwrote. A colorful collection that begins with loans to South America (that eventually led to the Baring crisis) and continues with loans to France, Germany, Belgium, Austria, Hungary, India, Iraq, Egypt, Italy, Japan, Portugal, South Africa and Turkey. The last loan before the First World War was a Belgian government issue. There follows a long interval until 1921 when the State of São Paulo Loan was issued. Loans for the Paris-Lyon-Méditerranée Railway, Brazil and Peru followed. The profitable loan business ended completely in the 1930's. The hazards of granting credit to foreign countries had become too great. Many merchant bankers suffered heavy losses. Barings no longer participated in such ventures.

Today government agencies provide the financial assistance that was once given to foreign countries by the merchant bankers of London. Like all other merchant banks Barings now finances mainly British industry. Occasionally, a foreign loan is issued. Last year Barings, in conjunction with their old friends the Rothschilds, Schroders and some banks on the Continent, launched a dollar loan for their old friend, Portugal.

THE GOVERNOR

One of the important Barings in our century was John, the second Baron Revelstoke, who joined the firm during the crisis of 1890, later took his father's place, and at the age of thirty-five was appointed a director of the Bank of England. He was a close friend of Montague Norman, a longtime governor. In 1929, Lord Revelstoke was one of the two British delegates at the Reparations Conference in Paris. (The German emissaries were Dr. Carl Melchior, of M. M. Warburg & Co., and Dr. Hjalmar Schacht.) On the last day of

the Conference, just after it had been decided to set up the
Bank for International Settlements, Lord Revelstoke died of a
heart attack.

The Barings have always served their country well. Evelyn
Baring, later the first Earl of Cromer, was Consul General to
Egypt in the early days of this century when Egypt was still
a colony of the Ottoman Empire. During the Second World
War, Sir Edward Peacock, a Barings partner, was entrusted
by the British government with the difficult task of liquidating British fixed assets in the United States, prior to the
passage of the Lend-Lease Act. Whenever important decisions are made in the no-man's-land between politics and
finance, chances are that a Baring is around. Until 1966
George Rowland Stanley Baring, the third Earl of Cromer,
was the hundred and thirteenth Governor of the Bank of
England. He was forty-three when he was appointed, the
youngest governor in the past two hundred years. In the City
of London many people still consider youth synonymous with
lack of experience and old age with wisdom. Lord Cromer's
appointment was much more revolutionary than the election
of John F. Kennedy as President of the United States, also at
the age of forty-three. In America youth is considered the
greatest asset of all.

Lord Cromer, a man of ability and charm, led the Bank of
England through a difficult period. He emerged as the keeper
of his nation's financial conscience and got himself in trouble
with the Labor government when he sounded solemn warnings against "indulging ourselves" by "an enlargement of
Governmental spending." During the 1964 crisis of the pound
sterling he kept a cool head and managed to raise, with
substantial help from the top officials of the Federal Reserve
Bank in New York, three billion dollars in twenty-four hours,
by making emergency telephone calls to the central banks of
eleven nations. One banker, according to the *New York
Times,* "was reached in a Turkish bath."

The golden days are over. Baring Brothers no longer acts
as agent for many foreign governments. Instead it deals in
acceptance credit, new issues, performs advising and investment services—it advises the pension funds of some of the
largest companies—and performs all conventional banking
services. The bank's professional ethics are very strict. Cer-

tain things might be done by certain merchant bankers but not by Barings.

"It is difficult to be explicit about this," a partner says. "The whole question is very much a matter of feel. The great thing in this business is to be right at least fifty-one per cent of the time."

SIEGMUND GEORGE WARBURG   141

4

Warburg: The Nonconformist

*"Progress in thinking is
progress towards simplicity."*
Siegmund George Warburg

SIEGMUND George Warburg is the most discussed and
least advertised among the great merchant bankers of
London. The City's gossip-filled bazaars reverberate with the
faint echoes of glorification and suspicion. No banker is more
glorified and more suspected than S. G. Warburg. His friends
admire him; his enemies distrust him; no one remains
indifferent at the mention of his name. The London *Sunday
Times* has called him "the postwar wonder of merchant
banking." Anthony Sampson, in *Anatomy of Britain*, names
Warburg "the most spectacular newcomer in the City." And
the *Statist* declared in 1961, "It would be hard to find in New
York a close parallel to the Warburg . . . success story."

An immigrant of relatively recent vintage who set up his
merchant bank as late as 1946, S. G. Warburg is considered
something of an upstart in the City's ultra-conservative
partners' rooms where some people may not remember that
their ancestors were upstarts once. Being very successful
makes Warburg only more suspect to the City's Old Guard
who like to forget how suspect *their* forefathers were to
British society in the early nineteenth century.

Whatever people may say about Warburg, and they say a
lot, they agree that he has done very much very fast. He
arrived in London one day in 1934 with less than five
thousand pounds to his name—admittedly a great, old name,
respected in the citadels of international *haute finance*, a
name carrying tradition and prestige which is an asset in

128

itself. In 1964, the profits of Mercury Securities Limited, S. G. Warburg's holding company, were about £2,300,000 before taxes. Mercury owns the whole equity of S. G. Warburg & Co., his banking subsidiary, and a diversified empire of enterprises ranging from insurance and metals to advertising and market research.

The Warburg legend has created the image of a dynamic, aggressive financial genius and go-getter who streamlined and modernized merchant banking, is said to never have lost a take-over battle, plunges with gusto into City fights, handles big international deals, commutes between London, the Continent and New York, is listened to respectfully in Whitehall and Washington, launches new companies, is always surrounded by secretaries and satellites, dictates while he is being driven out to the airport or on his way to the next appointment, casually makes telephone calls involving millions of dollars. And so on.

There is some truth in the legend but not the whole truth. The real Warburg emerges as a somewhat different man—diffident, doubting, soft-spoken, slightly stooped, with dark hair, a sensitive forehead, melancholy brown eyes, a melodious voice. He looks like, and might well be, a poet or philosopher. He reads Greek and Latin and often quotes in the classical languages. Speaking of a brilliant friend driven by impatience, Warburg was recently heard to say, "He is a man who doesn't know the difference between *kairos* and *chronos*." Such sentences puzzled his acquaintances, most of whom didn't know the difference themselves. *Kairos* is the right time; *chronos* is time in the abstract sense. Even Warburg's banking associates are often puzzled when he admits being prouder of his thorough knowledge of the classics, and of English and German literature, than of his widely admired skill in banking. Warburg is probably the only man in the City of London who has read Thomas Mann's *Dr. Faustus* three times—truly a feat of emotional discipline and intellectual endurance.

If this should give some people the idea that Warburg is a dreamer who lives in the clouds he will quickly set them straight. His associates say that he is just being practical: he considers a working knowledge of Greek and Latin a better preparation for merchant banking than a study of modern finance, management technique and economics.

"Classical education is a wonderful thing," Warburg has said. "It helps you to develop logical thinking and to perceive quickly and accurately what you read." He emphatically opposes the widespread belief that to think deeply means to think in a complicated way. "Deep" authors are often respectfully read and rarely understood. Obscurity is taken for profundity, ambiguity for wisdom. Warburg feels that symbolism is greatly overestimated these days and he quotes Kafka's definition, "A symbol is something that can be expressed only through a symbol and nothing else." Simplicity combined with thoroughness has helped Warburg more than anything else in life. "To think deeply means to think lucidly," he says. His motto is reflected by his words inscribed on his Ex Libris label, "Progress in thinking is progress towards simplicity."

Warburg has strong opinions about what to read and what to ignore. He reads books on history and philosophy; he loves good fiction and good poetry. He avoids business publications and ignores most newspapers. He used to read a lot of newspapers before the war but came to the conclusion that "newspaper reading leads to a gradual loss of memory since most people read the paper with the subconscious wish of trying to forget as fast as possible what they read." An interesting theory that may yet be scientifically proven some day. The very sight, and the weight, of America's Sunday papers are apt to frighten visitors to these shores who are not used to America's wealth (and waste). Warburg solves his newspaper problem by glancing quickly over the index, and discarding the rest. He allots himself ten minutes a day of index-glancing for the perusal of the leading newspapers from England, the Continent and America. Warburg's friends claim that this alone proves his wisdom. He spends many pleasant weekends reading and rereading the books he loves. He keeps his favorite authors on special shelves in his London apartment. When he goes to his secluded villa near Grosseto, Italy, his car is always filled with books.

People often ask Warburg how a modern, successful merchant banker can get along without a thorough, daily study of contemporary politics, economics and finance. He may shrug in his quiet way and answer, "I keep my ears open. People tell me everything that's important."

Such unorthodox views are characteristic of Warburg, who

is an enthusiastic nonconformist. Warburg wants to be right and he doesn't mind being different. In his scheme of things, theory and practice must always mesh. The life of the nonconformist is not always easy in modern society. Warburg doesn't mind paying the high price of unconventionality. He is quite certain that some potential clients who might otherwise have come to S. G. Warburg & Co. did not do so because they know Warburg to be an outspoken nonconformist.

Warburg often startles young men who come down from Oxford or Cambridge to be interviewed for a job, by asking, "Would you dare speak up against everybody if you didn't agree with them, or would you remain silent? Would you go it alone, be an outspoken nonconformist?" Quite a few of the candidates, mindful of the trends of faceless uniformity and uncritical adjustment in modern business life, give the wrong answer so far as Warburg is concerned.

The atmosphere at S. G. Warburg & Co. is distinctly nonsycophantic. Warburg does not like to be surrounded by yes-men. He has the quiet authority of the natural leader, the determination of the born executive, and he is boss in his bank, the master of his ship—a well-built ship with crisis-tight compartments and the latest safety devices to make it financially as unsinkable as possible. The crew is well trained, enthusiastic, hard-working and, by the competitors' almost unanimous consensus, brilliant.

There is a saying in publishing circles that "everybody has at least one book in him." Warburg has two books in him and he hopes to write them some day. One, which he calls "The Businessman's Book of Quotations," will be the outgrowth of his interest in epigrams. He collects and writes them all the time. Samples of Warburg epigrams: "Influence is more important than power. This applies both to nations and individuals." Or, "Life and imagination are in continuous conflict with each other. Imagination tears the material elements of life to pieces and creates a world beyond us which is in opposition to the world around us."

Warburg's second book, tentatively called "Education of the Adult," will deal with his favorite thesis that self-education relatively late in life is far more important than school education early in life. He is concerned about higher education in the Western world where many establishments of

advanced learning have become educational factories with
pedagogic assembly lines, turning out the latest student
models—students less concerned with acquiring knowledge
than with getting their degree. Warburg's interest in education, both in the sciences and the arts, has led to his generous
support of the Weizmann Institute of Sciences, in Rehovoth,
Israel.

Warburg is a man of many paradoxes. He loves tender
poetry and tough banking deals. He has not much hope in
the ultimate future of capitalism but leads his forces in
dramatic City battles with infectious confidence. He surveys
the state of the world with Schopenhauer-like gloom but feels
the West must fight on with firm determination. He is
sensitive about criticism in public but not in his own shop.
He is amused by occasional parodies which a staff member
writes about intramural goings-on at the bank.

Men of talent are often complex and hard to understand.
Warburg's complexity is heightened by much internal
conflict. Although he appears very sure of himself he cares
very much about what others think of him. He is said to be
dominating but his closest associates know that his dominating attitude is provoked by the wish of doing the best for
others. He knows the importance of publicity but gives orders
to avoid personal publicity. Mercury Securities owns, among
other companies, an interest in a successful advertising
agency in London but Warburg makes a sharp distinction
between his business and his private life. He was one of the
first people in Britain to perceive the future of commercial
television, and advised Associated Television, Britain's second
largest network, which is known for its "half American feel,"
as Sampson calls it, and for its close relations with American
programs. But Warburg rarely looks at TV himself.

He does not like to be interviewed. In fact, he agreed to
the exception in this case only after he had established a
rapport with this writer, and was assured that his story was
going to be one in a series about the world's great merchant
bankers, and that his was not the first that had been written.
Only then was he able to be convinced that there could not
be any possible suspicion of his seeking personal publicity.
That very day the London papers had headlines on their
front pages about a City battle in which Warburg figured
prominently.

YOUTH AND THE TEAM SPIRIT

Warburg's command post and the headquarters of S. G. Warburg & Co. are at 30, Gresham Street, London E.C. 2, just a short walk from the Bank of England. Merchant bankers never like to stray far away from the Old Lady of Threadneedle Street. Warburg's organization reflects his innermost belief in youth and the team spirit. "Youth" to Warburg means just that—men in their late twenties. He collects able young people with the same enthusiasm that other rich men show for old paintings. Of the firm's ten executive directors four are in their early thirties. The average age of the top people is well below forty—which makes S. G. Warburg & Co. in every respect the world's youngest merchant bank. Warburg calls youth "the greatest strength of our firm." (He rarely talks of himself, always of the firm, avoids the word "I" in favor of "we.") His son works as an accountant—but not at S. G. Warburg & Co. His father tolerates no nepotism.

Warburg's other creed is the team spirit. Ever since he entered the Warburg family bank in Hamburg as a trainee in the twenties, he has had definite ideas about the team he was going to build. The ideas have matured without any basic changes. In his statement of March 31, 1964, as retiring chairman of Mercury Securities, Warburg said:

My belief is that the priority task for private enterprise is to build up competent management teams. If we want to develop management teams with strong vitality and dynamism it is not sufficient to engage a group of individuals of good character and ability, nor is it sufficient in itself to mould them into a well-knit unit and to inspire them with courage and team-spirit. It is, above all, necessary continuously to change and develop the composition of such a team and especially to rejuvenate it. It is part of this process that the older members of the team must gradually move from the foreground to positions backstage and to advisory functions, making room for the younger members of the team to take over the lead in policy and management.

Warburg has dismissed people—unhappily and politely, pointing out that it may be better to part "in our mutual interest"—because they didn't get along with the team. He always reminds his older associates that it is their primary duty to act as a sounding board for the ideas of the younger men. Elderly executives who are not willing to give the younger people the benefit of their accumulated experience may find themselves in trouble with the master of the ship. A Warburg epigram says, "In order to build a good team of men the head of the team must in critical moments not only support the members of the team but must protect them." Teamwork is a two-way street at Warburgs. The members of the team can give their best knowing they are not only supported but even protected. They can also take a hint from another Warburg epigram, "The highest degrees of human potency are reached in enthusiasm, on the one hand, and in suffering, on the other." Team members at 30, Gresham Street admit that they've gone through very high degrees of human potency.

Obviously Warburg is a born teacher and never stops tutoring. He introduced what some people in the City call "the nursery principle" at his bank. One of the younger men must always be present at all important meetings. Afterwards he is asked to write a lengthy memorandum of the meeting. Often Warburg himself corrects the wording, as carefully as a professor going over his students' homework.

Warburg expects everybody to be as punctual, meticulous and well organized as he is. He freely delegates authority in big matters and shows himself as a man of vision and scope, but at the same time he can be pedantic about detail, a weakness that may be inherited from his German-Jewish ancestors. "Siegmund," says a famous merchant banker, "is the mixture of Jewish dynamism and German thoroughness—an unbeatable combination in modern merchant banking." Warburg fondly remembers one of his uncles, back in Germany, who used to say, *Der liebe Gott wohnt im Detail*"— the good Lord lives in the detail.

At S. G. Warburg & Co. every verbal promise, every telephone conversation, every oral statement must be confirmed later in writing. This is not due to any lack of trust on Warburg's part. On the contrary: his associates complain that he trusts people far too much. Only lately, at the repeated urging of his wife, he has become accustomed, on his frequent travels and in hotels rooms, to keep his attaché case with confidential papers locked. He likes people too much to be security-minded.

Warburg cannot stand incompetence of any kind, has no patience with people who don't know their job. Usually a mild-mannered man, he can get very irritated by a clerk at the airline's ticket counter fumbling with the vouchers. His serenity may be badly shattered by a sloppy waiter. His secretaries earn their money the hard way. Any letter containing a minor typing mistake or an unclear sentence must be retyped. Warburg is a fast reader who notices the slightest fault. He is very strict about clarity of style and lucidity of expression. Some people call this German *Gründlichkeit* (thoroughness). But the Germans are rarely lucid; many times they are merely vague when they try to appear deep; clarity of style is not at a premium among them.

Warburg was pleased when a director of the Bank of England once told him that he wrote better letters than many born-and-bred Englishmen. He is terrified at the mere thought of the gifted dilettantism and "ingenious sloppiness" that are widespread in the City. At Warburgs nothing is ever left to chance. He never loses a big battle because he is always prepared meticulously for victory. That doesn't mean that he doesn't have his failures. Most of them result from too much wishful or superficial thinking about human characters and their reliability.

Warburg's organization works almost with the precision of a Swiss watch. There is no touch of amateurism. This new attitude of tough and thorough professionalism is beginning to affect some of the older houses. Bankers now rely more on memoranda than memory, work longer hours, even talk shop during the once sacred lunch ritual.

"A PESSIMIST SURROUNDED BY RISKS"

Warburg is superstitious, always afraid of provoking the wrath of the gods—possibly the psychological aftereffect of his Greek education. He walks through life like a character in a Greek tragedy, forever expecting the worst to happen, the last man in the dead center of a hurricane, continually amazed that he is still alive. The frightful sound of the Erinyes is always in his inner ear—especially when all goes well. *That,* he feels, is the moment when one must watch out for the danger signals. As a banker, he is "a pessimist surrounded by risks." But there are degrees of pessimism. Warburg is a "white" or cheerful pessimist, not a "black" or even a "gray" one. His premonition of disaster is balanced by his faith in God and his fellow men.

He rarely enjoys the fruits of victory. After twenty-four hours, while his associates are still celebrating, Warburg is worrying again. At the beginning of a big transaction he always asks, "But what are we going to do if it doesn't work out?" He tells his associates that they must learn to listen to "hints of fate," and to react accordingly. He himself has learned "by painful experience" in the early 1930's in Germany that people in the banking world often foresee a crisis but do nothing about it.

When Warburg is away from his London headquarters, which happens frequently nowadays, he receives every day a large envelope with two files. In each file there are several mimeographed lists. File Number 1 contains the Management Mail and Memoranda List which mentions every conversation and important telephone call inside the bank, every incoming and outgoing letter, cable and other communication, with initials indicating the names of the executives who were assigned to the case and of those reading copies of the mail. The Management Mail and Memoranda List is the most important document of all. The file also contains press clippings of the day; a list showing all bonds and stocks bought or sold; minutes of the daily 9:15 A.M. meeting; possibly the minutes of the weekly investment meeting; a list titled Secret Memoranda; the travel schedules of all directors and top executives who happen to be away from London; a list of all luncheons given at the bank, with the names of guests; a list of all New Accounts; and the Daily Statement.

File Number 2 contains a list of Companies to be Kept Under Review; a list called Current Propositions (brief résumés of all pending matters); a list aptly titled Personnel Problems; a list of all Volunteer Trainees at the Bank (particularly close to Warburg's heart strongly beating for youth); and, finally, a list of all Money Dealings.

After glancing through his files, no matter where he is,

Warburg knows exactly what happened yesterday (or the day before) at his bank in London. This knowledge gives him a comforting sense of security and a pleasant feeling of good organization. He reads his lists as a conductor reads his scores. They are the blueprint of his creative thinking and inspire him to try new, imaginative feats in the artistry of finance. (He compares such feats to surgical operations or theatrical productions.) To him his lists are tangible proof, daily renewed, of the smoothly functioning mechanism of the team that he built and perfected in hard years of tutoring and training.

The team is a group of about twenty men who work as closely together as the members of a chamber-music group. Each member knows at any given moment what the others are doing, just as a good chamber-music player knows not only his part but also the parts of all his fellow players. The team is held together by "enthusiasm and suffering" and by loyalty, "the steel girders of the organization," and by the team's devotion to the master of the ship. There are bound to be invisible high-tension wires between able, ambitious people. Warburg cannot cut the wires but he tolerates no short circuit and remains the final arbiter when the fuses blow.

The team and several specialists—about thirty people in all —meet every morning at 9:15. During the meeting, which rarely lasts longer than half an hour, every important current transaction is reviewed, and all activities inside the bank are coordinated. Nowadays Warburg rarely attends the meeting —after years of training he feels that "they can get along without me"—but he carefully reads the minutes just the same.

New ideas which Warburg calls the bloodstream of a merchant bank" are informally discussed among the top executives and tested at the daily meeting. There is no "partners' room" at 30, Gresham Street, as in many of the City's older merchant banks. The senior directors have their own (small) offices. But the *esprit de corps* makes up for the physical contact of the conference room.

The Warburg organization is dominated by "the rule of four," a Warburg invention. In each important transaction four people must represent S. G. Warburg & Co.—one director and his deputy, and one chief executive and his deputy. In less important deals at least two people must be present. Warburg himself is not excluded from the rule. When he travels, usually alone, another member of the team joins him at his meetings.

THE CONTINENTAL INFLUENCE

Siegmund Warburg's emotional and intellectual makeup is dominated by three factors. First: he feels deeply as a European, and this is probably the reason that as an émigré he chose London rather than New York as the basis for his new life although he had strong family connections in Wall Street. Second: he is definitely the product of the ethical and intellectual heritage of his Jewish ancestors. Third: he never forgets that he was brought up in southern Germany. He feels at home in London and loves the City with its bizarre tribal customs. He became naturalized in 1939—his application was sponsored by several prominent merchant bankers— but never attempts to pose as a "genuine" Englishman in the manner of many who came a little late. He speaks correct English with an unmistakable German accent and doesn't try to hide it. He has close friends among the leaders of the City. He is fond of the English—and puzzled by their inscrutable ways. Inscrutable to a man from Central Europe.

There is, for instance, the predilection of the English for playing dumb. Warburg affectionately remembers an elder merchant-banking statesman, long dead, who would listen to one of Warburg's proposals and then would ask him, with a perfectly straight face but with that certain twinkle in his eyes, "Now do you *really* believe we should do it, Siegmund?" Actually the old fox, as Warburg knew well, had already made up his mind to do it.

Siegmund delights in asking his English friends embarrassing questions, and watching their reaction. There is often a long, slightly uncomfortable pause, and then the friend will say, "Well, Siegmund—let's cross that bridge when we come to it." At S. G. Warburg & Co. such answerers are called "bridge-crossers." Or he will tease his friends with the sort of question only a foreigner would ask, and is told, "Well . . . very interesting . . . there we are." End of conversation.

Warburg does not believe in the virtue of English understatement. His English associates often feel that he tends toward the other extreme—Continental overstatement. They are often disturbed by his tendency to step on highly sensitive English toes and implore him not to tell people the awful truth.

"No matter how tactfully you talk to them, you are bound to offend them," they say to Warburg.

He pays no attention to such admonitions. In Warburg's world there are two groups of people. One group (to which he belongs) wants to do everything right, even at the risk of an occasional conflict. "Many American and Scottish people belong to this group. The other group which includes many prominent City figures is so anxious to avoid any unpleasantness that they may occasionally do the wrong thing in order to circumvent conflict."

Warburg believes in strong praise and strong criticism—things that are "not done" in the City. He lavishly commends people for a job well done and mercilessly reprimands them for a failure. Where an Englishman will say, at the most, "I'm afraid, old boy, I don't quite agree with you," Warburg disagrees dramatically with the old boy. He is perturbed by the low standards of secrecy in the City, which is always filled with rumors, like any big marketplace. He holds a theory, based on the study of various psychologists, that gossip is a compensation for sexual incompetency. A serious study on the relationship between Bank Rate and libido may be overdue. There is less secrecy and more secret-sharing in today's merchant banks than ever before. In the old days the Barings, the Rothschilds, the Schroders, the Morgan Grenfells, the Hambros, the Lazards kept their secrets to themselves, and used them to their advantage. Warburg remembers his maternal grandfather's saying that there are three degrees of secrecy: in the first, a man promises to keep something to himself, but tells his wife; in the second, he doesn't tell the secret even to his wife; in the third, when he is reminded of the matter three years later, he no longer remembers that he ever heard of it before.

Among Warburg's favorite epigrams is the advice of an old friend, "Don't ever think of what you want to put into a letter—think only about the answer you might get to it." Another friend once told him, "Your strength in business is that you don't change your coat when you leave your home, you are always the same man." And he never forgets what

Felix Deutsch, once the head of AEG, said at the grave of the murdered German statesman Walter Rathenau, "Each man has the shortcomings of his merits but few have the merits of their shortcomings."

There is no doubt that the Continental influence is very strong at S. G. Warburg & Co. Young Englishmen have been known to arrive in traditional style, wearing bowlers and carrying umbrellas, but soon divest themselves of such paraphernalia of City conservatism. Some of them are quite surprised when the chairman of the board expresses a lively interest in their private affairs. Warburg feels that a man's private life affects his efficiency in business. They also note that he believes in giving a man a second chance (he has had some very good results with this theory) and harbors no grudges. They may not know that Warburg forgives, but never forgets, a mistake; that he won't mention an unpleasant experience, but cannot erase it from his memory.

A fellow merchant banker, Lionel Fraser, the former chairman of Helbert Wagg (now merged with Schroder and known as J. Henry Schroder Wagg & Co.) writes in his autobiography, *All to the Good*, "I admire Siegmund Warburg not only for his courage in starting a new life in this country and making an unqualified success of it, but for an almost monastic indifference to passing pleasures which seems to endow him with an unusual appreciation of the intangible, yet very real, things in life. I rate him high in the international banking fraternity."

Warburg discourages any attempt at show. He has never owned a Rolls Royce or a Bentley, once talked one of his directors out of buying one. Too conspicuous. He owns neither a yacht nor a town house. He breeds no racehorses, raises no orchids, shoots no grouse. In London, Warburg and his wife entertain ("more than we really like") in their apartment in Belgravia's Eaton Square. The apartment is furnished in quiet taste. The place is filled with books. They are everywhere—in the hall, in the drawing room, in Warburg's ascetic bedroom—a modern version of a Trappist monk's cell. The books are arranged according to languages and Warburg's preferences. Warburg likes to be with stimulating people and loves the forgotten art of conversation. His minimum standards of both stimulating people and good conversation are rather high.

Mrs. Warburg, the former Eva Maria Philipson, a slim, elegant woman of quiet charm, comes from an old Jewish banking family in Stockholm, Sweden. (The Warburgs, like the Rothschilds, are known as a Jewish house in the City, but on the board of S. G. Warburg & Co. Gentiles outnumbered Jews.) Mrs. Warburg passed the all-important test during their early years of exile when she told her husband more than once that if worse came to worst they would live in a two-room apartment with their two children, then six and three years old. Worse never came to worst. Warburg still discusses all important matters with her and frequently quotes her advice when he makes a decision.

Like many people who spent their early childhood years in comfortable circumstances and later lost their possessions, Warburg is relaxed about the attributes of wealth. He doesn't care much about food and drink, "stays with a dish" for days; on a recent trip to Frankfurt am Main he ordered boiled beef five days in succession. He doesn't experiment in food, only in banking. He says, "If orange juice were as expensive as champagne, people would serve it at elaborate parties." Orange juice is probably healthier than champagne, and Warburg strongly believes in the Healthy Life. Every second year he spends ten days or so in an expensive sanatorium in England where he pays a lot of money for a massage and a few glasses of orange juice a day. To ban the pangs of hunger, he plays bridge with his wife who diets with him though she doesn't need it. He loses ten pounds of weight and unspecified amounts of toxin, and feels happy and rejuvenated for the rigors of modern banking life, more boiled beef and an occasional glass of wine.

Money per se has no attraction for him. He remembers his grandfather, the late Siegmund Warburg, who said, "It was the Warburgs' good fortune that whenever we were about to get very rich something would happen and we became poor and had to start all over again."

A TALE OF SEVERAL CITIES

A great many things have happened since 1798 when the brothers Moses Marcus and Gerson Warburg founded M. M. Warburg & Co. in Hamburg. Actually the family's banking tradition is much older and goes back to one Simon von Cassel, a sixteenth-century ancestor who was a pawnbroker and money-dealer. (The prefix "von" has merely a geographic, not aristocratic, meaning; it denotes that Simon came *von* or from Cassel.) In 1559 Simon obtained permission to settle in the Westphalian town of Warburg from which the family later took its name. (Warburg, population 9500, is known for a twelfth-century "double church" with a Romanesque foundation, and a thirteenth-century church, St.-Maria-in-vinea.) This gives the Warburgs a clear historical lead over such early merchant-banking upstarts as the Barings who began their activities as late as 1717 in Exeter, and over the Rothschilds who became court factors to His Serene Highness Prince William, Landgrave of Hesse Cassel, and started doing business only after 1785.

Some Warburgs were known to have lived in the sixteenth century in Altona, near Hamburg. Altona was at that time under Danish rule. There the Jews—who gained full rights as citizens in Hamburg only in 1849—were allowed to be active as merchants and shipowners. One of the Altona Warburgs, Marcus Gumprich Warburg, moved in 1773 to Hamburg where the situation had become a little easier for Jewish merchants and bankers. He was the father of the two brothers who founded M. M. Warburg & Co.

Their timing wasn't very good. The year before, in 1797, the Bank of England had stopped its cash payments. Hamburg's trade in commercial bills had suddenly expanded, which created grave credit risks. Like London, Hamburg owes its commercial prominence to its port which then connected northern Europe with the Atlantic and the Mediterranean, and made Hamburg a fine base for merchant adventurers and bold entrepreneurs. Hamburg's status as a neutral, free city was another big asset. In time of war, Hamburg's merchants could, and did, trade with all belligerent parties. This aspect of neutrality has not changed in our day and makes neutrals suspect to others, who would like very much to be neutral themselves.

The new bank was less than one year old when, in 1799, the boom suddenly collapsed. Large overseas supplies had arrived in Portugal, England and Scandinavia, and there were sharp price breaks. In Hamburg alone over a hundred and fifty firms went bankrupt.

The Warburgs had been cautious and rode out the storm. In 1806 the French troops occupied Hamburg and seized some of the more substantial citizens as hostages. Among them was Gerson Warburg who was interned in Rothenburg, a small place in the Lüneburger Heide. According to a cherished Warburg family story, Gerson's brother Moses who had often quarreled with Gerson was rather reluctant to pay the high sum demanded by the French for his brother's release. He had to be severely admonished by the Jewish community before he agreed to redeem his brother. Even then he made a deal with the French and paid much less for Gerson than they had demanded.

In 1814 the French left Hamburg, and immediately the Hamburg Giro Bank began to replenish its silver stocks. M. M. Warburg & Co. helped to provide the silver supplies on which the new Mark Banco currency was based. The Warburgs were already dealing with N. M. Rothschild & Sons in London. In a letter of August 4, 1814, the Warburgs offer gold or louis d'or "for early delivery" and assure the Rothschilds that they are capable of handling business of this kind "as effectively as anybody in Hamburg."

After the death of the brothers the bank was taken over by Moses Marcus's son-in-law Abraham Samuel Warburg who remained in charge until *his* death in 1856. Money-changing and trade bill activities were the foundation of the firm. The Warburgs were the exception among the old merchant bankers: they were *not* merchants before they became bankers.

In 1863 the designation of the firm was changed from *Geldwechsler* (money-changers) to the more elegant title *Bankiers* (bankers). Five years later the *Bankiers* moved to their present address of Ferdinandstrasse 75. These were disturbing times. Prussian power began to threaten the small territory of the Free Hanseatic Town, and some people worried that Hamburg might lose its independent status as Frankfurt did, in 1866.

The firm had acquired great prestige in trading with commercial bills and foreign exchange—typical merchant-banking operations that demanded sound judgment and thorough knowledge. The Warburgs had good intelligence sources and a network of agents. They weathered the crisis of 1842 and the more severe one of 1857 which had started in

America with the failure of the Ohio Life and Trust Company. Its shock waves reached all the way to Hamburg where many merchants and bankers had accepted trade bills not based on genuine transactions. The Warburgs had endorsed many bills that came back to them under protest. There is no evidence that they had to impawn securities or commodities like many other local firms but it was not easy to meet all obligations. They were among the contributors to the "Garantie-Diskonto-Verein von 1857," a fund set up by the Senate of Hamburg to bail out firms in trouble.

By that time the firm was managed by Abraham's widow, Sara, a remarkable woman who piloted the bank through troubled waters, until she was joined by her two sons, Siegmund and Moritz. When Hamburg needed a silver loan of ten million Marks Banco, the Senate approached Prussia. The Prussians said no, and sent Hamburg an insulting answer. Then the Warburgs offered to approach Austria. A sister of Siegmund and Moritz was married to Paul Schiff, director of the Creditanstalt in Vienna. Schiff submitted Hamburg's request to Baron Bruck, the Austrian Minister of Finance. Baron Bruck went to see Emperor Franz Josef I and at once got permission to send a special train with silver ingots to the Hamburg Giro Bank. The silver was never needed and was returned—with interest—six months later to Vienna, the ingots still unpacked. Its mere presence spread calm and confidence in Hamburg and it served its purpose well. The crisis ended quickly.

Hamburg remained grateful to the Habsburgs and to the Warburgs who had engineered the transaction. The Warburgs' prestige increased. They were now known as a serious, reliable house. Both the Habsburgs and the Warburgs enlarged their respective empires through well-planned inter-marriages. The Warburgs became related to the Rosenbergs in Kiev, the Gunzburgs in St. Petersburg, the Oppenheims and the Goldschmidts in Germany. The five sons of Moritz Warburg later became known as the "five Hamburgers." Though less famous than the "five Frankfurters" (the Rothschilds) the Warburgs were doing all right. The oldest, Aby, studied humanities and became the founder of the Kulturwissenschaftliche Bibliothek Warburg, now known as the Warburg Institute, attached to the University of London.

Under Siegmund and Moritz Warburg the bank expanded,

floated loans, helped to set up the big commercial banks that
developed in the big cities of Germany around the turn of the
nineteenth century. Siegmund had close connections with
Baron Lionel von Rothschild in London. In a letter dated
May 31, 1871, the Warburgs ask for a share in the French
loan to be issued by the Rothschilds. The Warburgs had
arrived at the inner circle of international high finance. They
were involved in the second French postwar loan of three
billion francs. Floated by the Rothschilds in 1872, it was
twelve times oversubscribed.

Moritz Warburg, whose maxim was *labor et constantia*,
was a conservative banker. Like the great merchant bankers
of London he preferred to deal with big firms and important
banking correspondents and had no wish to have many
private clients. In 1878 the firm had only sixteen employees.
The offices were small and unpretentious; it was just as in
London, one didn't show one's wealth though one had friendly
connections with Baron Alphonse Rothschild in Paris, Baron
Leopold in London, Baron Albert in Vienna. Moritz's wife
Charlotte wrote her memoirs, as many Warburgs did. She
describes with great charm a journey to the Paris Exhibition
of 1878, and a visit to the Rothschild château at Ferrières,
still the family's famous showplace.

In a historical essay on M. M. Warburg & Co., a Hamburg
sociologist, Eduard Rosenbaum, quotes the advice given to
him in 1921 by Max M. Warburg when they discussed the
project of a history of the firm:

It should be shown [Warburg wrote], and I attach great
value to this, how much the development of such a firm
is governed by chance, and how the economic development anyhow is much more dependent on chance events
and inherent tendencies than on the so-called consciously aimed activities of the individual. The description
should be pervaded by a certain feeling of humility
towards these forces. For most people suffer from exagger-
ated self-esteem, and specially bank managers, when they
write their annual reports three or six months later are
inclined to adorn their actions with a degree of foresight
which in reality never existed.

Among the members of a family whose achievements in art, science and literature are as notable as in banking and commerce, Aby M. Warburg, the "Professor," as he was called, was one of the most gifted. As a young man he had half-jokingly renounced his right to enter the firm and asked his brothers only to support him in his scientific work—to pay for his books, as he put it. This turned out to be quite an expense, as visitors to the Warburg Institute in London will easily realize. Yet the "Professor" was no unworldly dreamer. He had a sort of sixth sense for an approaching financial crisis, the lingering premonition of disaster that never seems to leave his younger relative, S. G. Warburg.

Of the other "five Hamburgers," Max was an entrepreneur whose motto was *en avant*. Paul chose *in serviendo consumor* as his maxim. Paul and Felix were connected through marriage with the New York firm of Kuhn, Loeb and Co., which was then second only to the Morgans as an issuing house in America. The connection gave the Warburgs a special position in the international banking world.

Kuhn, Loeb & Co. had been founded in 1867 by two retired Cincinnati clothing merchants, Abraham Kuhn and Solomon Loeb, with a reputed capital of $500,000. It was a good time to start in business. The Civil War was over. The United States had just purchased Alaska from Russia. The Dominion of Canada had been established. Steel mills were built; telegraph lines went up across the continent; out west railroad crews were laying hundreds of miles of tracks.

Kuhn, Loeb & Co. financed some of the great American railroads. The firm's guiding spirit was Jacob H. Schiff, a Jewish immigrant from Germany. He became a partner in 1875 and spent forty-six years with the firm. He had faith in the country's economic future and realized that a banker's function is, above all, to be ready to help in times of adversity. When the Union Pacific got in serious trouble after the panic of 1893 and its reorganization was said to be impossible, Kuhn, Loeb & Co. achieved the impossible. The reorganization was approved by President McKinley in 1897. The new management was entrusted to Edward H. Harriman. The Union Pacific became so strong that it later acquired control of the Southern Pacific and bought over forty per cent of the shares of the Northern Pacific.

Felix Warburg married Schiff's daughter and joined the

firm. Paul Warburg married the daughter of founder Loeb and moved to New York in 1902. By that time the flow of credit was going in both directions. America was beginning to provide financing for Europe and the Far East. Kuhn, Loeb & Co. floated several Japanese loans during the Russo-Japanese War. The firm's position was established by Schiff who called the Russian (Imperial) government "enemy of mankind" because of its treatment of the Jewish population. When Lord Reading came to New York during the First World War to seek a loan for the British and French governments, Schiff demanded assurances that none of the benefits would pass to the Russian government. The Western Allies were unable to give such a guarantee, and Kuhn, Loeb & Co. withdrew from the sponsorship of the loan, although individual partners, among them Schiff's son, became personal subscribers. Bold individualism was still possible in the conduct of international financial affairs.

They were civic-minded people. Mortimer L. Schiff was president of the Boy Scouts of America. Otto H. Kahn was a power behind the Metropolitan Opera Company. In Felix Warburg's room the walls were lined with filing cabinets relating to his charitable activities. Paul M. Warburg in 1914 accepted an appointment by President Wilson to the Federal Reserve Board.

LA BELLE ÉPOQUE

In Hamburg the years prior to the First World War were *la belle époque* of private *Bankiers*. The balance sheet totals of M. M. Warburg & Co. had been 18,229,494 marks in 1891; 45,832,324 marks in 1900; and 127,325,616 marks in 1914. Warburgs was the leading German banker in the market of commercial bills which sometimes reached the amount of 50,000,000 marks. And they were strong in foreign-exchange. In 1900 Max and Paul Warburg placed a loan of 80,000,000 marks *Reichsschatzscheine* (treasury bonds) in America. Later the firm joined the select *Reichsanleihe-Konsortium*, the inner sanctum of German financiers.

The Hamburg Warburgs were invited by Kuhn, Loeb & Co. to participate in the floating of the Japanese loans which Max Warburg discussed in London with Korekiyo Takahashi, the Japanese delegate. Takahashi later became prime minister and a liberal elder Japanese statesman, and was assassinated in 1936. Warburg called him "the best arithmetician among all the finance ministers I ever met."

The Warburgs were now active all over the world. They took part in loan negotiations for the Chinese State Railways, increased their business with Scandinavia and America, set up a special department trading in copper, tin and lead. The firm survived the First World War and the astronomical inflation that followed in Germany, helped to set up the Hamburger Bank of 1923, which issued its own notes based on gold—and received the gold through the help of the Warburgs. The Hamburger Bank was the first German institute that was granted a dollar credit from the International Acceptance Bank in New York. Its chairman happened to be Paul M. Warburg. Sixty-six years earlier a crisis in Hamburg was ended by the arrival of Austrian silver; this time American dollars did the trick; in both cases the Warburgs had been the intermediaries.

Paul M. Warburg carried through the reorganization of the American banking system with Senator Nelson W. Aldrich. In 1928 the International Acceptance Bank was combined with the Manhattan Bank. Paul M. Warburg remained its chairman.

FULL CIRCLE

The Wall Street crisis of 1929 was felt in Hamburg the following year when depositors were beginning to withdraw large amounts of foreign money. Max Warburg went to New York and talked things over with his brothers Paul and Felix. The New York Warburgs took "a new financial interest" in the Hamburg house. The immediate danger passed. But the crisis deepened when the Austrian Creditanstalt in Vienna collapsed in 1931. Earlier, from December 21, 1930, until December 31, Warburgs had to repay eighty per cent of its foreign and fifty per cent of its German deposits. It is doubtful whether it would have come through without the help of the brothers in New York.

By that time two members of the younger generation had joined the Hamburg firm. Eric M. Warburg, the only son of Max, became a partner in 1929. And Siegmund G. Warburg was a partner from 1930 to 1936 (even after he had emigrated to London).

But the end was near, and the Warburgs knew it. Hitler had come to power. There was no *Lebensraum* in Germany for Jewish bankers. During the 1930's Max Warburg's number of directorships had fallen from over one hundred to eighteen. He tried to reason with Papen and Schacht, and he took dangerous risks to his personal safety. One day in 1938 Hjalmar Schacht informed Max Warburg that the firm was no longer a member of the august *Reichsanleihe-Konsortium*. The Warburgs had helped Hamburg in that city's critical days. Now no one helped the Warburgs in *their* big crisis. They were through. The firm was handed over to a group of banks and other firms. The name remained, at the express request of the Nazis, M. M. Warburg & Co., *Kommandit-Gesellschaft* (limited partnership). In 1942 the name was changed to Brinckman, Wirtz & Co. Brinckman had been an employee of Warburgs, Wirtz a client.

After the end of the Second World War, the firm became again a leading private bank in Germany. Members of the Warburg family were financially interested in the firm. Eric M. Warburg became a general partner in 1956.

And in July, 1964, S. G. Warburg of London acquired an interest in the private bank of Hans W. Petersen in Frankfurt am Main, and it was renamed S. G. Warburg. Once more the Warburgs are private *Bankiers* in Germany, just as in 1797. They have come full circle in the country where they started.

EPITAPH

Siegmund George Warburg is a banker by inheritance rather than environment. He was born on September 30, 1902, the only child of the late Georges Siegmund and Lucie K. Warburg. (The Warburgs, like the Rothschilds, almost always use the family's traditional first names.) Georges Siegmund, a "nonbanking" Warburg, a cousin of the "five Hamburgers," was a trained agriculturist who owned a large estate near Urach, an old town not far from Stuttgart, in the Swabian Alps. It is lovely country, with green hills and clear streams. Siegmund Warburg is fond of the region, sometimes goes back for a visit, and still feels somehow "at home" there.

This shocks some of his less tolerant Jewish friends. How can a man passionately devoted to the future of Israel and active in Jewish philanthropies even remotely feel "at home" in the country of Goebbels and Hitler?

Warburg tries to explain (he doesn't always succeed) that the Germany he thinks of when he goes there is the country of Goethe and Heine. Heine once wrote, *"Denk ich an Deutschland in der Nacht / So bin ich um den Schlaf gebracht."* ("When I think of Germany at night / I cannot sleep.") Warburg himself feels that way about Germany. But he dislikes easy labels and facile generalizations, no matter whether Jews or Germans, Americans or British are concerned. On his merchant banker's map of the world four countries—England, the United States, Israel and Germany —are "Warburg countries."

The Swabians are similar to the Scots, with their mixture of realism and romanticism, their love of lyric poetry and sober prose. Theodor Heuss, Germany's cultured, highly respected former Federal President, was a Swabian, a neighbor and friend of the Warburg family. So was Baron von Neurath who rose to international prominence as Hitler's Foreign Minister and *Reichsprotektor* of Bohemia-Moravia. Heuss, representing one Germany, remained Warburg's friend to his death. Neurath, who stood for another Germany, later played a brief, decisive part in Warburg's life.

Siegmund was devoted to his mother, a kind-hearted, selfless woman who taught her son the importance of self-discipline, and lived the way she preached. "If you see an ugly girl standing alone you should go and ask her to dance," she told her son as he went to his first dancing lesson. She came from Stuttgart (her maiden name was Lucie Kaulla) and was brought up under the strict, almost puritanical principles of her Jewish ancestors. Warburg often quotes her without being aware of it—when he lectures on the dangers of smoking (though he would like to smoke) or when he refuses to touch chocolates (which he loves). After his mother's death, in 1955, he wrote a moving epitaph, "mostly for my children," about the way his mother helped to shape his principles and his whole philosophy of life:

"My Mother told me that her father often used to say, 'My child, if you have to choose whch way to go, always ask yourself first which is the harder and choose it. It will be the right one.' She had a deep sense of duty which she managed to combine with cheerful serenity. Goethe and Beethoven formed her conception of life. Her home was a strict, almost Spartanic school, but at the same time a happy environment. What had to be done was done with absolute thoroughness; what had to be thought out was thought through toward the last consequence; what had been recognized as the important aim, was pursued with utter tenacity. . . .

"My Mother loved music and wrote some compositions. They express her feelings succinctly. One hears in them her happy dreams beyond all earthly conflicts and worldly problems. After her marriage she had to take care of a vast estate —a task for which she had not been trained and which sometimes severely taxed her frail constitution. In those years she developed an enormous willpower . . . When my Father became very ill after they'd been married over twenty years, my Mother kept away from him all work and worry. Despite my Father's prolonged illness and his deep depressions, there was great harmony in our home. This sense of harmony was the most important thing she gave me in my formative years. . . .

"She would always assist me with my homework, and she was very strict about it. If I made a small mistake, I had to write the whole page once more, and sometimes there were tears. She would repeat her criticism of something I'd done, again and again, until she was certain I would not forget it. Today I am deeply grateful to my Mother for being so strict with me . . . She made me pray every night but she was never dogmatic about religious matters. Once she told me that many religious forms seemed to her to contrast with the true faith; but she was tolerant toward those who did not agree with her. Until I became thirteen, she would always join me at my night's prayers; often she would come from downstairs to my room for a few minutes, even when my parents had guests that night.

"Later, when I was told to say my prayers alone, she would tell me, 'Before you pray, my child, ask yourself what you did wrong today and could have done better. All of us make mistakes every day. One must be critical about one's mistakes.'

"During my Father's sickness she had given up her music,

but a few years after his death she began to play the piano again, her beloved Beethoven sonatas and Bach fugues, and she took lessons and wrote more compositions. She got along very well with her grandchildren who adored her. She would say, 'The old people can learn more from the young people than the young from the old ones.' When she had to leave her beloved Swabian homeland and came to England, she settled down quickly to learn about her new country and its people. She admired their gentleness and fairness, their self-discipline and strong faith. She lived in London during the war and never worried much about the danger of the air raids. She was convinced that Hitler would be defeated because this was the battle of the good forces of mankind against the evil ones. But she was not sure that she would live to see the day of victory. She was seventy-three when she emigrated.

"Mother believed in the importance of real values, the things that matter. She had no patience with snobs and social life. She never stayed in her children's homes. 'An old mother is there to love and help, not to interfere and be a burden,' she would tell us.

"Once we discussed the difficulty of telling the truth to close friends—the reason why people often lie to each other because they don't want to hurt one another's feelings. My Mother would say that a lie always corrupts, even a well-intentioned one, that one must tell one's friends the truth, as tactfully as possible. And she would always tell us that one must never stop doing the best one can do for other people. She liked to quote Hofmannsthal, 'It makes much difference whether people live their lives merely as spectators, or are actively involved, suffering, enjoying, feeling guilty or happy with others: only such people really live.' Another favorite quotation of Mother's was:

> *Dein Glück, oh Menschenskind,*
> *Glaub es mitnichten,*
> *Dass es erfüllte Wünsche sind*
> *Es sind erfüllte Pflichten."*

That means, "happiness is not the fulfilment of desires but the fulfilment of duties," and accurately expresses Siegmund Warburg's philosophy of life. He is always conscious of his responsibilities—towards his family, his business associates, his clients, his friends, even his bridge partners. He plays the game with great concentration. He does not want to let his partner down.

Warburg remembers the day—he was hardly eight years old—when he came home with a chocolate bar that he'd bought himself out of his pocket money. His mother reproved him severely. He might spend his money on something worthwhile, perhaps a book, but not on chocolates! Warburg never forgot. Even now he often buys things for his family and friends but rarely for himself. And he hasn't forgotten the day when an elderly relative with a choleric disposition lost his temper. It was a painful experience and taught the boy self-discipline more than anything else has.

He went to the humanistic *Gymnasium* in nearby Reutlingen, and distinguished himself in the classical languages. After the *Abitur* (the final examination) he entered the Evangelical Seminary—a former canon chapter house in Urach, founded in 1479, where Eduard Möricke, the German nineteenth-century poet, had studied—and distinguished himself by consistently good marks. He was the first Jewish student in the history of that institution, where the teaching has a strong philosophical emphasis.

When the time came, as it does for all young Warburgs, "to go into the bank," a summons arrived from Max Warburg, one of his uncles, then the senior partner at the Hamburg house, who offered Siegmund a job as trainee.

Siegmund hesitated. He would have preferred to continue his studies. Later he wanted to teach. The Warburgs have always been scholars as well as bankers, students of art and of commerce. The family has produced some remarkable scholars—his American cousin James P. Warburg in New York is the latest of them—and Siegmund is convinced that if he hadn't become a banker, he would today be a university don or a scientist, a philosopher or a writer.

Max Warburg thoughtfully looked at the young man and said, yes, he understood, but how about coming into the bank for a couple of years, just to try it? If Siegmund didn't like banking, he could still become a scholar.

Siegmund agreed to try it. The rest is merchant-banking history.

THE FOREIGN MINISTER WAS AFRAID

Warburg's father had been a rich man before the First World War (his fortune had been estimated at about six million marks, *gold* marks) but like many other patriotic Germans, he invested nearly everything in *Kriegsanleihe* (war loans). After the lost war the German war bonds were not worth the paper they were printed on. But a Warburg has much even if he has nothing. The family was related through marriage to the other German banking dynasties. Warburg grew up among Rothschilds, Oppenheims and Mendelssohns. There were lavish parties and musical soirées at the house of the music-minded Mendelssohns in Berlin. Many German merchant bankers were prominent in politics, and literature, society and the arts.

Siegmund Warburg probably inherited his predilection for politics and literature from generations of politically interested and literary-minded Warburgs. Since 1905, when the firm had been involved in the Japanese loan, the Warburgs had kept close touch with the German Foreign Office. They were strongly interested in Germany's colonial enterprises. During the Morocco crisis in 1911, a member of the Warburg staff, Dr. Wilhelm Regendanz, was on board the cruiser *Panther* which the German Naval Command sent to Agadir at the request of the German Foreign Office. This was merchant banking in the twilight zone between politics and economics. Max Warburg had several talks with Lord Milner about the Anglo-German Bank in Morocco, and with Sir Edward Grey about a Warburg-headed syndicate trying to acquire the majority of the Nyasa Consolidated in the Portuguese colony of Nyasaland. In June, 1914, shortly before "the lights went out all over Europe," the Warburgs concluded agreements between Germany and England for a delineation of financial interest spheres in Turkey and Africa.

During the First World War, the Warburgs (together with most German Jews) loyally supported their country's precarious war economy. Dr. Fritz Warburg was named honorary commercial attaché at the German Embassy in Stockholm. Once he was authorized by the German Foreign Office to talk with a member of the Russian Duma, a man called Protopopov, about the possibility of a separate peace treaty with Russia. The talk remained without result. (Years later the Nazi demagogues revived the matter and called the Warburgs "pro-Russian.") Two members of the firm, Max Warburg and Dr. Carl Melchior, were delegates to the Peace Conference of Versailles. Both were against signing the peace treaty, and resigned in protest before the German National Assembly voted for the Treaty. (The Nazi demagogues ignored this fact when they raked up the Warburgs' past.)

In 1925, S. G. Warburg went to N. M. Rothschild & Sons in London as a trainee. The Warburgs and the Rothschilds had a long-standing family agreement concerning the exchange of their young men as trainees. Anthony Rothschild at one time worked in Hamburg. Later Warburg continued his training in Boston and New York. He worked in Boston with the accountants Lybrand Ross Bros. & Montgomery, and in New York first with the International Acceptance Bank and then with Kuhn, Loeb & Co. In 1930 he was taken as partner into the Hamburg firm. The following year he started a branch office for M. M. Warburg & Co. in Berlin.

The Nazi handwriting was on the wall. Warburg, the pessimist, did not choose to ignore the handwriting on the wall like so many others. He was haunted by the premonition of approaching disaster. One lives harder that way but perhaps one also lives longer. In March, 1934, after some of his Jewish and Catholic friends were arrested in Berlin (officially they were "taken into *Schutzhaft*," protective custody) Warburg did an impetuous thing and called on Baron Neurath.

In the pre-Nazi days the Warburgs had paid an occasional visit to the Neuraths in the Swabian Alps. After a suitable interval *Rittergutsbesitzer* ("manor's owner") Neurath would return the visit. When Siegmund returned from abroad, he would see Neurath, then a *Ministerialdirigent*, at the Foreign Office. Warburg would tell Neurath his impressions, and the able bureaucrat seemed to value the young man's reports for he always told him to come back.

Since then Neurath had become Germany's Foreign Minister, first in the caretaker government of Von Papen, and later under Hitler. Neurath received Warburg jovially. Well, well —had Siegmund come to report from another trip abroad? Where had he been?

Siegmund shook his head.

"On the contrary, *Herr Minister*. I've come to report on some happenings right here in Berlin which worry me a great deal. . . . Do you know that people are arrested in the middle of the night and sent to prison without any judicial procedure?"

Neurath, no longer his jovial self, admitted he'd heard that such things happened "occasionally." *Sehr unerfreulich,* really most unpleasant. And he mumbled about "the inevitable aftermath of the revolution."

"It's brutal injustice," said Warburg, with the directness of a young idealist of thirty-one. *"Ein Willkürherrschaft."* That means "role by arbitrariness," and was, under the circumstances, not exactly diplomatic language.

Neurath seemed very uncomfortable. He said that no one regretted these happenings more than he did.

"But after all," he said, "what can *I* do?"

Warburg knew his Weimar Constitution. He boldly suggested that the *Herr Minister* should see President Hindenburg. According to Paragraph 19, the *Reichspräsident* was authorized to dismiss the Chancellor (Hitler) who had committed an obvious offense against the Constitution. If Hitler were dismissed, the *Reichswehr* would firmly stand behind *Generalfeldmarschall* von Hindenburg.

"And it is well known, *Herr Minister*, that you have the ear of the President," concluded *homo politicus* Warburg.

Neurath admitted that this was true but said he couldn't do anything. And then he said, in his broad Swabian dialect, "I have to tell you, my young friend, that I myself am considered *national unzuverlässig* [politically unreliable] and must be very careful. Sorry, but there is nothing I can do. Good luck, and good-bye."

After leaving the Foreign Office Warburg did not go back to the bank. Instead he went straight home, and told his wife to start packing their bags. They were going to leave Berlin. Yes, at once.

"If the Foreign Minister himself has a bad conscience and is afraid, I have no doubt what will happen here to all of us sooner or later."

At the bank Warburg was called a defeatist. But looking back now he is convinced that his talk with Neurath was "a hint from heaven," like a powerful motivation in Greek drama. If he hadn't gone to see the Foreign Minister, he might have stayed in Berlin, until it had got late. Perhaps *too* late.

WINNING THE ALUMINIUM WAR

Early in April, 1934, Siegmund Warburg, his wife and their two small children arrived in London. He was convinced that war was unavoidable. He expected war to break out in 1936, when Hitler occupied the Rhineland, and again the following year. There seemed no point in starting a new banking business in London. It was like "building on sand." During the early phase of the war, when the Western Allies seemed almost paralyzed, Warburg was not sure they would win. But after Hitler invaded Russia, Warburg became convinced that this madness would ultimately lead to disaster and defeat.

Only at the end of the Second World War did Warburg begin to build a new life. But then he worked day and night. In 1939 he had founded a small firm, the New Trading Company. They had started with four employees; later there were six, then eight. In 1946, the name of the company was changed to S. G. Warburg & Co. (Like his predecessors, merchant banker Warburg was never a merchant but began at once as banker.) After merging, in 1957, with an old merchant bank, Seligman Brothers, S. G. Warburg & Co. became a member of London's Accepting Houses Committee —the City's elite, and the only *true* merchant bankers. There are only sixteen of them.

Looking back now at these early years, "the postwar wonder of merchant banking" is supposed to have said that it was a long, hard uphill struggle. The firm grew with the international expansion of trade. But even in the late 1950's Warburgs was not yet considered an important merchant bank. Just another house in the City.

The outcome of the "Aluminium War" of 1958-1959 changed all that. It was the most sensational take-over battle in the history of the City of London. In the Aluminium War, Siegmund Warburg was the Biblical David who defeated Goliath—the powerful phalanx of great, old merchant bankers and august "institutions." With one stroke Warburg moved right up to the top of the Big League. Prior to 1959 he was not loved and often ignored. He is still widely unloved, but he is no longer ignored.

The conflict started late in 1958 when two American aluminum giants—the Reynolds Metals Company of Virginia and Alcoa (the Aluminum Company of America)—were trying to get control of the British Aluminium Company, the largest British producer, and a highly strategic prize. British Aluminium had just completed a new reduction plant in Quebec that would fit in well with Reynolds's expansion plans. Britons are understandably sensitive about American take-over bids, which often create outbursts of a national inferiority complex and laments about the sad fate of "the poor relations." In the words of London's *Financial Times*, the Aluminium War was "a fight between two vast empires [Reynolds and Alcoa] for a distant province—almost like Russia and Austro-Hungary fighting in the Balkans in the old days." (A good thing that Kipling was no longer around to see the *Financial Times*, once a pillar of the empire, comparing the City to the Balkans.) The paper warned that the fight was "building up grudges which should not exist between leading institutions of the City."

Among the "leading institutions," two great merchant banks, Lazards and Hambros, acted as joint advisers for British Aluminium. They represented the "old" forces, guardians of the merchant bankers' glorious past. The press called them "Gentlemen." Reynolds was advised by S. G. Warburg & Co. Warburgs joined forces with Schroders and with Helbert Wagg, whose chairman was the late W. Lionel Fraser, a "self-made" banker, and thus also something of an upstart by conservative City standards. The press called them "Players."

Reynolds was told by Warburg to cooperate with a British firm to make the take-over bid less painful for the British public. Reynolds went into partnership with Tube Investments, one of the leading British industrial groups, owners of an aluminum rolling mill. Reynolds and Tube Investments, at the advice of Warburg, began to buy shares of British Aluminium, carefully and, in accordance with London Stock Exchange customs, "through nominees," which means anonymously. Thus they had a good headstart when the war erupted into the skirmishing stage. By October, 1958, they held ten per cent of the shares of British Aluminium.

"It was the best-kept secret in recent history," a merchant banker in the losing camp later said.

At British Aluminium they knew something was up and people had a feeling there was danger. Somebody was after their shares, but who? Such mysteries make life in the City of London forever exciting. British Aluminium's chairman was Viscount Portal of Hungerford, Britain's Chief of Air Staff during the last war. Its managing director, Geoffrey Cunliffe, was the son of a former governor of the Bank of England—a pair of "Gentlemen" if there ever was one. The cast of characters in this great financial drama couldn't have been more colorful.

Lord Portal and Cunliffe knew that their firm was a natural target for a take-over bid. Its shares had been around eighty shillings two years ago and were now as low as thirty-seven shillings. Their current earnings were small but their potential profits were considerable. They needed money to expand. Their own choice was Alcoa, with whom they had a "special relationship." While the buying of their shares by unknown, "sinister" forces went on, the board of British Aluminium counteracted the pressure by increasing the authorized capital from nine million pounds to thirteen and a half million. They were now in a position to issue four and a half million pounds' worth of new shares without consulting their own shareholders.

The war moved quickly toward a climax. On November 3, Sir Ivan Stedeford, the chairman of Tube Investments, met with Lord Portal and told him he would like "to have an association for future development." (The City has certain formulae for take-over bids, like marriage vows. The traditional phrases are politely uttered even while the antagonists are mentally rolling up their sleeves for the free-for-all.)

Portal and Cunliffe turned down the proposal—"stiffly," the papers reported—since they were already negotiating "with another group." Undaunted, Stedeford two days later made a definite, attractive offer for British Aluminium shares. Portal listened and later replied that he had reached an agreement with Alcoa and would sell them British Aluminium's four and a half million pounds' worth of shares, *unissued* shares. He refused to pass on Stedeford's *attractive* offer to British Aluminium's shareholders.

Stedeford summoned a press conference and spilled the beans. He would bid the equivalent of 78 shillings per share (half cash, half in shares) for all British Aluminium's shares. The shares would be vested in a United Kingdom company with a 51 per cent British interest. The fine merchant-banking hand of Warburg became almost visible later on, when it turned out that the hapless British Aluminium board had asked only 60 shillings per share as the price of issue to Alcoa.

Headlines exploded all over the front pages. Lord Portal and his advisers, Lazards and Hambros, were angrily criticized. Why hadn't the board of British Aluminium consulted its own shareholders before making such an important decision? Some commentators spoke of "an authoritarian attack against the shareholders' democracy." Lord Portal didn't exactly improve matters by declaring, "Those familiar with negotiations between great companies will realize that such a course would have been impracticable."

Further criticism was provoked when the British Aluminium board decided to jack up the 1958 dividend from 12½ to 17½ per annum. Many people in the City regarded this clearly as "an opportunist move."

By that time there was such excitement all over the City that no one took seriously the Lazards-Hambros claim that the Alcoa deal was "American collaboration" (one third of British stock to the Americans) while the Reynolds deal was "American domination" (forty-nine per cent of British stock to the Americans). Experts quickly and sardonically pointed out that one third of a company's shares is enough to give absolute control as long as the rest of the shares are widely spread.

Reminiscing now about the Aluminium War, Warburg is reminded of Churchill's description of the Second World War as "the unnecessary war." Warburg didn't anticipate a big battle when he advised Reynolds and Tube Investments. As the fronts began to stiffen and the distant thunder of heavy guns was heard, he became very worried. In fact, he went to see his opposite numbers, Lazards and Hambros, and pleaded for a compromise. He tried his best to convey the impression that he didn't suggest this compromise from a position of weakness. He did not succeed: Lazards and Hambros decided to call what they thought was Warburg's bluff. They decided to fight. There exist many parallels in world politics.

And so, on New Year's Eve of 1958, the Aluminium War moved from the boardrooms of the merchant bankers to spread all over the City. In a letter to British Aluminium's shareholders signed by Olaf Hambro, chairman of Hambros, and Lord Kindersley, chairman of Lazards, it was declared that the Reynolds-Tube Investments offer must be resisted "in the national interest." The two old merchant banks represented a formidable consortium that held two million shares of British Aluminium, and offered 82 shillings in cash —four shillings more than the other side—for any additional share. Many great merchant bankers had joined the consortium, among them Morgan Grenfell, M. Samuel, Samuel Montagu, Brown Shipley, Guinness, and Mahon. One banker was quoted as saying, "We must save British Aluminium for civilization."

A noble task, no doubt, but the consortium failed to perform it, though this was by no means certain at that time. For Warburg these were nerve-wracking weeks. In a takeover battle even great financial wizards don't know what the outcome will be until the very last moment. Big blocks of British Aluminium shares were held by the "institutions"— insurance companies, pension funds, the Church of England Commissioners—where now the truly big money is. The institutions' managers didn't tell the merchant bankers which way they were going to jump. Warburg admits that much of the power once wielded by the merchant has gone to the managers of these institutions whose holdings in the industrial giants are enormous and growing every day.

Gradually the fog began to lift, and the battlefield became visible. The institutions were beginning to sell large blocks of shares—not directly to the consortium but at the Stock Exchange. There, brokers for Tube Investments-Reynolds, alerted and organized by the Warburg forces, were buying up every share offered. Happy days were here again for British Aluminium shareholders. In a single week, 1,300,000 shares were traded—at over four pounds per share! Happy days for Warburg too. Nine days after the battle had begun, Tube Investments-Reynolds held eighty per cent of the shares. The consortium had suffered a crushing defeat. The managers of several institutions later said they had been disgusted by the consortium's attitude, and decided to dump their British Aluminium shares.

The war was over, but for some time the grudges remained. Lord Kindersley of Lazards was heard to mutter at the mention of S. G. Warburg, "I will not talk to that fellow," and several merchant bankers were seen crossing the street to avoid meeting other members of the fraternity.

All this is now forgotten and today Lazards and Warburgs have close relations. "Big people will forgive others though they may never quite forgive themselves," is a favorite Warburg epigram that fits the occasion. Some of his erstwhile adversaries have now become Warburg's friends. There are "big people" in the City of London.

SHOCK WAVE IN THE CITY

S. G. Warburg's personal concept of merchant banking—"the fluctuating nature of activities by a group such as ours," as he said in a statement to the shareholders of Mercury Securities—has sent shock waves through the City. Many of his competitors now reluctantly follow the new trend. Warburg considers the traditional function of the merchant banker as money-lender outdated. In a statement made as retiring chairman of Mercury Securities, among the firm's activities, "advisory services to industrial clients in England and abroad" came first, followed by "management of investment accounts" and "issues of foreign bonds and domestic issues." Only in fourth and last place he mentioned "credit and money business."

Warburg sees the modern merchant banker as the trusted adviser to financial and industrial enterprises. He compares the merchant banker to the family doctor who calls in specialists when needed—accountants, lawyers, engineers, efficiency experts. He doesn't see a paradox in the fact that the merchant banker often knows more about the client's industrial organism than the client knows himself. A good family doctor often knows more about his patient's body than the patient does. And talking to a firm with financial problems is like X-raying a man's body. Warburg gets great personal satisfaction out of giving constructive advice. Occasionally he is consulted by statesmen and political leaders. He is gratified to see that his advice is accepted.

"Basically, merchant bankers do what lawyers in America do, only more so," a Warburg teammate explains. "Lawyers in the United States act mostly under instructions. We act more like friends who help the clients to formulate the instructions. We try to reconcile differences between companies. It's not strictly a scientific business but full of intangibles. Often it means doing the right thing at the right moment. Suppose two partners in a firm are not on speaking terms but each has a friend. The friends sit down and try to straighten out the partners' differences. We are the friends. A thorough, financial knowledge is necessary but not sufficient. One can read many things out of a balance sheet—but the intangibles have to be guessed. Management is made up of people, and people are unfathomable. You would be surprised how many big corporations are badly managed. When they are faced with serious financial problems, their boards are utterly helpless and often make the wrong decisions. We offer a thinking service, acting as a group of advisers. Often we move in as a team, sit down with the management, diagnose the problems, try to find solutions."

When Warburgs advised Chrysler on the projected merger with Rootes (which was advised by Lazards) the advisers got together and tried to reconcile the inevitable differences. A member of the British government who had watched the negotiations with some misgivings—it was another "symptomatic" case of an American firm taking over a British firm—said, "If Siegmund has his fingers in that pie, it will come out all right," and it did. There was a basis of mutual trust. Much water had run down the Thames since Warburgs and Lazards had fought against each other on the battlefields of the Aluminium War.

"First one tries to bridge the basic differences. Then there is some involved give-and-take until one reaches a meeting ground somewhere in between. It is very important to make one's own client listen. That often takes a long time. Only then can we make decisions for the client. At that point the accurate science of finance enters the field though no one can really explain precisely how it is done. The technicians take over. The deal is made."

KNOWLEDGE THROUGH PAINFUL EXPERIENCE

S. G. Warburg acquired his merchant-banking knowledge through "painful experience," a recurrent expression in his private vocabulary. He will never forget the lesson of the crisis of 1929-1930. In Vienna, the Bodenkreditanstalt, Austria's largest agricultural institution, had got in terrible trouble. At the personal request of the Federal Chancellor, Baron Louis von Rothschild agreed that the (Rothschild-controlled) Creditanstalt, Austria's largest bank, take over the Bodenkreditanstalt's liabilities. As a result, the Creditanstalt itself had to suspend payments the following year. This time even the Rothschilds couldn't prevent the *Krach*.

"It was fantastic," Warburg remembers. "People everywhere had said it couldn't happen. Well, it did happen. The fall of the Creditanstalt started a terrible chain reaction all over Europe. Many other institutions collapsed. People withdrew their deposits and the liquidity of many banks was endangered. That's the sort of experience one never forgets. Sometimes I try to explain this to my young people at the bank but I don't really succeed. They listen politely—and forget. No theoretical teaching equals the value of painful experience. There were brilliant people all over Europe who did foresee the great crisis—but did not act accordingly."

Could something like 1929 happen again? Warburg doesn't think so. The teachings of John Maynard Keynes have taught people a great many things, given them confidence that capitalism can be made to work, that a violent depression can be averted by skillful manipulation. Warburg now worries about different problems—the population explosion in Asia and Africa, and the rapid expansion of Red China.

Warburg, the tutor, always tells the young men at his bank that a good merchant banker, like a good doctor, must rely on a blend of idealism and knowledge, common sense and applied psychology. The most important single component is idealism. "A banker and a surgeon must not think of money when they start to operate." This also answers the question about the merchant banker's function in the future. There will be larger hospitals as the world's population increases, but there will always be a need for good doctors and surgeons. Warburg tells his associates, "The satisfaction of rendering a good service is more important than the size of the anticipated bill." The great merchant bankers whom he met as a trainee after the First World War never thought of money as the primary purpose of banking. "For most of my colleagues in the City merchant banking is a constructive achievement, an intellectual sport."

There is hardly a technical problem in merchant banking that cannot be solved, but there will always be the nearly insoluble psychological problems. Just as well: Warburg is fascinated by the challenge. When he advises a client about a projected merger, he always tries to find out what the other side is thinking. This is the tactical part of the problem. Then comes the strategic question: do the people really mean what they say? This is where "the occult powers of the successful merchant banker" come in.

"Every good doctor will admit that a cardiogram tells you a lot—but not everything. The rest is a matter of instinct, *Fingerspitzengefühl*, extreme sensitiveness that comes with knowledge and experience. Even sound instinct, however, won't prevent the merchant banker from making mistakes."

When Warburg is asked by a young man how to train for the profession of merchant banker, he points out that he can suggest only the technical part of the training. In England it's accountancy, in America a few years' practice in a good law office. Some good American bankers started out as lawyers. Warburg is not impressed by many economists who spend their time and energy redefining definitions and renaming terminologies.

Mergers and amalgamations have become an important activity in merchant banking. In this era of mass production industrial units are getting bigger, and the trend toward bigness continues. Warburg is against bigness for the sake of bigness, but he realized at the end of the last war that Europe would have to follow the American trend of amalgamation and rationalization, or Europe would be eased out. In these bigger units the merchant banker must act like a living cell, creating new ideas. To the outsider such mergers are often mysterious riddles of high finance camouflaged by enigmatic figures. To Warburg the operations are necessary, simple and lucid. At Warburgs they didn't invent the art of the merger and the technique of the take-over. It is true that the firm has never yet actually lost a take-over battle. But defeat in battle can often be avoided only by slow or quick retreat, "prior to irrevocable involvement in an acute struggle." This certainly applies to take-over battles no less than to military battles. Warburgs has on several occasions retreated from such battles when it came to the conclusion that the price to be paid was too high.

In the past years Warburgs has acquired so much experience in take-over operations that it has made almost a science out of it. A very profitable science. Fees usually range from one half to two per cent of the amount at stake, and these amounts are often very large. Fees are not mentioned in the City until the operation is completed. A great surgeon first saves a millionaire's life and then sends him his bill. The merchant banker often saves a millionaire's financial life. At S. G. Warburg & Co. advisory fees now account for a growing slice of profits. Merchant banking remains a profitable business, though for different reasons.

DRAMA IN FLEET STREET

Warburg, the student of history, has always closely followed the changing trends in merchant banking. As a trainee after the First World War he was taught that the merchant banker's primary obligation was to give credit, to issue domestic and foreign bonds, to arrange large loans. As the shadow of Nazism darkened the Continent, credit became restricted and finally stopped flowing out of Europe altogether as it began to come from the other side of the Atlantic.

At the end of the war, as Warburg started to build up his new business, the established merchant bankers of the City were picking up the pieces and trying to reestablish old connections. Warburg was way behind, and he had the added handicap of being an upstart at the starting post. But he perceived, perhaps a little earlier than his colleagues in the venerable old houses, that the role of the merchant bankers was changing fast in a changing world. In the "era of the migration of capital" (a Warburg expression) the issue of bonds, the credit business, even the management of accounts became mere sidelines. Merchant banking became a service business, and the merchant banker a combination of doctor-consultant-financial-engineer-friend-and-adviser.

In those early years Warburg's primary concern was to get customers. He felt like a doctor, who is not permitted to advertise and must wait until the patients come in. As they began coming in and more experts were needed, he started to build up his team of specialists, headed by Henry Grunfeld, a cool-headed banker from Berlin who shrewdly assessed people, figures and risks. Business kept expanding but Warburgs was ready. The team spirit was a reality at the bank. There were complicated financial constructions, great amalgamations, involved transactions. They didn't mind: the more complicated, the better. The modern merchant banker must always be one step ahead of the big commercial banks if he wants to survive.

In the late 1950's the Warburgs—the team—were known among knowing insiders as brilliant advisers. "It is always pleasing to a man's vanity for his services to be sought by opposing interests at the same time," writes Lionel Fraser. Warburgs has had several pleasant experiences. As adviser to Roy Thomson, the Fleet Street tycoon, Warburgs engineered the smooth, painless transfer of Kemsley Newspapers—including the *Sunday Times,* England's great Sunday newspaper—from Lord Kemsley into the hands of Roy Thomson for four and a half million pounds.

A big deal and a symbolic change. Instead of the old gentleman who had a ticker tape in the hall of his country house, where important news items were brought in on a silver tray by an impeccable butler, the son of a poor barber from Toronto walked into Kemsley—sorry, Thomson House, in Gray's Inn Road—shook hands with everybody, and went on to collect more newspapers as philatelists collect stamps.

The transfer was a complex operation. Aside from the shares held by the Kemsley family there were one and a half million shares in Kemsley Newspapers held by the public. All shareholders, it was agreed, must have the opportunity of selling their shares for cash at the same price as the price received by the Kemsleys. Eventually all shareholders had a chance to sell at a price of ten pounds and ten shillings, the same price as the Kemsley family received.

At a later stage, Warburgs became "temporarily and reluctantly" the opponents of Roy Thomson. Odhams Press, one of the largest British publishers of magazines, trade journals, and also owners of *The People* and the *Daily Herald*, saw the danger signs of being taken over by Cecil Harmsworth King, the big Fleet Street entrepreneur. It hastily contacted Thomson about a possible merger.

When King heard of the "secret" negotiations, he hit the ceiling. The situation became extremely delicate for Warburgs. It had advised King for years, before it had become adviser to Thomson. Cecil King, a cultured man with a great ambition for power, had been one of S. G. Warburg's first important clients. They had met in the early 1950's, several years after King had taken over the *Daily Mirror*, which now has a circulation of over five million, and calls itself "the largest daily sale on earth." It is probably the most successful venture in tabloid publishing.

King had been in need of financial advice. He approached a great old merchant bank and was turned down. The "Princes of the City" wanted to have nothing to do with the unconventional Mr. King. Warburgs, which likes nonconformists, became King's adviser.

After Odhams Press started to negotiate "secretly" with Roy Thomson, Cecil King quickly issued a counterbid which was much more attractive to Odhams' shareholders than Thomson's bid. When it became clear at 30, Gresham Street that there might be conflicting interests between King and Thomson, Warburgs informed Thomson, regretfully, that on the principle of seniority of client relationship it was acting for King in this matter. Thomson understood and called in a famous merger expert, Kenneth Keith of Philip Hill, Higginson, Erlangers.

The fight for Odhams Press developed into a big drama. Lionel Fraser, who jointly with Warburgs' Henry Grunfeld looked after King's interests, later wrote that "financial blood, newspaper blood, and labour blood" was spilled in the process. The battle ended with a clear victory for King who found himself after a tense week in control of the biggest newspaper empire in British history, "to the astonishment of Parliament, the Prime Minister and most of Odhams," as Anthony Sampson reports. Happiest of all were Odhams' shareholders whose shares went up from 40 shillings when the talks began to 64 shillings when they ended. Cecil King now controls about 38 per cent of Britain's daily newspaper circulation, and 40 per cent on Sunday, and has reached his ambition of being the biggest newspaper publisher in the world.

For Warburgs it was another spectacular success. But what pleased them most was that Roy Thomson, the loser, came back to them after the battle was over. Today Lord Thomson of Fleet, another very big and powerful publisher, is an important client of S. G. Warburg & Co.

RISKS ARE CAUSED BY PEOPLE

People who meet Warburg for the first time sometimes wonder how this quiet man with his dreamy eyes and soft voice is able to argue with tough tycoons and brilliant bankers, and come out on top.

"Siegmund's greatest asset is his inner authority," says a friend who often watched him during intricate negotiations. "There are other men with exceptional minds in the merchant banking fraternity. Siegmund has the brilliant mind and also the conclusive force that comes out of a man's innermost conviction. I've seen him enter a room where some of the world's great industrialists were assembled. Men of authority, used to issue orders, to be listened to respectfully. Siegmund would sit down and they became silent. They paid attention to him because they'd learned that Siegmund will not utter a single superfluous word. Big people gladly pay a premium for lucidity of thought and economy of expression. Warburg clarifies, never merely simplifies, complicated matters."

What the friend calls Warburg's inner authority comes out of Warburg's sense of duty, his Spartan self-discipline. He is never playful, neither with ideas nor with words. He approaches every matter with complete intensity. When he wastes an hour, he has pangs of conscience. He was brought up in the belief that to waste an hour of one's life is a sin. He applies the same rigorous standards to everybody else. He has no use for people who tell him light-heartedly that something can't be done. "If you want to do it, you can do it," Warburg may answer. He believes that energy and perseverance can move mountains, even in business. He talks to an apprentice in his bank with the same intensity that he displays to persuade a member of government that devaluation is no cure for England's economic ills. And why not? The apprentice may become a member of government himself and will remember the talk with S. G. Warburg as a milestone in his life.

Great bankers are said to have the minds of calculating machines. Warburg is also a keen observer with a highly trained memory. No detail, no matter how insignificant, escapes him. He notices the different hairdo of a stenographer whom he hasn't seen for months, or the worn heels of a man's shoes. Because nothing is unimportant to him, he discovers quickly people's hidden strengths and little weaknesses—an indispensable talent of a merchant banker whose job is to assess risks. "Risks," Warburg says, "are caused by people."

His associates, clients and friends rely on his reliability. "When Siegmund says that he's going to call you on the seventeenth of December, at four P.M., you know he's going to call you," a prominent client says. "There may be a war, a blizzard, an earthquake, the lines may be down, there is a general strike—but Siegmund is going to get through. In this unreliable world of ours his attitude is a source of great comfort. You know there is at least *some*body left on whom you can rely absolutely. He never forgets a promise. It took the people in the City a long time to realize that Warburg never utters these conventional phrases as we English so often do, without really thinking what we say. Warburg means literally what he says, which is a phenomenon in this loosely talking age. People who don't like him accuse him of being too intelligent—'clever,' you know—which is always somewhat suspect here. Those who know him well realize that his attention to detail, in thought and in word, comes out of his sense of inner duty."

Warburg never makes a promise if he isn't certain he can fulfill it. He can be very tough when he feels that somebody was treated unfairly. He once flew to the Continent and spent several days there because somebody he hardly knew had been wronged. He can also be very tough with people who are unfair to him. He doesn't mind being disliked, envied or justly criticized. But he gets angry when people accuse him of something he hasn't done.

Warburg in action is precise, effective, polite and always skillfully conveys the impression that the other fellow thought of the great idea first. Masters of the hard sell are often captivated by the melancholy charm of this master of the soft sell. He is one of the world's best-organized men. On his trips he has everything for weeks ahead arranged beforehand, down to meals, appointments, things to do. "Siegmund knows whom he's going to have dinner with three weeks from now," says a friend. "He knows he must call up a widowed aunt at five-fifteen in the afternoon." In Warburg's simple private office at the bank in London a red light is installed to keep people out when he is occupied with other matters, but he rarely uses the red light. People wander in and out all the time. Warburg interrupts his dictation, talks to the caller, makes a couple of telephone calls, turns back to his secretary, and continues to dictate his letter in the middle of the sentence, exactly where he had stopped. He applies his meticulous sense of organization where it matters most—to himself. Before he goes into an important meeting, he prepares himself for every contingency, every possible objection, and thus is ready to counter every argument. As a congenital pessimist he always expects the worst to happen, and is perfectly prepared for it. He is not as flexible as many merchant bankers, who make a fetish out of flexibility. Once Warburg has taken a line of conduct he follows it strictly and completely concentrates on whatever he is doing. Everything else becomes unimportant for the time being.

He is not jealous of his competitors. The merchant-banking fraternity has its prima donnas who react not unlike prima donna sopranos, prima donna baseball players, or prima donna field marshals. Warburg admires people who know something better than he does. He hates bad bankers, of whom there are quite a lot. His sense of justice sometimes gets him in trouble. Once he got into a terrible argument with a ticket collector in the London Underground. The man accused him of having traveled one station too far with his ticket. Warburg said he had asked for the right ticket and hadn't noticed that he was given a ticket that cost three pennies less. He was upset for days, wanted to go to court to prove his innocence, and was persuaded by his terrified associates only after long and painful discussions that arguing publicly with the London Underground (and making headlines in the tabloids) would hardly help the image of one of the world's leading merchant bankers.

"What can you do with a man who likes to pay his taxes before they are due and won't let you bring in a small bottle of perfume without declaring it to the customs?" says a friend. "Siegmund will declare *any*thing. He's been brought up in Germany where people always unconditionally surrender to authority, *any* kind of authority."

But he is also a practical man who does much for people he likes and nothing for those he doesn't like. He may spend days at the bedside of a sick relative but he doesn't waste any time with funerals. He feels, perhaps not unreasonably, that his time is more useful for the living than for the dead.

A STUDENT OF GRAPHOLOGY

Warburg's intellectual curiosity embraces a wide range of subjects—literature and philosophy, politics and psychology, the arts and music; and modern currency problems have long been a favorite hobby. He is convinced that money is becoming worth less all the time. He speaks wistfully about the wise law of Solon in Athens that all debts not paid back within seventy years must be canceled. People who contract debts pay the interest. But with the development of the means of production people inevitably want to pay back their debts—and the money they pay back is always worth less. Only during the second half of the nineteenth century and the early years of the twentieth century were the world's leading currencies tied to gold. Since then the values of all currencies have gone down, slowly and inexorably.

The gradual devaluation began much earlier though. The great fortunes of the eighteenth and nineteenth centuries were not made by people lending money but by those who owned and developed land, traded with raw materials, built railroads and utilities, and creatively financed industry. They considered obligations a short-term investment only. Warburg's "painful experience" after the First World War, when bondholders lost nearly everything while shareholders who didn't sell eventually came out all right, has formed his basic investment philosophy.

Next to currency problems, his main extracurricular interest is the science of graphology, "which some people unfortunately still consider something akin to astrology." Several years ago, when he worried about an associate with some emotional problems, he sent a page of the man's handwriting to a noted graphologist in Zurich. He received a lengthy character analysis which convinced Warburg that the graphologist knew more about the man (whom the graphologist had never seen) than Warburg did after talking to the man every day for years.

Warburg endowed the European Foundation of Graphological Science and Application which is now attached to the University of Zurich. The Swiss, sober-minded, analytical people with an inborn sense of precision, seem especially gifted for the exacting science of graphology. At the opening of the Foundation in April, 1963, Warburg explained why he endeavored to further the development of graphology though he considered himself merely a dilettante.

"My experience with graphology convinced me that graphological analysis enables us to gain insight into the psychological structure of other people, to find out more about them than years of personal acquaintance or spontaneous, intuitive impression will tell us. . . .

"I learned that the handwriting of a person contains signs of tension that tell more to the expert graphologist than that person's facial or muscular or verbal expressions tell to the rest of us. If we don't take people for granted but always try to strengthen the forces of good, we must find the direct way that leads from psychological knowledge to psychotherapy. Graphology helps us to understand certain psychological connections and to undertake the solution of complicated psychological problems. If I were indiscreet I could tell you of many experiences when, at the advice of expert graphologists, I changed my attitude about difficult psychological situations, and adopted a different course of action so that seemingly insoluble problems could be straightened out in a new, happier way.

"I realize that many people still consider graphologists to be cranks and eccentrics. Actually graphologists pioneer new segments of psychological knowledge. Many sciences have started as myths. The knowledge of the stars began as astrology and only gradually became the accurate science of astronomy. Today no one would call an astronomer a crank. Eventually, I am convinced, graphology will become *hoffähig*

—presentable at the court of profound knowledge, comparable to the earlier sciences of astronomy, chemistry and physics . . ."

"A LIVING FORCE OF ITS OWN"

Of all the great merchant bankers of London, only Baring Brothers & Co., founded in 1763, and S. G. Warburg & Co., founded in 1946, have their names in the telephone directory without any description, such as "bankers," "merchant bankers," "merchants and bankers." Both firms consider themselves well enough known in the City to dispense with any title. The atmosphere at S. G. Warburg & Co. contrasts strongly with the Dickensian mood at Barings. (Sir Edward Reid, the chairman of Barings, is a personal and business friend of S. G. Warburg's.)

There is nothing Dickensian about 30, Gresham Street, a rather functional structure with simple, modern lines that could stand in Wall Street or in Frankfurt am Main. They have a grandfather clock and many old prints there but these old-fashioned appurtenances are canceled out by electronically steered elevators and automatic machines, and by the marked absence of ancestral portraits and coal fires in grates.

This is obviously Modern Business. Big Business. Long, white corridors with functionally divided rooms on both sides. Of the two hundred and fifty employees, few are visible. Everybody walks with a brisk pace. The doors of the individual rooms are closed, and there is a sense of secrecy. The rules of the game are severely enforced at S. G. Warburg & Co. No merchant banker would use advance knowledge of an intended merger for personal gain. That's elementary—a man might just as well steal silver spoons. One doesn't even talk about it. Except at Warburgs where they do everything differently. There they do talk about it. Anybody suspected of the slightest infringement of the unwritten rules will be summarily dismissed.

From the start, the firm has acted as a catalyst in international business. In 1947, Warburgs with the Banque Nationale pour le Commerce et l'Industrie formed the British & French Bank. A very important transaction, that for the first time in years brought British and French business together again. During the following years Warburgs also made a specialty of repatriating companies that had been uprooted during the war. It brought back to England from the United States a twenty-five per cent interest in Associated Electrical Industries that had been acquired by General Electric; a number of London office buildings that had been purchased by an American group were returned to British ownership; the Brazilian Warrant Company, a coffee plantation and trading firm, was transferred from Britain back into Brazilian hands; and the International Telephone & Telegraph Company's twenty per cent interest in the L. M. Ericsson Telephone Company, which make telephone and other communication equipment, was sold back to European investors. Warburgs also advised the Timken Roller Bearing Company when it bought up all the shares of its British subsidiary, and the bank introduced a number of foreign securities on the London Stock Exchange, including Chrysler from the United States, Farbenfabriken Bayer and Hoechst from Germany, Finsider from Italy, and the Discount Bank of Israel. Warburgs also floated a number of private companies that became public companies.

In the past years Warburgs has built up a worldwide web of manifold interests. It advises British firms expanding on the Continent, and American firms expanding in Britain and Western Europe. It financed Austria and floated a fifteen-million-dollar loan to develop Italy's *autostrade* (superhighways). It has had its fingers in many British pies, from hire-purchase (as the British call finance companies) to television. In Switzerland it placed an issue of bonds of the International Telephone and Telegraph Corporation, of British Aluminium, of Reed Paper Group. In Canada it has had an investment trust and a finance company since 1953. And in the summer of 1965, S. G. Warburg & Co. opened a branch in New York City.

In his last statement as chairman of Mercury Securities, Warburg said that while the circle of clients expanded slowly during the early years, in recent years the expansion proceeded "at such a pace that we are having continuously to increase the size of the departments concerned." He admitted that the increased business volume might lead to a deterioration in the quality of service, and exhorted everybody to

make "special efforts to maintain the personal style and
character which we consider essential for a merchant-banking
house."

Last year S. G. Warburg decided to step aside "before the
doctor told me I had to stop." He would no longer continue
as chairman but would remain a member of the Board "to
render whatever contribution I can to our Group's further
progress." A favorite Warburg epigram says, "Good organization means to make oneself dispensable."

In his final statement Warburg said,

> Leaders in industry and finance are often inclined not to
> step down before the decline of their capacities becomes
> manifest, holding on too long to their positions and thus
> preventing the formation of a strong chain of potential
> successors. It has all along been our principal aim in the
> Warburg-Mercury Group to achieve a management
> structure in depth, self-recharging, free from nepotism,
> and based on integrity and humility, on imagination,
> courage and efficiency.

A characteristic Warburg statement, placing old-fashioned
virtues ("integrity and humility") ahead of the "courage and
efficiency" that are constantly preached today. It was as
forthright as unorthodox, and provoked angry mutterings in
paneled boardrooms and vintage banking parlors where
"leaders in industry and finance" still "hold on too long to
their positions" although "the decline of their capacities" has
long become manifest to everybody but themselves.

Yet it expressed nonconformist Warburg's conviction that a
well-made organization must go on, irrespective of its
members. The team is more important than the totality of the
individuals who form it. Of the twenty-five names on the
letterhead of S. G. Warburg & Co., ten are "executive
directors" and fifteen are "directors." Among the latter is S.
G. Warburg.

"This division on the board is very important to me,"
Warburg says. "It does not mean that some of the 'directors'
do not work just as hard as those called 'executive directors.'" "Director" S. G. Warburg certainly works as hard as
anybody else in the organization. On a recent business trip to
Frankfurt am Main, he had his first appointment at nine A.M.,

spent most of the day in seven different meetings, and had a long talk about business matters until shortly before midnight. Merchant bankers never retire—they just work a few hours more every day.

The division on the firm's board between "executive directors" and "directors" means that when some of the executive directors reach a certain degree of seniority they should move from the executive side to the advisory side. "They should become, to use the Japanese expression, wise elder statesmen," says Warburg.

He hopes that in due time the "wise elder statesmen"

> will want to make room for other colleagues well trained to follow them. Thus I am convinced that my stepping down as Chairman will not weaken but on the contrary strengthen our Group. Over the years our team has developed into an organism which is now a living force of its own. This organism is today stronger than the sum of the individuals who compose it.

Which echoes the wise words of Walter Bagehot, the great Victorian banker, economist and critic, "The business of a great bank requires a great deal of ability and an even rarer degree of trained and sober judgment."

5

Mattioli: The Master of Paradox

*"A good philosopher can
always become a good banker."*
Stendhal

THE first time I saw Raffaele Mattioli—rising to greet me from behind a large desk, and dismissing a blue-uniformed usher, who had shown me into his office in Milan —I found myself wondering why he looked familiar. Then it came to me. He is a big, powerfully built man, and his face— with full lips, a Roman nose, deep-set eyes that are full of fire, and a high forehead under a shock of gray hair—had instantly called to my mind one of the timeless old men who live in Michelangelo's frescoes. I felt that I was in the presence of a Renaissance patriarch on temporary loan to the twentieth century.

My impression was not altogether preposterous, for, like the great figures of the Renaissance, Mattioli is a man of varied interests and accomplishments. Readers of poetry know him for his translations into Italian of many sonnets of Shakespeare and Coleridge's "Kubla Khan." As owner of the distinguished firm of Casa Riccardo Ricciardi, which issues Italian classics in beautiful editions, he occupies an important position in the publishing world. He has attained considerable stature in academic circles as an economist and historian. And a vineyard he has developed over the years (he gave it to his daughter after her marriage a few years ago) is known throughout Tuscany for the high quality of its Chianti. (It is no secret that a great many wines being sold today as Chianti are not actually made from the grapes of the district, but Mattioli's Chianti is; he is proud of his wine and most of it is sold to a venerable firm in England whose standards in such matters are as high as his own.) Mattioli seems to have excelled at every activity he has ever embarked on, and he got into the one he is best known for almost by accident, at another man's suggestion. He is many things to many people in Italy, but principally he is the chairman of the board of directors of what is generally recognized in financial circles the world over as Italy's foremost banking establishment. This is the Banca Commerciale Italiana, or B.C.I., whose destiny he has guided for more than three decades.

It has been said that Mattioli proves Stendhal to have been right when he wrote that "a good philosopher can always become a good banker." Mattioli would be the first to point out that the converse hardly holds true. He himself doesn't look like a banker, nor does he behave like one or talk like one. He has no use for the pomposity in which some of his international colleagues indulge, and even on fairly formal occasions he will appear in a baggy flannel suit, a colored shirt, a tie with a thick knot, and a wide-brimmed hat of the *fin-de-siècle* Montmartre variety. His private office at the bank's headquarters, in Milan, is a large, wood-paneled chamber that seems always to be in a state of glorious disorder. I have never seen such an office in any other bank. There are books everywhere—on shelves along the walls, on a round table in the middle of the room, on almost all the chairs, on the floor, and on the desk, where they are carelessly flung down on top of balance sheets and confidential reports. Some of the books are on banking, finance, or economics, but most of them are works of poetry, history, or philosophy. The windows of the room look out on the Piazza della Scala, which is dominated by Magni's monument to Leonardo da Vinci. Mattioli called my attention to the fine view he has, right from his desk, of the Teatro alla Scala, which he naturally characterized as the world's greatest opera house. He also informed me that the world's greatest composer of operas, Verdi, had died nearby in the Grand Hotel, while people wept in the streets below, and he pointed out that only a few steps from the Piazza, through the Galleria Vittorio Emanuele, is to be found the Duomo, which is one of the three largest churches in Europe. The bank's location obviously delights Mattioli, and he expressed deep satisfaction that Italy's great powers—the Church, music, the arts, politics, and finance—are neighbors in what he called a microcosm of the whole country and its history.

Mattioli's home, I learned, is a large apartment just around the corner from the bank in an old *palazzo* on a street that bears the name of one of his favorite writers, Alessandro Manzoni. And when Mattioli is neither at home nor at his bank, he is apt to be at his publishing house, which is conveniently situated just a few doors away. In fact, all three buildings are in the same block, so days can go by in which he doesn't need to cross a street, and, Milan's traffic being what it is, this is another source of satisfaction to him. I gathered that Mattioli's daily routine is as unorthodox as everything else about the man. He told me that he rarely gets to the bank in the morning before eleven. At one, he walks home for a quiet lunch with his wife, and after that he takes a siesta. He returns to his office at around five in the afternoon, and stays until ten or later. Those hours in which the bank is empty except for night watchmen are the time to do some really constructive banking, he said enthusiastically.

Even a brief conversation with Mattioli reveals that he is fond of paradox, and leads to the suspicion that he enjoys confusing people. He is a brilliant practitioner of the art of irony, which has always been highly regarded in the country of Goldoni, Machiavelli, and Pirandello. Friends of his have told me that they are often unable to tell whether he means what he is saying. A good many people, it appears, are often unable to understand him at all, but this doesn't appear to bother him. In a recent annual report, he included a statement about the bank's responsibilities in the management of credit that may be translated, "Ours is a practical activity of a purely intellectual kind; it seeks to reconcile an abstraction of a mechanical order with a reality of a biological order." Some of his associates asked him if he would clarify this a little, since some recipients of the report might find it rather cryptic. Mattioli replied that those who didn't understand it should simply reread it until they did.

When I remarked on how unusual it was to find a banker who was also a genuine man of letters, Mattioli's face took on an expression of sardonic merriment, and his voice took on a histrionic resonance as he replied. "I see no difference whatsoever between a poem and a balance sheet," he said. Our conversation was in English, for the most part, but Mattioli, who is at ease in French and German as well as Italian, borrowed freely from any of these languages when it suited his purpose. His hands were in constant motion as he developed the theme: "At best, each is a work of art, and I approach both in the same way. When I look at either a poem or a balance sheet, I try to see the center of gravity, the focal point. I read and I judge. How are things grouped around the center? Is there a natural equilibrium? What is the weight of the various components? Will the foundations support them? I ask myself these questions whether I am studying a profit-and-loss statement, a Shakespeare sonnet or the Gothic structure of the Duomo or the fugue at the end of Verdi's *Falstaff*. One always looks for the source of truth—wasn't it Mommsen who said that? It applies to history, philosophy, poetry—and also to banking, which is a little of everything."

Mattioli's face suddenly became almost solemn, and he said quietly, "A banker must always remain in command of money. If he ever permits money to take command of him, he's in trouble. And a banker should never forget the words of Cardinal Borromeo—that there can be no authority without service to other people." He paused—it was a calculated pause, I thought—and then, smiling ironically, continued, "To say that we are at the service of our country is to utter a cliché with a faint trace of self-glorification. But, if I may invoke another authority, a banker's work, like a government's, should be 'of the people, by the people, and for the people.'"

Mattioli went on to say that although he deplores the tendency of bankers to calculate all transactions in terms of profit, he does not regard his own approach to questions of finance as a romanticized one. A prominent Wall Street investment banker, he said, had confided that he saw himself in the role of "one empowered to convert dreams into reality with the help of a little money." Mattioli smiled. "That's not the way I look at it," he assured me. "To me, banking is an abstract art in an abstract world."

More specifically, Mattioli sees the function of a banker as that of a mediator between two distinct but interdependent economic entities—deposits and loans. This is much more than a simple exercise in arithmetic, because granting credit in effect creates new capital and stimulates the formation of new deposits in the banking system; no money is actually drawn out of a depositor's account when a bank uses his savings as the basis of a loan, which may then be invested in a business that brings in money to other people. "The management of credit is a great responsibility," Mattioli declared. "It's certainly no job for a bureaucrat. It takes imagination, and a thorough understanding of the fact that a bank exists to lend money and that money is lent to be used." For many years, the Banca Commerciale Italiana was known as the bank of big business in Italy—"the licensed breeder of pachyderms," as Mattioli put it—but in recent years the emphasis has been shifted and today the average business loan is only about twenty million lire, or thirty thousand dollars.

"Italy's problem of problems is a very old one—we need more capital," Mattioli told me. "All our other economic problems revolve around it, including the conflict between public enterprise and private initiative—one waits for the other to make a decision, and both of them excuse themselves for doing nothing by asking where the money is to come from, although everyone knows that money put into sound and healthy production makes more money. Everywhere you look, the demand for credit is greater than the available resources. Selecting the right people to get credit among so many possible borrowers is very difficult."

Mattioli takes a characteristically skeptical view of his country's economic growth in the postwar years. "Nearly all the economic index figures have tripled, but our very prosperity has called attention to a number of serious imbalances, particularly in the fields of education, hygiene, and communications," he said. "We've got something like full employment for the first time in history, and one unavoidable consequence of that has been an impatient reinforcement of the bargaining power of the trade unions, which, in turn, has affected the stability of our politics. There has been a sharp rise in consumption, a demand for goods that the domestic market cannot satisfy, and the increase in imports has kept us worrying about our balance of payments." Italy's economic situation is further complicated by what Mattioli calls "the paradox of depressed areas." He pointed out that money invested in a depressed region may not really benefit that region very much. Large amounts have been invested in the

Mezzogiorno, the impoverished southern part of the Italian peninsula, with the result that many people there are now able to buy radios and washing machines, motorcycles and automobiles, nearly all of which are manufactured in the prosperous northern part of Italy. Consequently, a good deal of the money sent to the south for development purposes is flowing back where it came from. Only about twenty-four per cent of Italy's total population lives in the northern industrial regions of Lombardy, Piedmont, and Liguria, but that same per cent earns fifty per cent of the national income. To correct this imbalance, the government has initiated a long-term program to improve education, housing, and community development in the Mezzogiorno and to establish refineries, chemical factories, and other industrial enterprises there. Several big northern companies—including the Montecatini chemical company and the Olivetti business-machines company—have expanded into the south. But there is still a great shortage of skilled workers in the region, and Mattioli made it clear to me that he does not consider the problem of the Mezzogiorno even half solved. "There are two ways of helping the development of depressed areas," he told me. "One is to hand out direct aid and aid in the form of subsidies, low-interest loans, tax exemptions, and privileged investment quotas. But all this only perpetuates the harmful split between protector and protected. The other way, which is much more difficult, is to make the entire economic system of which the underdeveloped area is a part grow and prosper by modernizing and strengthening its productive equipment and renewing its institutions. Eventually this method can put Italy into the proper relationship with her Mezzogiorno, Europe into the proper relationship with Italy, the industrial nations of the world into the proper relationship with the poverty-stricken areas. The problem is so much more than a mere matter of local maladjustment that it might defeat even Prospero and all the spirits at his command."

Mattioli walked over to the windows and stood looking over the activity in the Piazza. "So I was left rather cold by all the international applause for what some people called Italy's economic miracle," he said. "We were told that we were the smartest boys in the class, that we had won first prize for our strong currency, our rate of production, the sacks of gold piled up in our vaults. But when admiration is colored by surprise, we must reject it. In a hundred years, will the combined resources of all the nations of the world be sufficient to provide even the minimum of well-being for the swarming population of our planet? That is the miracle we must pray for. And the problems that still beset us right here in Italy are so many that if we don't use our available resources wisely to increase our ability to produce, there will be no miracle. We might as well put up a sign like that one forbidding God to work miracles in the cemetery of Saint-Médard—'De par le Roy défense à Dieu, / De faire miracle en ce lieu.'"

I asked Mattioli how he went about determining the use of the available resources of his bank; that is, how he decided who should get credit.

The question brought a frown to his face. "A great many elementary questions go through my head at the same time," he said. "Naturally, I ask myself if I can trust the man who wants credit—will the money come back? But there are a lot of other matters to consider. Does he submit the elements of a sound proposition? Does he give me all the necessary data? Is he keeping anything back from me, either knowingly or—this is much worse—unknowingly? And, most important of all, what is he going to do with the money? I try to determine both what use he expects to make of it and how it will *really* be working—which may not be the same thing. What will the money produce? Will it merely sustain the client, or will it further his economic growth?" Mattioli is contemptuous of bankers who rely heavily on statistics and computers in making decisions. "Machines can be helpful as long as they are used only for information, but no statistics can replace the singular operations of the human mind," he said. "The great danger with machines is that they ignore the human element. They reduce people to figures, and that makes trouble. The banker's profession, if exercised conscientiously, calls for hard work and perception, worry and courage, enthusiasm and calm nerves. Admittedly, this is a preposterous mixture of contradictory qualities and emotions. But without them we are nothing but bureaucrats."

Mattioli looked around in a conspiratorial fashion and said, "Bankers like to appear the picture of dignity, the image of noblesse. Don't be fooled. They are merely trying to cover up their inconsistencies and doubts. Between success and bankruptcy there is a margin no wider than a razor's edge. You know, in my younger years, when I worked for the financial press, I used to write amusing articles about bankers. I was like a second-rate music critic. It is easy to be sarcastic about people who compose music, to make fun of those who perform it. Well, today I am a banker, and I myself must write and perform the sort of financial music I used to criticize. That is not so easy." He was silent for a moment, and then went on, "We bankers, like the members of some other professions, are fond of pretending that we know everything. I always try to remember the advice of my father, who told me that a man should never be afraid to admit that he doesn't understand something—particularly if he knows all about it." The recollection caused a beatific smile to illuminate Mattioli's face.

Mattioli's father, from whom, it appears, he inherited his predilection for paradox, kept a small general store in the town of Vasto, south of Pescara, in the Abruzzi Apennines, a wild mountain range where the Mezzogiorno begins. Mattioli described the Abruzzi to me as being in about the same latitude as Rome but centuries behind it. He was born in Vasto on March 20, 1895, and went to school in the town of Chieti, a few miles away, so he had ample opportunity during his childhood and early youth to observe the economic problems of the Mezzogiorno. Although he has spent all of his adult life in the north, he loves to reminisce about village life in Vasto, and at times he has been known to lapse into the dialect of the south, at least long enough to make use of some of the colorful expressions for which that part of the world is noted. (The rich diversity of the Italian peninsula is a source of pride to Mattioli, and his desire to see the economic institutions of all its regions modernized is balanced by a conviction that the modernization must not entail the imposition of cultural uniformity. In a recent report, he declared that the "essential characteristic of our country, which consists in the subtle diversity of the situation in each area and in each sector . . . should not be eliminated—planning should not mean leveling—but should, on the contrary, be defended, extolled, encouraged, and protected.")

The storekeeper's son from Vasto went north to study at the University of Genoa, and soon decided that he would like to stay in the academic world, studying and teaching economics. "Economics appealed to me because it is part history and part philosophy, and its philosophy, however abstruse, is always connected with the miseries and hopes of humanity," he explained. "And I found that I loved teaching because when you teach, you are also taught." His ambitions were temporarily diverted by the First World War, during which he served as a junior officer in the Italian Army, was wounded, and was decorated. While the disposition of the Hungarian port of Fiume was being debated at the Paris Peace Conference, Mattioli joined the poet Gabriele D'Annunzio, another native of the Abruzzi, in his melodramatic attempt to seize and hold Fiume for Italy, and he is convinced that the ignominious ejection of the invaders strengthened his natural preference for realism over romanticism in the conduct of public affairs.

When he left Fiume, Mattioli decided to settle in Milan, the commercial and financial center of Italy. At first, he worked on a financial-magazine. (This was the period in which he says he wrote sarcastic articles about bankers.) In 1920, having received a doctorate in economics from the University of Genoa for his dissertation on "the stability of money," he was appointed an assistant professor at the Università Commerciale Luigi Bocconiv, in Milan, Italy's foremost center of economic studies. The appointment was a great honor for a young man of twenty-five, but when, in 1922, a public competition was announced for the post of general secretary of Milan's Chamber of Commerce, Mattioli decided to take the examination—partly out of intellectual curiosity. "I thought I had had enough theory for a while," he told me. "I wanted to find out whether theory matched practice in economics."

Mattioli won the competition and got the job, but almost before he could begin to look into the relationship between theory and practice in economics he was offered an opportunity to conduct his investigation on a much higher level. The opportunity was provided in 1925 by Giuseppe Toeplitz, a native of Poland whose ingenious speculations had made him a legendary figure in European financial circles, and who was at the time the head of the Banca Commerciale Italiana. Mattioli had met Toeplitz several times and had taken a great liking to the man—a round little figure with a goatee and an expansive gusto for good living—and now Toeplitz told him that after looking around for some time to find just the right person for the job he had decided to invite Mattioli to become his private secretary. He indicated that the job might have interesting possibilities, since he wanted to start training a successor. Mattioli hesitated. He liked his new job at the Chamber of Commerce, which offered him a good deal of freedom. Still hoping that he might teach again some day, he wanted to write and do a lot of reading. Working for Toeplitz would mean keeping long, regular hours and adapting himself to the demands of a large business organization. He was only thirty, and he wasn't sure that he was ready to make such a final commitment as the job seemed to require. In explaining to me why he ultimately accepted Toeplitz's offer, Mattioli said that he may have been swayed by the simple fact that for him banking was terra incognita. It didn't remain so for long. Signor Toeplitz's young private secretary showed an astonishingly quick grasp of banking problems, and one old-timer at the bank told me that from the first the tall, lean young secretary was feared as "le dauphin." "After a couple of years, Mattioli knew more about banking than his competitors," my informant told me. "Toeplitz remained the gifted entrepreneur playing his hunches." Mattioli added to me: "Toeplitz was not only a great banker but a delightful, unforgettable man."

For a country with financial houses that can claim to have been open for business since the sixteenth century, the Banca Commerciale Italiana is practically an upstart, having been founded in Milan in 1894. Those who founded it were not Italians. The kingdom of Umberto I had close economic ties with the empire of Wilhelm I, and a group of German bankers who had observed the rapid industrialization of Italy in the last decades of the nineteenth century became convinced that the country could use a new bank. Accordingly, the Deutsche Bank, the Disconto Gesellschaft, the Darmstädter Bank, the Berliner Handelsgesellschaft, and A. Schaaffhausenscher Bankverein became sponsors of a new institution that they named the Banca Commerciale Italiana. Within a few years, however, the young Italian bank had achieved complete independence and was demonstrating its national character by opening branches throughout the peninsula. During the years before the First World War, the bank participated in the financing of Italy's new hydroelectric and textile industries, and of its shipyards, railroads, and heavy-machinery plants. The program was an ambitious one, and B.C.I. soon became Italy's leading bank. Throughout its early years, and especially after the First World War, B.C.I. was expanding in all directions, but in Italy, as elsewhere, not all the economic expansion of the 1920's was entirely sound. The bank's official history contains the cautious comment: "One may now have second thoughts on the policy then pursued, which may not have been wholly in keeping with the tenets of banking orthodoxy." At any rate, in 1931, when the shock waves of the Wall Street crash of 1929 forced the formidable Creditanstalt, the Rothschild family's great bank in Vienna, to suspend payments, disaster quickly spread throughout Europe. In Italy, B.C.I. found itself on the point of failure, for it had billions of lire tied up in what appeared to be irrecoverable claims, and almost no cash on hand to meet the demands of depositors.

Here was a practical lesson indeed for a student of banking philosophy, and Mattioli, having witnessed the collapse of the old entrepreneurial system of banking, soon had an opportunity to take part in the creation of the carefully regulated institutions of a modern mixed economy. In the early thirties the government stepped in to bail out what were legally known as the nation's three "banks of national interest"—the Credito Italiano, the Banco di Roma, and B.C.I.—and new laws enacted to protect depositors in the future changed the very structure of the big banks. Until that time, B.C.I. had been what the Germans call a "mixed bank," not only holding money on deposit but also carrying out all the customary operations of a merchant bank: financing industry; granting acceptance credit as a means of guaranteeing bills of sale; launching new stock issues; and acting for clients in many investment and commercial activities. After the crisis, a strict division was made between merchant banking and commercial banking. As in the United States, where the Glass-Steagall Act of 1933 required bankers to choose between merchant banking and commercial banking, Italian bankers were henceforth forbidden to do both. In the course of the banking reorganization in Italy, the government set up and financed a vast central holding company, the Istituto per la Ricostruzione Industriale, or I.R.I., and this now controls nearly all the shares of the three "banks of national interest." Despite their common ties with I.R.I., they are completely independent in their day-to-day operations and compete freely with one another—and also with several banks that are not controlled by I.R.I. but are owned directly by the state—most notably the Banca Nazionale del Lavoro, which is now the biggest bank in Italy in terms of deposits. The three "banks of national interest" function almost exactly the same way as privately owned banks throughout the world, except that they need government permits to open branches in urban centers where they are already represented. The Banca Commerciale Italiana now has almost three hundred branches in Italy, and in recent years it has been known as the most dynamic of the three, in large measure because of the dynamic qualities of its chairman.

Amid the disasters of 1931, no protests were heard when Toeplitz announced that he was ready to retire. It was decided that the bank should have two top administrators. Raffaele Mattioli was named to be one of them. The other was an older man named Michelangelo Facconi, and people in the bank were saying:

> *"Con Michelangelo e Raffaello*
> *Certo ogni cosa andrà a pennello."*

That is, "With Michelangelo and Raphael, everything will go as with a brush"—meaning very smoothly. Given the difficulties facing the bank, that prediction seemed absurdly optimistic, yet, as Mattioli still likes to boast, B.C.I. survived the great crisis with no damage to its depositors. It was touch and go for a long time, but in the end not a single depositor lost a single lira. Facconi retired in 1936, and then Mattioli, at forty, was sole head of the bank. He had never made a secret of his views on Fascism, but by now his importance in the financial world had put him beyond the reach of Mussolini's bullies. He gave a number of other anti-Fascists jobs in the bank, and during the war he secretly helped various employees whom he knew to be members of the Italian resistance. One Jewish executive whom I met in Milan told me that early in the war he suddenly was transferred to Lima, Peru, to set up a research department for which there seemed to be no pressing need.

According to the banking laws that Mattioli has operated

under since the early thirties, B.C.I. must confine its business to the servicing of commercial accounts and the granting of short-term credit—that is, loans to be repaid in no more than twelve months. Under special conditions, it may lend limited amounts for longer periods, but Mattioli's urge to be involved in the financing of great new ventures has often required the exercise of great ingenuity. After the Second World War, he helped set up the Banca di Credito Finanziario, better known as Mediobanca, because it grants what is known as "medium" credit (loans to be repaid in from one to five years), together with "financial," or long-term, credit. Mediobanca is controlled by the three "banks of national interest" and, in effect, conducts their merchant-banking operations for them. For example, the three commercial banks may lend money to Mediobanca, and Mediobanca may, in turn, underwrite a new stock issue, which the commercial banks themselves would not be permitted to do. Mattioli does not feel particularly bothered by the legal restrictions imposed on banking in his country—Italians, as he pointed out, have always managed to live with their enormous bureaucracy—and he considers himself, both by training and by inclination, a merchant banker. B.C.I. is far ahead of any other Italian bank in the field of foreign trade, and Mattioli has assembled a staff of experts well qualified to help Italian merchants and manufacturers expand their businesses nearly anywhere in the world. Mattioli has been particularly active in establishing new contacts for the bank in Latin America, in the Near East, and in the new countries of Africa. According to S. G. Warburg, a friend of his who is one of London's great merchant bankers, "Mattioli considers it his chief object to advise his clients on, first, their aims and, second, their methods of operations. In these respects, Mattioli is a merchant banker in the best sense of the word, for he serves his clients as consultant and father confessor."

Unlike most of the large merchant banks in London and elsewhere, B.C.I. does not maintain a special advisory service. Mattioli and his associates advise their clients constantly, personally, informally. "In any sort of conversation, one is giving and taking advice all the time," Mattioli explained to me. "We grant credit, and it is clearly our duty to advise our clients on how to use this credit. No special department is needed for that. People in need of credit come in and want us to look at their plants. So we go and look at their plants, at their machines, at their books. But, above all, we look at the people, and at the relationship between the people and the machines in their plants. This is what really matters. Machines do not make profits. People make profits with the help of machines. The best machinery is useless without the right people handling it."

Mattioli has chosen his own people—those who work with him in the bank—with great care. He does not tolerate any yes men around him, and one of his managing directors confided to me that he always thinks twice before saying that he agrees with the boss, because the consequences can be very unpleasant. "I don't like people who deliberately try to think in my way," Mattioli told me, with some heat. "If I turn out to be right, the other fellow will say he was right, too, but if I am wrong, he will say it was all my fault. Besides, why should I pay a man for thinking the way I do? I can do that for myself. It would be a waste of money." He drives his associates in the bank hard, and they are well aware that Sundays and holidays mean nothing to him. He tends to become even more caustic than usual when any of his executives indicate that they would like to take a vacation. He is likely to tell them that they will have all the time they want when they retire, and recently when one man broke a leg on the last day of a long vacation, Mattioli proclaimed the accident an act of poetic justice. And he will telephone bank employees after midnight whenever he has a problem on his mind. In spite of such autocratic treatment, all his associates are clearly devoted to him; on the other hand, the wives of some find the chairman's attitude exasperating, and have been heard to mutter that he just likes to have an audience available day and night. Manifestly, there is some truth in this, for most of the important decisions reached in the bank are the result of a lively interaction between Mattioli and his staff. At weekly meetings with his top associates, he systematically challenges any proposals that may be up for consideration. "Sometimes I don't understand what they plan to do, and I tell them so," he said. "That makes them sit up and think a little harder. They may know that I am just testing them, but we play a continuous and complicated intellectual game here. A game like that is very healthy for bankers."

Some people have come to feel that Mattioli loves contradiction for the sake of contradiction. After a long and unproductive conference with him, a prominent American banker once told him, "You know, you're so dead-set against any kind of orthodoxy that I don't think you care what you do as long as it's unorthodox." After telling this story with some amusement, Mattioli went on to say that in many ways he envies the international bankers he deals with, including his friend Warburg. "What a pity that the Italian money market is so small!" he exclaimed. "Sometimes I think I have it in me to do big things."

Although Mattioli certainly has done some big things, his point about the Italian money market is well taken, for despite the fact that the Medicis were among the first great financiers, as we have come to understand the term, Italy's financial practices today are quite unsophisticated by modern standards. The shares of only about a hundred and twenty firms are listed on the Milan Stock Exchange, and of these only about half are actively traded. Many large Italian businesses are still owned by the descendants of the people who founded them, and very few mergers or amalgamations take place in the private sector of the economy. A long history of poverty has made those Italians who do possess capital extremely wary about taking any sort of risk with it. The only bank that many of them will trust to keep their money for them is a savings bank, and as a result the volume of deposits that a commercial bank like B.C.I. has at its disposal is rather drastically limited. In a tone of some irritation, Mattioli remarked, "The depositor doesn't seem to realize that his most effective safeguard is not the bank's own resources but the soundness of its judgment in making advances."

When it comes to soundness of judgment, Mattioli's own record is unrivaled, yet he is by no means timid about taking chances on men with new ideas. As he sees it, the unorthodox investment often proves to be the soundest investment of all. That certainly holds true for B.C.I.'s association with the brilliant industrialist Enrico Mattei, who first approached Mattioli at the end of the Second World War. Mattei had an opportunity to take over a large company for the exploitation of Italy's natural-gas reserves, and he needed money. After sizing up the situation and the man, Mattioli lent him a billion lire. The venture was a spectacular success. By 1962,

when Mattei died, he had transformed the company—a
government-controlled monopoly called the Ente Nazionale
Idrocarburi, which he ran much in the manner of a *condot-
tiere*—into one of the world's leading oil-and-natural-gas
enterprises; the empire that Mattei built now includes
refineries and distribution systems on four continents and is
worth almost two billion dollars. Mattioli's bank currently has
a considerable stake in two giant pipelines that are being
built by the Ente Nazionale Idrocarburi—the five-hundred-
and-forty-six-mile Central Europe Pipeline that will ultimately carry twelve million tons of crude oil annually from Genoa
to Switzerland and Germany, and the Trans-Alpine Pipeline,
linking the port of Trieste with refineries some three hundred
miles away in Germany, which will be able to carry more
than forty million tons of crude oil a year. Mattioli's eyes
gleamed as he described the second gigantic project, and, in
response to a comment from me, he conceded that even in
Italy a banker who has it in him can sometimes do big things.

"Money means nothing unless it is being used," Mattioli
remarked at one point. "I use one man's money as the basis of
a loan so that another man can make something. This is my
responsibility and at the same time my wealth—for banking
has not made me rich. But I have three sons and a daughter,
and I have given them a good education. They have given
me grandchildren. I have enough to eat and my books. What
else do I need? My work, and I have work that makes me
happy."

There can be no doubt about that. Indeed, as far as I could
determine, no division exists between Mattioli's work and his
play, and, just as he may spend an evening studying a
banking problem at home, so he is apt to spend an hour or
two in the afternoon listening to music in his office. Once, as
I sat with him listening to a Bach cantata that was coming
full blast out of a large radio he keeps there, a piece of paper
was placed on his desk by a tiny, fragile-looking man in his
late seventies, who had previously been introduced to me as
Valentino Bona, his private secretary. (A white Russian
émigré, Bona is able to handle correspondence in a dozen
languages, by Mattioli's reckoning, and is said to be the only
man in the bank who can occasionally establish some order in
the magnificent chaos of the chairman's office.) Bona made
signs indicating that the paper concerned a matter of great

urgency, but Mattioli made a spiraling upward motion with his right hand to express impatience at the interruption, and then, having hardly glanced at the message, told Bona to pull up a chair and do some real work. "Immerse yourself in the music!" he thundered. The three of us sat there for fifteen or twenty minutes, working on Bach.

Aside from music, Mattioli has few hobbies, though he says he is fond of films, especially American Westerns. One thing he unquestionably likes is books; in fact, toward them he reveals an attitude that might be taken for avarice. He loves beautiful editions, and he has taken a personal hand in the design of the typography and binding of the masterpieces of Italian literature that have been put out by his publishing house. He is an enthusiastic collector of rare editions, and specializes in the works of early writers on economics. Shortly after the last war, Mattioli discovered a rare edition of *Responsio ad Paradoxa Malestretti* (*Réponse aux Paradoxes de M. Malestroit*) by the sixteenth-century French political philosopher Jean Bodin who gave a rational explanation of the revolution of prices in his century and showed that the amount of money in a country is no accurate gauge of its wealth. Bodin was one of the first economists who realized the futility of prohibiting the export of gold and silver. No wonder Mattioli was delighted with his book which had a particularly beautiful binding that made it very rare. He proudly showed it to his friend and fellow economist, fellow publisher and fellow collector Luigi Einaudi. Einaudi owned a copy of the book but he was excited by the beautiful binding of Mattioli's treasure.

Mattioli was very pleased. "Nothing makes a bibliophile more attached to a book than the knowledge that another bibliophile covets the same book," he later wrote in a short monograph on the memorable experience.

When Einaudi became President of Italy on May 11, 1948, Mattioli went to the Quirinale Palace in Rome to pay his respects to his old friend. They talked for a while, and the President of the Republic casually inquired whether Raffaele still owned that beautiful edition of Bodin's *Responsio?*

Indeed, he still had his little treasure, Mattioli said, with that twinkle in his eye that appears when he enjoys himself.

Well, asked the President, would Raffaele now consent to sell it?

Mattioli reports in his monograph, "I obstinately but respectfully said, 'Now less than ever, *Eccellentissimo Presidente.*'"

Seven years later, the term of Einaudi's presidency ended. And so, in May, 1955, Mattioli once more made the journey to the Quirinale Palace, this time to say goodbye to the departing President.

"Almost mechanically, without giving it any thought, I put the small book in my pocket. . . . The following day, a great many people in very high places who had also been at the Quirinale asked me, '*Dottore* Mattioli, what did you give to the *Presidente?* He seemed so very happy yesterday.' What could I answer? What would my answer mean to these people? How could I explain to them what a triumphant satisfaction was there for me in that short, fleeting moment, the sudden smile of gratefulness, the sparkle in Einaudi's eye that repaid me generously for my little sacrifice."

6

Abs: The Organist

*"A banker must always know
the extent of the risk."*
Hermann Josef Abs

FOUR hundred and fifty years ago Martin Luther, the implacable social critic, called Frankfurt am Main *"das Geld-und Silberloch,"* the hole full of money and silver. Luther was right and the people of Frankfurt didn't mind. The "hole full of money and silver" was always a Lutheran city although the Catholic emperors were elected and crowned there.

Frankfurt's greatest native son, Goethe, who was baptized in the Protestant St. Catherine Church and called himself "the merry Protestant," had as much respect for money and silver as everybody else in town, and never enough of either. *"Armut is die grösste Plage/Reichtum ist das höchste Gut,"* he writes in one of his famous poems. Yes, poverty seemed the worst plague to him. He earned up to ten thousand taler a year but tried to get out of taxes amounting to a mere hundred and fifty taler. When Frankfurt taxed him for mortgages that he had inherited from his grandfather, Goethe angrily asked "to be dismissed from the citizens' community." At the age of sixty-nine, the greatest Frankfurter of all gave up his native city.

Frankfurt emerged as a great financial power in the second half of the sixteenth century when both Antwerp and Lyon began to lose their eminent positions, owing to internal trouble and religious wars. Historically, geographically and geopolitically, Frankfurt was destined to become a hole filled with money and silver. The great European trade route, leading from Holland to Venice by way of the St. Gotthard, led through Frankfurt. Today the Continental banking centers of Paris, Brussels, Amsterdam and Zurich are but a short jet ride away. Nearby is the industrial Rhineland, once again the fast-beating metallic heart of modern Germany.

Frankfurt's Rhine-Main Airport has become the Continent's busiest turntable. Sooner or later everybody who needs money or wants to invest money winds up in Frankfurt. The big money is there, and money always flows toward money, like water toward water.

Goethe's Frankfurt must have been a lovely town—hard to believe now—with quaint streets, picturesque gabled houses, dreamy squares. It was an independent Republic in the Holy Roman Empire of the German Nation. Its stock exchange was already prominent in the eighteenth century. When the French conquered the Netherlands, Amsterdam was wiped out as a financial center and Frankfurt took over.

At the end of the eighteenth century, forty-five banks were doing good business in Frankfurt. In 1804 twenty-six different state loans were quoted there. And the following year the banking house of Johann Mertens, founded in 1605, celebrated its second centennial.

In 1803, the Rothschilds, "coin-changers down in Jew Street," moved their *Wechselstube* out of the ghetto into more elegant quarters in the city and became—almost—respectable Frankfurt bankers. The move caused some exasperated comment. One can well believe that the Mertens, the Neufvilles, the Golls, the Metzlers, the Bethmanns and all the other, long-established, distinguished bankers turned up their aristocratic noses at the newcomers. But the newcomers were here to stay. Within two decades they had all but taken over the Frankfurt stock exchange and were right in the center of the city's financial scene. The Rothschilds made Frankfurt the greatest money power on the Continent and gave the city its golden era.

More merchant bankers have come from Frankfurt than from any other city on earth—the Bethmanns, the Ladenburgs, the Erlangers, the Sterns, the Seligmanns, the Schiffs, the Speyers, to name only a few. Frankfurt financiers became as famous as French chefs and Italian tenors. Ex-Frankfurters attained powerful financial positions in Manchester and London, Amsterdam and Brussels, Milan and Madrid, Constantinople and Alexandria, even in New York. The international arbitrage business—the exploitation of the difference in quotations on several stock exchanges—started in Frankfurt.

It was a glorious time but it didn't last long. Frankfurt became rich, saturated with self-glorification, and narrow-minded. The local banking aristocrats tolerated no competition from the outside. When the first joint-stock banks were set up in Germany, Frankfurt ruled against their having any branches in the city. In 1854 a local state bank, the Frankfurter Bank, was founded. The Senate decided that only those citizens of the Free City of Frankfurt who were entitled to the vote could subscribe for shares. Such laws always seem to be expressly made for the purpose of being circumvented. Enterprising speculators promptly hired strong young men who had both the right to vote and the elbows to push themselves through a large crowd of would-be subscribers.

Frankfurt had always been outspokenly anti-Prussian, and when Prussia went to war against Austria in 1866, the Frankfurters wholeheartedly supported Austria. After Austria's defeat, the Frankfurters paid heavily for backing the wrong horse. The independent Republic lost its sovereign status. The victorious Prussians severely punished their traditional enemy. They added insult to injury by transferring even the provincial authorities from Frankfurt to nearby Wiesbaden, a small, insignificant town. Berlin became the capital of the new German empire. A new currency was introduced. Frankfurt was completely left out in the cold.

Consequently, anti-Prussian feelings became even stronger along the Main. The resentful bankers refused to participate in any financing that might further the industrialization of Germany in the 1870's. That turned out to be a fateful mistake. Bankers must never permit their personal emotions to interfere with their business decisions. The bankers actively opposed the young joint-stock banks that had been set up in Darmstadt, Dessau, Meiningen. The foolish citizens of Frankfurt didn't even permit the introduction at their local stock exchange of the shares of any railroads located in Prussia.

By the time some cooler heads in Frankfurt realized that they might have made a mistake, it was too late. Their city's financial supremacy was lost. Berlin had become the political and banking capital of Germany.

The decline of Frankfurt was followed by the inevitable exodus of able people toward greener pastures. Frankfurt's best financial brains left for London, Paris, New York; some even went over to the enemy in Berlin.

The end came one day in April, 1901, when a circular was sent out which began:

> It is our sad duty to inform you that in consequence of the decease of Baron Wilhelm Carl von Rothschild, the banking house of M. A. von Rothschild & Söhne will go into liquidation. . . .

Today Frankfurt am Main is again the richest city in Western Germany—and the ugliest. Frankfurt's new opera house looks like a department store, and a department store there looks like a supergarage. The Frankfurters themselves say, "If the word OPER were not written in big letters on the façade of our opera house one would think it had been built by OPEL."

Frankfurt was badly destroyed during the Second World War and decided to rebuild itself in a sort of pseudo-American style, which might better be described as "West German nouveau-riche." Tall, functional boxes of glass and steel stand next to anachronistic buildings from the *Gründerzeit*. Automobile traffic is channeled through a devious system of one-way streets. It often takes longer to go somewhere by car than to walk.

Frankfurt's most important buildings are its banks. They have a soulless, heartless, anonymous appearance. In America the big banks have outgrown the childhood diseases of their functional period and are now trying to acquire the Human Look: paintings, rugs, neo-baroque interiors, cozy niches for writing checks, and luxurious powder rooms for the female customers.

The banks in Frankfurt haven't reached that phase yet. They rely more on the hardness of their currency than on the softness of their interiors. The Germans have not forgotten that some very distinguished-looking banks went down to defeat during the hectic 1930's.

At the end of the last war there were no banks left. The circulating medium of exchange was American cigarettes.

Even Germany's versatile bankers' banks haven't learned yet to deal in tobacco.

Today everybody makes money in Germany. The new crop of depositors doesn't care about the appearance of its banks. They know that their currency is backed by a larger percentage of gold than is the once almighty dollar. No one in Germany likes to be reminded of the past. The big banks intentionally made a visible break with the past. They want to look as no bank in Germany ever looked before.

UPS AND DOWNS OF THE DEUTSCHE BANK

Through the windows of his private office, Hermann Josef Abs sees an immense structure going up across the street. Men with blue steel helmets climb over steel girders. Cement mixers grind noisily. The screeching sounds are not pleasant for Abs who loves classical music, especially the music of Johann Sebastian Bach, the greatest architect of vast musical structures. But somehow Abs doesn't mind the noise, which symbolizes the economic renaissance of Germany in which he has participated as one of the main architects. He ascribes the miracle to a combination of various components—foreign help and confidence, German determination and industriousness, the contribution of twelve million refugees, Erhard's courageous laissez-faire policies, and Adenauer's successful efforts to make Germany again a respected member among the world's nations.

Abs's deceivingly modest official title is Speaker and Member of the Management of the Deutsche Bank. But the Deutsche Bank is Germany's biggest, Abs runs it, and he is doubtless Germany's leading banker.

The Deutsche Bank has had its ups and downs since it was founded in 1870. (In 1929 the Deutsche Bank incorporated the venerable Disconto Gesellschaft that had been set up in 1851.) In the 1870's the Deutsche Bank was not an elegant establishment. It occupied one floor in an old, dilapidated house in Französische Strasse (now in East Berlin, a few yards from Checkpoint Charlie). The stairway was dark and "almost dangerous," and the directors' offices, tiny rooms, faced a dim courtyard.

In spite of such humble beginnings the Deutsche Bank had

an auspicious start. It was founded at the right time. The 1870's saw the big change in Germany, the development from an agricultural to an industrialized economy. The joint-stock banks helped to prepare the conditions that made Germany eventually a great industrial power. The Deutsche Bank considered itself a pioneer in international trade. It financed very large industrial projects and participated in international issues.

In England it has always been said that a banker must never try to be an industrialist. Industrial ventures include risks far beyond the banker's knowledge. But the German banks became great entrepreneurs in the late nineteenth century. Many of the activities of the Deutsche Bank had an expansionist, sometimes even imperialist flavor. An early memorandum defines the primary aim of the bank "to develop and to facilitate commercial relations between Germany and the other European countries and overseas markets."

This declaration carried a considerable element of risk. The Deutsche Bank accepted deposits, competing with Germany's large savings banks. At the same time it was an acceptance bank, a commercial bank, a discount house, an industrial bank, an investment house. And it did many other things, even dealings in real estate.

The risks were not unknown to either bankers or law-makers. According to German law an *Aktiengesellschaft* (limited company) is legally represented by the *Vorstand* (the board of managing directors) whose members are known as *Vorstandsmit-glieder*. This is the policy-making body. There also exists the *Aufsichtsrat* (the supervising board) which is a controlling organ. Its function is to supervise the *Vorstand*. It is concerned with personnel problems and with smooth succession. It tries to find talented people who might be the managing directors of tomorrow.

The dualism has often been criticized. As early as 1863 the *Banker's Magazine* in London wrote about the situation in England, where they had their own problems, "The directors are all honorable men; the manager is an honorable man; the shareholders, they too, are all honorable men (unless women and children); and where such honor and excellence prevail, it is surely unreasonable to identify any man, or class of men, with that invidious and troublesome attribute—responsibility."

The great German banker Ludwig Bamberger, one of the founders of the Deutsche Bank, once said, "in conjunction with an efficient manager the supervising board is superfluous, but with an inefficient one it is helpless."

Bamberger, one of the most brilliant German bankers, came from Mainz, went into politics, got in bad trouble in 1848 for his liberal ideas, was sentenced in absentia to prison and later to death. He spent twenty years in exile in London and Paris. (Heinrich Heine and Richard Wagner went into exile at the same time and for similar reasons.) Bamberger joined the great private bank of Bischoffsheim und Goldschmidt, was one of the founders of the Banque de Paris et des Pays-Bas, returned to Germany after the amnesty of 1866, became a liberal statesman and champion of free trade, and, with Adalbert Delbrück in Berlin, cofounder of the Deutsche Bank. The name, incidentally, was Bamberger's idea. It appealed to the Germans' national instinct and remained a prime asset of the bank. Bamberger also helped to establish the gold standard in Germany. He once made the classic statement, "People lose their wits and go mad about two things, love and bimetallism."

From 1870 to 1900 the Deutsche Bank's guiding spirit was Georg von Siemens who built it into the greatest financial establishment of Germany's Wilhelminian era. He was a man of strong opinions who bitterly fought control by his supervising board, and he won the fight. "When twenty-four men manage a bank, the result is the same as when a girl has twenty-four admirers," he said. "None of them marries her, but at the end she has a baby."

Once he stood up in the Reichstag and declared proudly, "We are in a sense leaders of the spirit of enterprise of the nation." He went even further in a letter to his wife when he wrote, "I think that with every year I am drawing nearer to my object of making German import and export independent of England; the attainment of that object will be a national achievement, as important as the conquest of a province." It was a clear, concise statement concerning his private banking policy as well as the general policy of the German banks at the time prior to 1914.

Many people abroad criticized this expansionist policy. Was Germany wealthy enough to be able to afford such aims? Could the Deutsche Bank dare invest both at home and abroad? In England it was said that the German banks were not constructed for rainy days, and it was cautioned that they should limit their activities.

Perhaps some of this criticism was caused by professional jealousy. Siemens had established a branch of the Deutsche Bank in London which at first met with considerable difficulties. It was said to underbid the local rate of commissions and to do "business at a loss in order to acquire valuable information from the study of its acceptances." But the Deutsche Bank was the only foreign bank in London permitted to contribute its share at the time of the Baring crisis. Its acceptances were always considered first-class.

The greatest overseas venture was the construction of the Anatolian and Baghdad Railway—an enormous project, 1560 miles, from Constantinople to the Persian Gulf. The great railroad opened up Asia Minor, the vast territories around the Euphrates and the Tigris. Mesopotamia was given over to civilization.

(History is quickly forgotten. During the severe political crisis between West Germany and the Arab states, caused by Walter Ulbricht's visit to Cairo in 1965, the German embassy in Baghdad was burned down by an angry mob. Apparently no one remembered there that the country had been "given to civilization" by the Germans.)

The Deutsche Bank also had a share in the issue of the Northern Pacific's six per cent first-mortgage bonds. The president of the Northern Pacific was Henry Villard, formerly known as Heinrich Hilgard in the German Palatinate, where he was born. He was a real entrepreneur—journalist, financier, railway magnate, a man with many friends and many enemies.

Villard invited his friend Georg von Siemens to come over for the opening ceremonies of the Northern Pacific, "to celebrate the new link between two oceans." Siemens went to America in 1883. Unfortunately the program of the festivities was disturbed by an unforeseen attraction. Villard's opponents used the opportunity while he was away from New York to attack his share position.

Villard returned at once and fought like a lion but it was too late. He had to give up his position. During the power struggle the common stock of the Northern Pacific fell from 57 to 23, and the preferred stock from 90 to 56. The security of the bonds of which the Deutsche Bank had a large block was endangered. Siemens immediately helped with the reorganization of the Northern Pacific and the German bondholders suffered no loss.

WHERE THERE'S A WILL . . .

At the end of the Second World War the big German banks were in terrible shape. In the Soviet Zone of Occupation their branches had been liquidated. In Berlin they were closed. And in the three Western Zones they were handicapped by a noncurrency that had lost its primary function as a medium of exchange. Mindful of the dangers of concentrated power, the military governments of the three Western Allies broke up the remaining structure of the Deutsche Bank into ten branch institutes. It was the absolute low point in the long history of the big bank.

The tide turned in 1948 after the currency reform. "As if touched by a magic wand, new forces became active in the economic life of Western Germany," the Deutsche Bank's official history reports. "The sudden rise of production created a sudden change in the situation of the banks." The big slogan was reconstruction. Even visionaries—and good bankers should be men of vision—didn't then think of an "economic miracle."

In the history of the Deutsche Bank these years are known as "the interregnum." It ended in 1952 when the bank's ten local branches were amalgamated into three regional limited companies in Hamburg, Düsseldorf and Munich. These were the so-called "succession institutes." The Deutsche Bank's reserves of 140 million marks were divided up 20 to 40 to 40 per cent. Instead of ten small banks there now were three medium banks.

Even then the thought of "reunification" was always in the minds of the managers although they didn't talk about it when American, British or French officials happened to be around. "Reunification" in this case meant the final merger of the three succession institutes into one big bank.

"One tried one's best to remain together so far as the law permitted," the official report says. "That wasn't always easy, but the leading people in Hamburg, Düsseldorf and Frank-

furt had the same will and the same direction of thought."
Where there's a will, there is usually a way; the managers of
the three banks met regularly and made sure that the three
institutes were directed by the same policies.

For big financing transactions that went beyond the resources of any one single institute the managers used the
form of the consortium. One of the three institutes would act
as leader and the two "sister banks" were asked to join.
Complete coordination had already been reached in questions
of policy and personnel. The trend was irresistible but there
were still some naïve souls among the Western officials who
preferred not to notice it.

The state of affairs was at last legalized late in 1956, when
all restrictions were abolished by law. On March 5, 1957, the
three "sister banks" were merged into the new Deutsche
Bank. The aim of the merger was "to combine the advantage
of both centralized and decentralized organizations and to
avoid their disadvantages." This is banker's language for
having your cake and eating it too.

The legal seat of the bank is now in Frankfurt am Main,
the three central offices are in Düsseldorf, Frankfurt and Hamburg. Each central office has several members on the common
management board. Eventually, it is hoped, the Deutsche
Bank will again be active in reunited Germany "in the spirit
of the old Deutsche Bank."

The Deutsche Bank is a typical German postwar success
story. The balance sheet has gone up from 6.4 billion marks
in 1954 to almost 16 billion marks in 1964. The bank has
over 23,000 employees and is now about the twentieth-
largest bank on earth. Though not officially called a merchant
bank, it carries out nearly all merchant banking operations.
Josef Hermann Abs rightly considers himself a merchant
banker. He has larger resources at his disposal than any other
merchant banker in the world.

PRIMUS INTER PARES

Officially Abs is only a member of the ten-man management board, and its "Speaker." Actually, he is *primus inter
pares*. Abs (who knows London quite well) compares the
Deutsche Bank to "a mixture of Barclays and Hambros." He

thinks of Barclays, biggest of the big British banks, in terms of deposits, and of Hambros as representing the philosophy of merchant banking. It is merchant banking on a gigantic scale, financed by enormous deposits.

Abs is not boasting. The Deutsche Bank does both commercial and investment banking; it does nearly everything with the exception of long-term credit exceeding four years. The most important activities are in the field of short-term current credit. The Deutsche Bank takes deposits in its six-hundred-odd branches in the big and almost all the small towns of Western Germany. It does its own brokerage business (which Barclays or Hambros is not permitted to do). It gives acceptance credit but keeps the acceptances in its own portfolio. There is practically no discount market in Germany.

Abs is a student of history who has not forgotten the sins of the distant—and the not so distant—past. He was around when Dr. Schacht, then the head of the Reichsbank, omitted interest payments due on German obligations and instead used the money to buy back the cheap obligations. Abs is acutely aware of his responsibilities, of the enormous size, scope and possibilities of his bank, and of the inherent dangers. He knows that he is being watched by many people outside Germany and is somewhat allergic to criticism. When *Fortune* magazine, in its June, 1964, issue wrote that

. . . in several respects the German business and banking systems are peculiarly permissive of, and conducive to, a kind of mismanagement . . . In the current capital-investment crisis, the role of the big German banks, in which there is no separation of the banking and brokerage functions, is, to say the least, unhelpful. . . .

Abs wrote a letter which the magazine later published:

I would not contend that the German business and banking systems do not offer a possibility for reform; we are constantly endeavoring to make improvements. However, as long as in countries where the banking and brokerage functions are separated, business failures occur which are definitely more far-reaching and more serious than those which happened in the Federal Republic, I cannot see in such a separation a means to prevent greater failures in my country. . . . He who considers the failures of Borgward, Schlieker, Hugo and Otto Stinnes as a sign of beginning instability of the West German economy, could in the same way regard the case of Allied Crude as "symptomatic" of an unsound financial structure of American enterprises. . . .

Bankers don't have the eminent social position in Germany which they enjoy in England or America where they are considered pillars of their communities. Too many German pillars have turned out to have brittle foundations. Abs is under the close scrutiny of his own countrymen. At a recent television interview he was asked, "How does a man with such power control himself? Have you a method of permanent self-control?"

"I learned to control myself as a partner in a private bank in Berlin," Abs answered. "I was one of five partners. No important decision was taken without the consent of all five partners, and each was responsible with his personal assets."

Abs often says that a banker must learn to control himself before he can control others. "He must have a healthy sense of balance between courage and caution, particularly when he works with funds that were entrusted to him by others." To demonstrate courage and caution at one's own risk, working with the funds of one's own bank, is not the spirit of enterprise. But to work with foreign money, to use foreign interests in the pursuit of an idea—that is a different matter. That proves a genuine sense of enterprise.

"My colleagues on the managing board of the Deutsche Bank have the right balance," he says. "A man with too much caution and no courage wouldn't be helpful in the long run. And a man with too much courage and not enough caution would be dangerous. In the old days the management told the shareholders little. We tell them nearly everything. We know the importance of *diligentia*. But no patent of a concept excluding any crisis has been invented so far. And we are hampered by the attitude of many Germans who still think as if they were bureaucrats under the Kaiser."

Abs conveys a banker's impression of rocklike assurance and elegant dignity but there is no doubt that he is a deeply concerned man. Like so many other Germans whose personal conscience is clear, Abs carries his individual burden of a vast, national guilt. Some Germans try to conceal their feelings by pretense, bluster, joviality; Abs is too intelligent to even try. He knows the sins of the past, both as a human being and as a banker. Sins against humanity and sins against the banker's sacred code.

A thoughtful man who is constantly aware of the past wouldn't want to take sole responsibility for Germany's largest bank. The bank which Abs informally calls "my bank" has no general manager, no titular head. The *Vorstand* is ruled by the *Kollegialprinzip*, on the collegial principle. Its ten members function as a team although each man has his separate duties and regional functions. All important policy decisions, and all decisions concerning deals over one million dollars are made by the team's unanimous consent.

The ten members now meet twice a month, for two daylong sessions, a change from their former schedule of Tuesday and Friday afternoon meetings each week. If one member objects to a planned undertaking it is quietly dropped. The members know, as in the times of Siemens, "that in the long run only such transactions are profitable that are good for the common weal."

HERMANN ABS'S WANDERJAHRE

At sixty-five, Abs is a tall, erect man with a quiet voice, an ironic smile, a dandylike moustache, and a sardonic wit. An ardent Anglophile, he could be a German actor playing an Englishman. He wears English suits, is fond of English understatement and the English sense of humor. He would dearly love to establish the Dickensian atmosphere prevailing in Hambros's partners' room in the large, functional conference room of the Deutsche Bank, which has no atmosphere whatsoever. On the big oval table are cigarettes and cigar boxes, and there are writing pads and pencils, nondescript furniture and wall-to-wall carpeting. Hambros was never like that.

Frankfurt is efficient and thorough and very Teutonic in spite of its thin pseudo-American veneer. Understatement and half-sentences are not for the Germans who are intent, unrelaxed and have a mania for thoroughness. They use a long paragraph when an English banker would use half a sentence. They try to be searching rather than probing. Abs now realizes, wistfully, that at the Deutsche Bank they will never do it as they do it at Hambros. He can console himself with some cold facts, however. They do a lot more business at the Deutsche Bank than at Hambros.

Abs is not a household word in Germany (such as Krupp) but he is well enough known to have been X-rayed several times in his life, by non-Germans and Germans. The most thorough X-raying was done by his fellow citizens in the last few years. The pictures show no trace of political illness. Abs never was, and isn't, a member of *any* political party. It's a great luxury for a man in his position, which he calls "one of my little vanities."

He makes no secret of his political sympathies, however. He is a practicing Catholic, and was a close adviser to Konrad Adenauer. The trade unions respect him as a fair negotiator and one of the leading capitalists who favored giving the workers a voice in the management—the *Mitbestimmungsrecht* (codetermination law) that has been the basis of Germany's generally good management-labor relations. One third of the Deutsche Bank's supervising board is made up of representatives of the employees. (In steel and coal enterprises the ratio is fifty:fifty.)

Owing to his good relations with both management and labor, and his great gift for compromise, Abs has been mentioned as a possibility for very high office in Bonn. Not surprisingly, he is one of the most bitterly attacked West Germans in East Germany.

During the last war, when Abs attended an international conference in Switzerland as a representative of Germany, he was once asked whether he didn't suffer from the inner conflict between being a good Catholic and a good German.

He answered, "This problem never existed for me. I was always a Christian first and a German afterwards." Abs is a dedicated *Weltbürger*, a cosmopolitan "citizen of the world," like Goethe. He hopes for a future supernational Europe, "a sort of cultural Atlantic community that may revive the ideals of the Greek-Roman era." He is not sure though that people and nations will be able to overcome "the narrow confines of nationalism."

Abs was born in 1901 in Bonn, then a somnolent, small university town. No one dreamed of the town's future world prominence. Abs's mother come from the *gutes Bürgertum*, the upper-middle class. His father had been a poor boy who worked his way up to the *gutes Bürgertum*. From his mother Abs inherited a sense of security and belief in himself; from his father ambition and curiosity about the outside world. His father had spent many years abroad as a tutor and later became an official interpreter in French and English. He taught his son the importance of learning foreign languages and about the mentality of other people. Abs speaks English, French, Dutch and Spanish almost as well as his native German and he gets along especially well with foreigners because he understands them.

A boy from the *gutes Bürgertum* would go to the distinguished *Städtisches Gymnasium*, the best local secondary school. There Abs studied Latin and Greek. He was seventeen when the First World War ended and the world he had known came to an end. Abs does not regret it.

"A world set up today like the world before 1914 would again destroy itself," he says. "Much of it was façade and lie."

The old *Ordnung* was gone. Prior to 1914 the son of a *gutbürgerlich* family was expected to study at the university, become an *Akademiker* and graduate as *Herr Doktor*. Abs caused considerable comment during his final year at the *Gymnasium*, when he asked his teacher to insert a note in his final report that he'd finished his studies "in order to become a merchant."

The school authorities were shocked. They said that the word "merchant" had an undignified sound. His classmates, his teachers and the director of the school asked Abs not to insist on the doubtful expression. It would disgrace not only him but the distinguished *Gymnasium* as well. If he would at least consent to have the phrase changed to "in order to study economics," or "modern sciences." That was bad enough because a proper *Gymnasium* graduate was expected to continue with the classical studies.

Abs was a stubborn fellow even then. He didn't give in and received his report with the phrase "in order to become a merchant." He was told that this was the first time such an awful thing had happened in the glorious history of the school.

Abs shattered more illusions when he quit Bonn's Friedrich Wilhelm University one year after he'd begun his law studies there. He felt bored at the august institution and instead decided to take the modest job of trainee at a bank. His father, who had become a prominent lawyer, was not happy but he didn't oppose the idea provided it was only for a while.

Abs never quit banking. Today he says his decision was made that fateful morning when he had an appointment with the owner of Delbrück von der Heydt, a distinguished merchant bank in Cologne. While Abs was waiting for his interview (and to present his much discussed report card) he read a book that was lying in the waiting room. It was the history of an old bank, Bankhaus Gebrüder Schickler, that had been founded in 1712 under the name of Splitgerber & Daum and later became the private bank of Frederick the Great. (This firm was later amalgamated with another house and became Delbrück, Schickler & Co.)

Abs was so impressed that he decided right then and there to become a partner in the firm. It was a somewhat premature dream of glory considering the fact that he had not yet been accepted as a trainee, but he was to achieve it fourteen years later. Anyway, he started as a trainee.

The interim years were well spent and gave Abs his cosmopolitan outlook, that today serves him so well. He spent the depressing postwar years away from Germany. While the country was rocked by the astronomical inflation, Abs had the fascinating job of currency dealer in Amsterdam and got an inside view of the other side of inflation. Later he worked in London, in Paris and in the United States.

He returned in 1928, an ardent "citizen of the world," and became an employee at the Berlin private bank of Delbrück, Schickler & Co. Founder Adalbert Delbrück, a prominent theoretician and lawyer, later became cofounder with Bamberger of the Deutsche Bank. His son Ludwig Delbrück had formed Krupp into a limited company and was appointed banker to the Imperial Privy Purse.

It was a house with great traditions that had weathered many storms and Abs felt at home there. Six years after he'd started to work for them, he was made a partner of Delbrück,

Schickler & Co. He now attributes his fast climb to what he calls "the banker's three cardinal qualities." First, to be able to put oneself into the situation of the customer, or of the person with whom one negotiates. Second, courage as one approaches a certain task. Third, caution—to know the extent of the risk. Abs had studied the history of German banking, a history of too much courage and not enough caution, of underestimated risks and bitter failures. He knew what had happened during the banking crisis of 1931 when too many people had not considered the extent of the risk.

He is still worried on that account. Recently he was asked whether he thought there were some firms in Germany today whose managers didn't carefully evaluate the extent of the risks.

"Definitely," said Abs. "That's one thing that really frightens me."

INTERROGATION

Two years after he'd been made a partner in Delbrück, Schickler & Co., Abs was offered the opportunity to join the *Vorstand* of the Deutsche Bank. The job paid only half as much as the partnership in the private bank but he accepted.

At the end of the last war Abs was interrogated by the Americans, who asked him why he had given up a very lucrative job to become a member of the management of the Deutsche Bank. Abs answered the question with an anecdote, "When my organ teacher joined the army in the First World War, his younger brother and I took over the teacher's duties as regular organist in the large Cathedral and in a smaller church. The job in the smaller church paid much more but I decided to play the organ in the Cathedral. There they had a five-manual organ with seventy-two registers, compared with the two-manual organ with thirty-six registers in the small church. Playing that powerful big organ had always been my dream." He still enjoys playing the big money organ of the Deutsche Bank.

The Americans also wanted to know why he hadn't left Germany after the advent of Nazism. Abs had good connections abroad, and could have gotten a good job.

"I had started to work at Delbrück, Schickler during the

banking crisis. Later I was made a partner. It wouldn't have been right to give up the responsibilities of the partnership. And there were personal reasons. I had a family, my children were born in Berlin. I decided to stay."

Abs was terrified, but not really surprised, by the spread of nationalism and Nazism between the two world wars. He had always been concerned by the failure of his fellow Germans to merge successfully their private and political lives.

"The Germans were never able—and still haven't learned —to form a harmonious whole out of their various spheres of activity—politics, social life, work, hobbies, home life, literature, the arts, and to acquire a complete personality through a natural synthesis. There is a lingering sense of immaturity which persists even today."

Abs didn't join a resistance group but he had close friends among several men who were arrested on the twentieth of July, 1944, and later executed. At one time he was involved in secret negotiations with some people in the West. But a good banker knows "the extent of the risk." Abs knew his responsibility toward his family—his wife repeatedly asked him to be careful—and toward his bank, being a member of the management. Abs makes a careful distinction between the authentic hero who plans his mission, following it through to the bitter end, and the Don Quixote who gets involved in an adventure without giving any thought to how it is going to come out.

When Abs applied for a visa to the United States in 1949, he was asked by the American Consul in Frankfurt, "In your questionnaire you did not state that you ever joined a resistance movement against the Nazis. This does not quite tally with our information. Why didn't you admit that you were active for the group of the twentieth of July?"

"A man who was not hanged or shot by the Nazis should not be considered a resistance fighter," said Abs. "Too many called themselves members of the resistance because they had once told a joke about Hitler and were briefly interrogated by the Gestapo. I didn't want to belong to them."

He was granted the visa.

TURNING PRISON INTO PROFIT

Abs's postwar career was as unusual as his prewar one. Soon after the end of the war he had been sought out by the English as an adviser in currency problems. Later he was jailed by the English. Not long ago Abs was asked by a German reporter how it was possible to be a trusted adviser one day, a common prisoner the next, and a free man ninety days later? Wasn't there something fishy about it? The old story perhaps—the little fish get caught but the big ones always get away?

Abs said, "I had been consulted by the British, who knew me. As so often in those days the British and the Americans were divided in their plans for the future Germany. The Americans wanted a new currency issued by the different Länder [states] of Germany. The British accepted my proposal for a currency that would be issued for the whole of Germany by the Reichsbank in Hamburg. I even suggested two men for the job. This irritated the Americans who insisted upon the execution of the so-called 'automatic arrest.' And thus I was jailed for ninety days by the English at the demand of the Americans."

Abs spent three months in the prisons of Altona and Nenndorf. An able banker turns every experience into profit. Abs made penetrating studies of his fellow prisoners whom he discovered "in their utter nakedness—some turned out to be miserable heels and others were fine men."

After his release he was permitted to return to his estate near Remagen. Then the French wanted him as an adviser but the English didn't permit it. "The dissensions between the Western Allies were one of the phenomena of the postwar years," Abs remembers drily.

In 1948 Abs was elected the first president of the Bank deutscher Länder but was not permitted to take on the job because he'd submitted certain conditions. Later the Marshall Plan authorities assigned him to help organize the Kreditanstalt für Wiederaufbau, the credit institute for the distribution of counterpart funds. He was appointed deputy chairman, and has been chairman since 1959.

"And thus Abs was once again on top, together with the

other big fish who had been on top at the end of the war, and even earlier, in 1933," a brash German reporter said to him during a TV interview.

"Yes," Abs said. "But the big fish started work with one employee, one secretary, and one old retainer."

NO TIME TO GO TO THE DINING CAR

Banking was Abs's third choice of profession. He really wanted to study mathematics and music. He admits now he might have become a second-rate mathematician or musician. By general consent, he is a first-rate banker.

The Germans are hard-working people. Even among his hard-working fellow citizens Abs is known as an especially hard worker. His energy is almost unlimited. He is known to have come out of a ten-hour conference not looking visibly tired. He has robust health, needs little sleep. A typical Abs day begins early in the morning and ends late at night. He thrives on the tensions of his job and is happiest in the middle of a full-sized crisis. While the shells explode all around him, Abs demonstrates poise and sangfroid. A virtuoso in financial brinkmanship, he makes a specialty of bailing out companies whose managements have gotten themselves into trouble. He nearly always succeeds. He is rarely nervous; his staff has never heard him raise his voice. He is supremely confident that everything will come out all right.

"It's like playing patience. If you do it well, not a single card must be left in the end."

Abs has been elected to the supervising boards of over thirty companies, most of them publicly owned (Siemens, Badische Anilin, Daimler-Benz, etc.), some partly or wholly state-owned (the German Bundesbahn, his present "problem child No. 1," and Lufthansa, a former problem child). Abs admits, tongue in cheek, that he always gets elected because his name happens to always come up at the beginning of the alphabetical list of candidates. As a member of the *Aufsichtsrat* (governing board) of these companies, he is mainly concerned with succession problems, trying to find able men who will be the general managers in ten or fifteen years. A difficult job. A whole generation of potential candidates has not come back from the battlefields of the war that Hitler started.

"I won't advise a company that does nothing about its succession problem. And I make it a rule never to get involved with two competing firms. I am on the board of only one electrical concern, one chemical concern, one engineering firm, and so on."

Abs has a banker's memory for figures and a banker's ability for glancing over a balance sheet and spotting the one wrong figure. He probably knows more than any other German banker about the inner workings of the top German firms. He is an expert in bringing together a difficult problem and the best available expert for solving it. He moves with apparent effortlessness from one job to the next, feels lost in a vacuum when an appointment is suddenly canceled and he has "nothing to do" for an hour.

Every moment must be used. On long train rides Abs's associates join him in his private compartment for carefully scheduled conferences. One man rides with him from Koblenz to Bonn where he gets off while another man gets aboard who will stay on until Düsseldorf. There is no time to go to the dining car; besides, Abs hates dining cars. Snacks are bought on the station platform while the train stops for two minutes. If you've seen a man looking like the Speaker of the Deutsche Bank at the delicatessen counter, asking the girl for two rolls with sausage, but hurry up please, you were right: it was Abs. After a day of long meetings and a late dinner discussion on business, Abs summons his secretaries and dictates for a couple of hours, leaving everybody exhausted except himself.

His associates have learned that it takes a long time to understand him. Abs's style is characterized by a profusion of thoughts. He assumes that everybody understands what he is talking about, doesn't realize that he often knows more about the subject than anyone else. He delegates authority freely, doesn't bother with detail. Perhaps the secret of his success is that he enjoys what he is doing, doesn't worry about current problems, has no doubts about his ability to cope with them.

Like Konrad Adenauer, whom he has always admired, Abs has demonstrated a remarkable gift for self-education and a talent for self-discipline. He has taught himself to be absolutely unemotional about everybody and everything concerning his business. An invisible shell of detachment seems to surround him which makes him a formidable fighter in a coolly analytical profession. Abs's friends consider his detachment his greatest strength. It must have taken an iron will to reach that point.

Abs accompanied Adenauer on the Federal Chancellor's first trip to England in 1951. Adenauer's ideas about England at that time were basically not very different from what he'd learned about "the perfidious Albion" in school in the Wilhelminian era. He had never made an effort to understand the English. Getting off the plane in London Airport he made a short, improvised speech which puzzled his guests and terrified his advisers.

After they got to their hotel, Abs sat down with the Chancellor and gave him a thorough two-hour briefing on England and the English. Adenauer was always a fast learner. That night, speaking at a dinner given in his honor by the Prime Minister, the Chancellor delighted his guests and surprised his advisers. He'd skillfully incorporated the gist of Abs's briefing and completely projected it as his own conviction. It was a masterly performance, and the beginning of improved English-German relations.

Later Adenauer went back to London for the funeral of King George VI. By that time he'd learned something about the British people and was deeply impressed by their admirable self-discipline, their devotion to tradition, their sense of fairness, their lasting belief in democracy.

BACH AND GOETHE'S CHESTNUTS

Abs is known in high financial circles for his sardonic sense of humor. It has been said of him that he would rather lose a good friend than a good story. He himself thinks he has mellowed. "Besides," he says, "a man who has no personal enemies rarely has any personal friends."

He does not believe in the supremacy of economic over political forces, as so many businessmen do. On the contrary, he thinks politics should come first. He considered it a political rather than a financial success when he single-handedly launched the first foreign bond issue in Germany since 1914. This happened in 1958, and even some of Abs's associates thought it was much too early. But Abs had correctly guessed the new strength of the German capital market and the issue was a success. In April, 1959, the Deutsche Bank floated a two hundred million mark loan for the World Bank, at five per cent, at par. Abs set the price at 98 for the bonds when they were quoted officially, four months later.

"Of the two hundred million we repurchased one hundred thirty-seven million on our own," he says with quiet satisfaction.

Since then Germany has been a major capital-exporting country. In 1964 German issues amounted to 945 million marks. Abs now propagates European "parallel" loans—the simultaneous issue of several loans by one issuer in several European countries in the respective home currencies through national consortia. The terms and conditions of all parallel issues should be as uniform as possible. The coupon rate should be the same. Different prices bridge the difference in the interest levels in the various countries of issue.

Abs is a man of many hobbies. He loves music and often invites artists for an evening of Bach at his home. He supports young painters. In the garden of his home, in Kronberg, a small town in the Taunus mountains near Frankfurt, he grows strawberries and has some beautiful, old chestnut trees. The trees were already there in the days of Goethe, who was fond of chestnuts. Abs likes to think that Goethe's mother picked some chestnuts from the old trees in his garden and sent them to her son in Weimar.

7

Lehman Brothers: The
Money-Magicians

ADMITTEDLY, Wall Street people feel more at home among the noble temples of finance in the City of London than visiting Citymen do between the anonymous skyscrapers in the canyons of Wall Street. In the City the making of money has always been thought of as an art, or at least a highly developed technique, with the custom-made product tailored to fit closely the individual need. Wall Street produces money in a much bigger, more impersonal way.

"It's a little like the difference between a handmade Rolls Royce and a production-line Cadillac," an English banker says. "But the deeper truth is that many Englishmen simply cannot forget that a generation ago London was the financial center of the Western world. Today it's Wall Street. That hurts."

American bankers and businessmen walk through the City of London with the comfortable assurance of men who know that everybody is just a little richer back home. That's the way American art collectors now feel in the old museums of Europe. They admit that the New World owes a great deal to the Old—history, culture, tradition, taste. But Americans are learning fast and have the means of satisfying their ambitions. The world's great collectors—the men who amass paintings, money, factories, art treasures, businesses, corporations—are now in the United States. Wall Street will never have the quaint atmosphere of the City of London. But Wall Street has the power.

Basically, there is little difference between the financial districts of London and New York. The English do things more gracefully. The City is smaller, more intimate. American businessmen dealing with London's great merchant bankers admire the efficiency and speed, facility and graceful manners of the practitioners of *haute finance*. The fees of these artists are rather modest compared to the bills of the leading New York investment bankers.

Size is really the only distinguishing element. A London merchant banker may launch a bond issue of £300,000 or £500,000. A big Wall Street firm cannot be bothered with such a trifle. Its issues probably start at $5,000,000. Wall Street investment bankers rarely deal with individual owners of firms, but mostly with boards, often with the boards of very large corporations. There are always many people involved, the machinery is cumbersome, everything is quite complicated. People try to avoid responsibility, and it takes much longer to get a decision. There are too many partners, too many meetings, too many experts, too many lawyers, too many analysts. The stakes are higher, and so are the rewards. It is easier to get rich in Wall Street than in the City of London.

Otherwise, both sides agree that things are much the same on both sides of the Atlantic. There is much competition between the members of New York's banking fraternity, and at the same time much give-and-take. Just as in London. It is often said that Wall Street is tough. So is the City though there the toughness is sometimes camouflaged by a thin veneer of Old World courtliness. But when survival is at stake, the graceful trimmings—polite phrases and congenital smugness, studied understatement and gentlemen's agreements—disappear as fast as yesterday's ideas. Then "the rough and vulgur structure of English commerce," as Walter Bagehot called it, becomes apparent.

The City is traditionally proud of its high standards of integrity, of the emphasis placed on trust and verbal promise. But Wall Street is just as honest. Almost all trading of securities is done orally; immense deals are closed over the telephone, only later confirmed in writing. Wall Street's standards of integrity may be different from London's, but they are not lower. The City exercises self-control. Wall

Street is policed by government controls. Wall Street's controls are much stricter.

America is said to be the land of unlimited opportunity. The City of London is noted for its conservatism. But Wall Street's "unlimited opportunity" is restricted by government controls. And London's "conservatism" is more myth than fact.

Wall Street has greater respect for the public investor, tells him much more than they do in the City. American bankers are often shocked by the reticence of their City confrères. Americans still remember what happened in the earlier decades of our century. They often grumble about the restrictions and regulations that surround them like barbed-wire fences but they admit that such controls are necessary to protect the investor. They have learned to live with their fences. They have not forgotten that many people were swindled during the Depression.

Americans go from extreme to extreme, usually remedy one extreme by another. The English, too, have had their critical moments but avoid therapy by extremes. In the past hundred years many investors have been cheated in London, but the English still don't force their bankers to tell the investor everything in order to obtain his money. Public companies in the United States, especially those whose shares are listed on the New York Stock Exchange, are subject to public disclosure of their accounts, to periodical interim reports and many other regulations. After the Bloom case, there was talk in London of imposing similar disclosure requirements in Britain. It's not true, however, that "something like the Bloom case couldn't happen in Wall Street," as some people there claim. It could, but would probably be followed by many law suits and be investigated by the authorities.

Unlike the City, Wall Street is not internationally minded. Americans have had bad experiences with investments abroad; by and large they are not interested in foreign securities. The British, the French, the Germans, the Swiss, the Japanese know a great deal about American companies whose shares are traded at their stock exchanges. Americans know little about European or Japanese companies. They have an instinctive distrust of anything foreign—foreign customers, foreign governments, foreign securities.

Once I saw on the desk of a prominent Wall Street

investment banker a beautifully bound volume. The title was *What I Know about Foreign Securities*. The banker was the author. He handed me the book, with a smile. I opened it. All its pages were blank.

"We've just sent a man to Lagos, Nigeria, on a glamorous, pioneering mission," he explained. "The expenses will be large and the profit will be small. If we'd sent him to Philadelphia on a nonglamorous deal, it would be the other way around—small expenses and large profits. The streets of America are still paved with gold, why go abroad? Instead of spending all that energy on the Lagos job we could have placed a ten-million-dollar bond issue for an American company, right here at the office. Obviously, there is no genuine incentive for international deals. There is little money in it, and we don't need the prestige, the romance, the glamor. I suppose we are spoiled brats. As long as things go well in this country, no one wants to venture out into an uncertain future in foreign lands. Besides, we have neither the education nor the experience of the British."

Wall Street's big sources of money—insurance companies, pension funds, banks, savings and loan associations—have become disillusioned by foreign investments. Many of them have less than five per cent invested outside the United States. The English who know they must trade or perish had an early headstart in the new countries in Asia and Africa— countries for which many Wall Streeters have basic contempt.

There is plenty of lucrative adventure at home. When Macy's and Gimbels are among your customers, why worry about an obscure department store in Lagos, Nigeria?

Different attitudes do exist in the world's two great financial centers. The City of London secretly loves a successful eccentric. In Wall Street individualists are suspect, conformity is the rule. A sort of premium is paid for organization men with the "right" connections, members of the "right" clubs who sit on the boards of the "right" corporations and play golf with the "right" people. No one wants to wear a different shirt.

A few years ago an old, respected Wall Street investment bank decided to have its history written. One of the partners, a former historian, was given the task, and a task force. They went through the firm's archives and discovered some very amusing stuff. Alas, the best stories were not deemed fit to print. The august partnership thought that the merry exploits of the founder-adventurers might not suit the present, dignified image of the firm. As though a respected house couldn't afford some smiling skeletons in its corporate closet! The book was written—a dutiful, rather dull house history.

Americans were brought up to be receptive to high pressure and tough salesmanship. The City of London values low pressure and the soft sell. Paradoxically Americans often show more conservatism than the City's intrepid entrepreneurs. Postwar Wall Street knows no such success stories as the City's S. G. Warburg & Co., or Philip Hill, Higginson, Erlanger (who went all the way to Nigeria to set up a branch).

The City is always looking for greener pastures. Wall Street's pastures have been luxuriously green for a long, long time. And they are very, very large.

Merchant banking in the classic sense of the word came to an end in Wall Street during the Depression. The Glass-Steagall Act of 1933 required bankers to choose between underwriting and the commercial-banking business. They were no longer permitted to do both. Wall Street's "merchant bankers" are investment bankers. Most American investment firms are partnerships but there are also some corporations and their number is increasing. Nearly all of them are privately owned. In the City of London, all merchant banks except N. M. Rothschild & Sons are public companies.

When the great merchant bank of J. P. Morgan split, Morgan Stanley became the underwriting branch of the stately establishment. Morgan Stanley still enjoys a unique position in Wall Street, owing to its history, prestige and bluest-chip clients: General Motors and Standard Oil of New Jersey, the world's largest and second-largest industrial firms; United States Steel, sixth largest, and Du Pont, the eleventh, as well as a rare collection of foreign governments, banks and insurance companies. Morgan Stanley represents "the long-established manufacturing companies," and is not interested in anything "new," though they have graciously consented to deal for International Business Machines. In terms of the City of London, Morgan Stanley might be called a mixture of

Rothschilds, Barings and Lazards, of course minus the merchant bankers' commercial-banking operations.

There are other prestigious houses in Wall Street backed up by a comforting sense of superiority that comes from knowing that one belongs to the small elite of a large financial community. The First Boston Corporation, domiciled in New York despite its name, is a publicly owned company, the respected leader in the government bond business; skilled professionals who avoid all speculative investments and don't even have their own advisory service. A similar hegemony in the competitive-bid utility bond market is conceded to Halsey, Stuart who often buy a whole issue for their own account.

Goldman, Sachs is the uncontested leader in the handling of commercial paper ("acceptances" in City parlance) and represents Ford and General Electric. Lazard Frères is the American branch of the worldwide Lazard establishment, also very important in London and Paris. The Wall Street firm is known for healthy aggressiveness and shrewd judgment. One could go on and on. Kidder, Peabody has a fine history and a strong position in mutual funds. Smith, Barney has made an impressive record on behalf of the service industries. White, Weld & Co. helped to make the publishing industry a *Wunderkind* of Wall Street. Kuhn, Loeb is still respected for its great position under Jacob H. Schiff when it helped to finance the expansion of America's railroads and steel mills.

And there is Lehman Brothers, which has achieved the greatest postwar growth in Wall Street. *Fortune* calls Lehman Brothers "one of the biggest profit makers—many believe the biggest—in the business."

In Wall Street today's success may be tomorrow's failure. People are not easily impressed with success itself but they admire Lehman Brothers for its integrity, philosophy, aggressiveness and, above all, for its methods. Lehmans has a reputation for making money consistently and in a big way.

"Everything these fellows in William Street touch seems to turn into money," a member of the competitive investment-banking fraternity admitted to me the other day, and he sighed. "Many houses are better known for raising money than for making it. Lehmans *makes* money."

The House of Lehman combines old prestige with new authority, ancient traditions with modern skills. Its operations are characterized by "ingenuity," a word that is constantly used by Lehman Brothers' partners. They are a bunch of brilliant entrepreneurs, unorthodox without being unconservative, tied together by their dedication to the firm and their devotion to Robert Lehman, its head. The partners have great enthusiasm for their job—which, basically, as one of them said, is "to buy something for a dollar and try to sell it for two."

At Lehman Brothers the word "adventure" does not have a dubious sound. Individually or collectively, the partners will listen to almost any intelligent proposal. They have a sure sense of timing which is so important in the artistry of high finance. Unless a good idea comes along just at the right moment it may turn sour.

Lehman Brothers is not afraid of risks. "The biggest risk sometimes is to take no risk at all," says Robert Lehman, a cautious-looking banker who doesn't give the impression of ever taking any risk. The partners often come up with ideas which they don't mind calling "deals." Protocol and language are not as strict as along Bishopsgate in London, home of some ancient merchant bankers, where no one would ever utter such words as "risk" or "deal."

American bankers think in much shorter terms than do their English colleagues. Lehmans may buy something, sell it profitably after a while, and that's that. They care more about profits than about "control" of a business. They don't participate in industries, as the London merchant bankers do. Lehmans considers itself an intermediary between those who have big money and others who need it.

Lehmans has no objection to making a fast buck, preferably a million bucks. It underwrites bond issues and distributes stock issues, does much commission business, charges very high advisory fees, arranges mergers, provides risk capital for new ventures, privately "places" million-dollar notes, manages two large investment trusts.

Above all, it seems to know what Robert Lehman calls the secret of "sound" investing, "to put your money in the right place at the right time." Which sounds easy, like writing a good poem or singing a glorious high C. But very few people are able to do it.

The secret of sound investing was impressively demonstrated by the early activities of the Lehman Corporation. "Closed-end" investment trusts, invented by the wily Scots in the 1850's, became as fashionable in Wall Street in the 1920's as bootlegged liquor—and were about as healthy. In one year alone—1927—over one hundred and forty investment trusts were formed. Most of them led a short existence.

An exception was General American Investors which was jointly underwritten in 1927 by Lehman Brothers and Lazard Frères. Lehmans did so well in this venture that it decided to underwrite its own investment trust. The Lehman Corporation was launched successfully in September, 1929. The Corporation's initial offering of one million shares of $100 par value were sold to the public for $104. The partnership of Lehman Brothers had bought one hundred thousand shares for its own account. Within a few days the shares had climbed to $136. Everybody was getting richer by the minute.

The Crash came a few weeks later but fortunately it did not come *too* late for the lucky Lehman Corporation. Much of its new cash had not yet been invested in securities. The first wave of selling ended in November, 1929. There followed the usual reassuring statements by the great, respected leaders of the financial community. Many "experts" decided to buy. Lehman Corporation, ably managed by Partner Monroe C. Gutman, did not buy. Then came the second big wave of selling, followed by a dreary, long period of disaster. Afterwards no one dared make any reassuring statements.

While stock prices fluctuated wildly, Gutman and his analysts did what Robert Lehman now calls "putting your money in the right place at the right time." The right place, they decided, was the Lehman Corporation. With the cash they still had they began to buy back the Corporation's own shares which had plummeted from $136 to about $36. They certainly were "sound investors." They knew that the Lehman Corporation's assets in cash, bonds and preferred stocks were worth a great deal more than the low market price of the Corporation's shares. This was bargain-buying on an "ingenious" scale.

By 1932 they had repurchased and retired almost one third of the original issue, at the same time providing a steady and healthy market for the Corporation's own shares. When the storm was over, the Lehman Corporation emerged as the only trust linked to a major investment house that rode out the Depression with its prestige left intact.

The Lehman Corporation is an organization distinct from Lehman Brothers. It has its own independent board of directors and a wide public ownership. Many people confuse the two organizations but neither one seems to mind since each is a credit to the other. The partnership of Lehman Brothers advises on the purchase and sale of securities, makes the policies, guides the operations, and places its facilities at the disposal of the Corporation. For these services Lehman Brothers receives $225,000 a year from the Corporation. Individual partners who serve as officers and directors of the Lehman Corporation do not receive any additional compensation.

The Lehman Corporation maintains its own research staff. Its assets are now about $400,000,000. It has never missed a dividend payment. Among its shareholders women outnumber men by one third. Monroe C. Gutman, seventy-nine and still in charge, hopes that some of the original shareholders kept their shares. Encouraged by the success of the Lehman Corporation, Lehman Brothers sponsored a mutual fund in 1958. The assets of One William Street Fund are now about $250,000,000.

Even official Washington was impressed by the record of the Lehman Corporation when, after the Depression, an investigation was made into the operations of investment trusts. Lehman partners were listened to respectfully. Some of their recommendations later became law. Trusts must now report all stock commissions paid to brokers, the cost and market value of all securities in their portfolio, and divulge other details.

In 1950 the government brought an antitrust suit against seventeen investment banks whose cooperative syndicate transactions and give-and-take "conspiracies" had long focused the attention of Washington's trustbusters. Counsel for Lehman Brothers, one of the seventeen defendants, argued convincingly that "Lehman Brothers' special attitudes form a continuity of character that is impossible to confuse with the modes of business of the other sixteen defendant firms. The investment banking activity of the firm is but a part of its completely independently conceived relation to industry."

At first sight this looks like a clever semantic argument, placing "special attitudes" against "modes of business" but the fact is that these "special attitudes" do exist. (On the other hand, the government lawyers pointed out, quite rightfully, that investment bankers rarely snatch away from each other a client who has been with another house for a long time. Such things may be done in Madison Avenue, but in Wall Street they are "not done," just as they wouldn't be done in the City of London.)

The "special attitudes" are hard to define and pin down but the expression is dear to the partners' collective heart. It's comforting to know in this competitive age that there are certain things which others don't do at all, or not nearly as well as they do them at Lehman Brothers. The City of London considers making money an art; Wall Street considers it a business; Lehman Brothers considers it a virtuosity. It "generates" new business all the time. It takes an old business and "revitalizes" it. And it was and is always looking for "the wave of the future."

At a time when no dignified investment banker would have anything to do with department stores, airlines, cigarettes, electronics, textiles, and, God forbid, five-and-ten-cent stores, Lehman Brothers had the imagination *and* courage to tackle such ventures. Years ago, it embarked upon a thorough study of the potash industry which lasted for months. Highly paid experts finally decided this was a "wave of the future." Then Lehman Brothers cautiously developed the American Potash and Chemical Corporation and nursed it along until a very attractive bid was made by the Standard Oil Company of New Jersey. The wave of the future had come in.

Right now oil shale is considered another wave at Lehmans. Neither oil nor shale, oil shale is a mineral deposit. When the rock is mined, crushed and heated to a temperature of about 1000° F. it gives off vapors and gases that can be condensed and purified. The end product is, for practical purposes, indistinguishable from crude oil. At Lehman Brothers they admit that the wave is still very speculative, "at the imagination-cum-courage stage." But so were many other projects which since have become "sound investments." Lehman Brothers is proud of its record as successful oilwildcatters in the Southwest. Its special oil department has been very active in the past twenty years. Wall Street believes that Lehman Brothers now knows more about oil than does any other investment bank.

A "special attitude" that turned into a veritable bonanza for Lehmans was their legendary deal with Litton Industries. In the summer of 1953, Charles B. Thornton, vice president and general manager of Hughes Aircraft, left the unpredictable Mr. Hughes. So did several scientists and executives. They decided to strike out on their own, with Litton, then a small electronics company. Naturally, they needed money, and Thornton approached one of Lehman Brothers' senior partners, Joseph A. Thomas, for backing.

Thomas, an exuberant Texan with exuberant personal and political opinions, is known around Lehman Brothers as "the deal person." There was a lot of discussion and then it was decided to raise $1,500,000 for Litton. The Thornton group sold Lehman Brothers 75,000 shares of common stock, "at prices ranging from ten cents to one dollar."

After the first nine months of operation, the skepticism of the Lehman Brothers' partners seemed justified. Litton was struggling badly. Sales were only $3,000,000, and earnings were a measly $154,000. It looked as though this wave of the future would never reach the shore.

What happened later is a page out of Lehman Brothers' Collected Fairy Tales which "sound," rich investors will read as bedtime stories to their kids someday. Last year Litton's sales were $110,000,000, profits over $4,000,000. The shares are now worth at least $800,000,000. In 1965, the shares were traded as high as $150—which isn't bad if you paid ten cents for them.

"Funny thing," Partner Thomas said recently, thoughtfully smoking his cigar. "The hardest things to raise money for often turn out to be the best."

Could another Litton miracle happen today? The cautious optimists in the partners' room say, "yes—under certain conditions." A few years after the Litton deal had become a success, four executives left Fairchild Semiconductor and joined Signetics Corporation, a California outfit making miniaturized circuits. Lehman Brothers, perhaps not unmindful of Litton, loaned Signetics $1,000,000. Then Corning Glass Works told Lehmans it was interested in the integrated circuit field. Lehmans said, fine, they had just the company for them. Corning put another $2,000,000 into Signetics which now has sales of "several million dollars."

Thomas remembers another investment of $29,000 which is now worth $5,000,000. "An exception, to be sure, but if you have enough of them, you're sitting pretty. It's not a question of being smart or lucky, as so many people think. We make mistakes like everybody else. But we always try to be open-minded. We happen to be curious people. Fellow came in the other day and asked me, 'Do you know how many people live in the United States? How many of them have shoes? More than one pair of shoes?' And he went on and on, with a lot of fascinating figures. I was quite impressed until I realized he wanted us to back his invention, a new shoelace made of rubber. We don't like inventions too much here."

Another celebrated Lehmans' *specialité de la maison* was the Hertz deal. The Hertz Corporation was originally the Omnibus Corporation, with subsidiaries operating bus lines in New York, Chicago and other cities. In 1924, John D. Hertz, a Chicago entrepreneur, bought a controlling interest in Omnibus. Later he sold his car-rental business to General Motors. In 1934 he joined Lehman Brothers as a partner.

In 1952, the Omnibus board of directors approved a Lehman Brothers' recommendation to quit the bus transit business and switch to more profitable activities. When General Motors decided to sell the Hertz System, the highest bidder turned out to be no one else but—Omnibus. Strange and devious are the ways of Big Business. Two years later, Omnibus changed its name to Hertz Corporation. At Lehman Brothers, Partner Frank J. Manheim kept plugging the car-rental business that seemed to develop into a worldwide wave of the future. Under his guidance, and with Lehman Brothers' backing, the Hertz Corporation began to repurchase Hertz franchises which General Motors had sold to independent owners. Hertz began to acquire local outfits around the United States and then expanded abroad. Today "Hertz" is almost a household word on several continents.

Partner Manheim, who foresaw the expansion and designed the overall strategy, is a former college professor who taught French literature and history before he joined Lehman Brothers. He considers literature and history excellent approaches to investment banking. He says, "I get tired of people who think that banking is accounting. Banking is imagination."

The Hertz record is regarded as another proof of Lehman Brothers's "ingenuity." The market value of Hertz's common stock has gone up from $7,000,000 in 1953 to nearly $100,-000,000 in 1965.

"The Hertz deal," says Manheim, "should help to deflate the Wall Street myth that the investment banks 'run' America's industries. On the contrary—they *serve* America's industries."

Lehman Brothers had some spectacular postwar successes in the oil field. In 1950, Partner Edwin L. Kennedy heard that Jergins Corporation, a West Coast oil-and-gas company, was up for sale. A big Wall Street firm had tried to find a buyer, and failed. Several prospects had been deterred by Jergins's half-ownership of California's San Ardo field which was shut down because there seemed to be no market for its thick, low-viscosity oil.

The experts in Lehman Brothers' oil department didn't share this pessimism. They were sure there might be a market somewhere for such oil. They figured that Lehman Brothers might eventually make nine million dollars' profit on Jergins's $29,000,000—if the company's assets were sold piecemeal. Nine million dollars ain't hay, even for Lehman Brothers.

Now the wheels of high finance began to turn with clockwork precision. Partner Ehrman raised $10,000,000 from the partnership, from Lehman Corporation and other Wall Street houses. Then he borrowed $19,000,000 from the Chase Manhattan Bank. The Chase Manhattan won't lend nineteen million to the first fellow who comes along but they trusted Lehmans' oil experts.

Jergins was bought by the group and renamed Monterey Oil. Within eighteen months Monterey sold an office building, a gasoline plant, and a small electronics firm—which later became Beckman Instrument Corporation and turned into a special success story of its own. Monterey was able to pay back five million to the Chase Manhattan and another five million to the investors. Monterey still owed $19,000,000.

By that time some people began to realize the potential of the long-neglected San Ardo field—exactly as Lehmans' oil experts had predicted. Lehman Brothers could afford the luxury of declining several excellent offers. ("It was like in Hollywood when a 'property' is getting very hot and the price goes up overnight," a partner remembers.)

At last Lehman Brothers accepted an offer from General Petroleum, a subsidiary of Socony Oil, of $18,200,000 for San Ardo. Now Monterey was able to pay off the Chase Manhattan and the remaining five million to the original investors.

Within two years, to the astonishment of the financial community, Lehman Brothers had raised and paid back $29,000,000, and still owned Monterey Oil's assets, then worth about $28,000,000. Today Monterey Oil is worth a great deal more. Lehman Brothers, Lehman Corporation and individual Lehman partners still hold most of Monterey's two hundred thousand shares for which they had originally paid nine cents a share. Last year, the shares were traded as high as $45 at the New York Stock Exchange.

If Daddy had bought a thousand nine-cent shares of Monterey sixteen years ago for ninety dollars, and *if* he had kept them, his ninety-dollar investment would have grown into forty-five thousand dollars. For a mere nine hundred dollars Daddy could have bought himself a fortune worth almost half a million dollars. Yes, miracles still happen in Wall Street.

And now turn out the lights, kiddies, and sleep well.

By the severe standards of the City of London where the modern financial age begins circa 1694 A.D., when the Bank of England was founded, Lehman Brothers, the oldest continuing partnership in American investment banking, is not very old. When Lehman Brothers was founded in 1850, Baring Brothers was over ninety years old, Rothschilds over fifty.

All three came from Germany which contributed to classical merchant banking as much as to classical music. The Barings came from Bremen in the north, the Rothschilds from Frankfurt in the center, the Lehmans from Würzburg (Bavaria) in the south. All three were, and still are, a family business.

In 1844, Henry Lehman, the twenty-two-year-old, enterprising son of a Würzburg cattle merchant, arrived in America. Like many other immigrants he began his career as an itinerant peddler. He was honest and hard-working, and the people trusted him. A year later he settled in Montgomery, Alabama, and hung out a small sign, H. LEHMAN, outside his little shop on Commerce Street. By 1850 he had been joined by his younger brothers, Emanuel and Mayer, and the three brothers formed a partnership called Lehman Brothers. The Montgomery directory listed them as "grocers." Actually the store supplied clothes, utensils, food, and a great many other articles needed by the local cotton farmers.

Business was excellent in booming Montgomery where the war cry was "Cotton is king!" Many customers paid in raw cotton instead of cash. The Lehman brothers were resourceful traders. They first made a profit when they acquired the cotton and then resold it again at a profit. A shrewd sense of profit-making is characteristic of the beginnings of all merchant-banking dynasties. These men prospered because they were just a little smarter than the next fellow. Gradually Lehmans' retail trade became less important as it devoted more energy to the cotton-brokerage business.

Henry Lehman was known as something of a hypochondriac. He was always haunted by the fear that he was going to die of yellow fever. People said he was going to live until ninety. When the dreaded disease broke out in Montgomery in 1855, Henry hurriedly left town and went to New Orleans where Lehman Brothers was going to have a branch office. A few weeks after he arrived there he caught yellow fever and died, at the age of thirty-three.

In 1858 Emanuel Lehman opened an office in New York where the big opportunities were. But Emanuel was, above all, a Southern patriot, and when the Civil War broke out, he hurried back to Montgomery, the Cradle of the Confederacy.

The Lehmans served the South well. Emanuel fought in the Confederate Army. Later he helped to sell Confederate bonds in London, and then he went on to the Continent, trying to sell cotton. It was a great chance for an ingenious merchant who was not afraid of running the blockade. He could buy cotton in the South cheaply and sell it in Germany at ten times the price. It may not have been very patriotic; it may even have involved him in some smuggling. But what about the earlier activities of the Barings and Rothschilds during the Continental blockade? Didn't the Barings help in getting the silver treasure of King Charles IV of Spain out of Vera Cruz, Mexico, and into the hands of Napoleon, Britain's arch enemy, with the help of American merchants, and with special permission of the British government? Didn't the Rothschilds organize big shipments of British guineas and French napoleons d'or right through the enemy lines to supply the army of the Duke of Wellington then fighting in Spain? Today the descendants of the great merchant adventurers are understandably proud of such exploits. When the deals are big enough they become *coups* and wind up in the history books.

Emanuel Lehman's brother, Mayer, stayed in Montgomery, was active in war work, and was called "one of the best Southern patriots." He had powerful friends in high Confederate circles, among them Governor Thomas H. Watts of Alabama and Hilary A. Herbert, later Secretary of the Navy under President Grover Cleveland. In December, 1864, he was appointed to a special committee that tried to raise funds to aid Confederate prisoners in the North.

Certainly a worthwhile endeavor. Mayer Lehman had an idea that he might have borrowed straight from the Barings or Rothschilds. Suppose the Committee were to send half a million dollars which the Alabama Legislature had authorized in shipments of cotton to cotton-starved New York? There the proceeds of the sale would be used to buy blankets, medicaments and other provisions. The shipments would have to go right through the battle lines—exactly as in the earlier days of the Barings and Rothschilds. Some 1500 bales of cotton were actually shipped to Mobile pending Union permission for transportation through the lines.

Mayer Lehman personally carried a letter from Governor Watts to President Jefferson Davis. Dated December 14, 1864, the letter outlines the project and warmly recommends the bearer. "He is a foreigner but has been here fifteen years and is thoroughly identified with us," wrote Governor Watts. "It will be necessary for him to go through the lines. I ask that he may be furnished with the proper passports and endorsed by you as the agent of the State of Alabama."

Jefferson Davis complied, and on January 14, 1865, Mayer Lehman sent a written request to General Ulysses S. Grant, commander of the Union Armies, for safe conduct through the battle line.

"We well know that a gallant soldier must feel for those brave men, who by the fortunes of war are held prisoners exposed to the rigors of a climate to which they are not accustomed, the severities of which are augmented by the privations necessarily attendant upon their condition," Mayer Lehman wrote persuasively. But there was no answer, and two weeks later Mayer wrote again.

Permission was never given. Late in February, President Davis was told that General Grant refused to open the battle line to Mayer Lehman. Washington had decided that relentless attrition would end the war quickly. Six weeks later General Lee surrendered. Mayer Lehman's scheme had become meaningless. Before the arrival of Federal troops in Montgomery, 88,000 bales of cotton were put to the torch, part of which were assets of the Lehman Brothers.

In 1866 Emanuel Lehman went to New York to operate a cotton-brokerage business at 176 Fulton Street. Two years later Mayer followed him there and they moved to Pearl Street where they stayed ten years, when they moved again to larger quarters, at 40 Exchange Place.

Another parallel with the Barings and the Rothschilds who left their serge and linen stores in Exeter and in Manchester, and went to London in search of bigger opportunities.

Lehman Brothers prospered during the economic and industrial expansion in the United States in the second half of the nineteenth century. They kept their original firm in Montgomery until 1912. The New Orleans branch lasted until 1936. But they concentrated their energies in Manhattan. Emanuel remained the firm's conservative "inside" man, while the more aggressive Mayer saw the outside contacts. For many years the two brothers alone managed the affairs of the firm. They were among the founders of the New York Cotton Exchange, became members of the Coffee Exchange and of the first New York Petroleum Exchange. In 1887 the firm acquired a seat at the New York Stock Exchange.

Toward the end of the century, Lehman Brothers, still primarily a commodity house, began to engage in enterprises which led to investment banking. It acted as "private bankers" to industry, and was appointed Fiscal Agent of the State of Alabama. It sold the state's bonds (not an easy job in view of the South's bad credit rating) and serviced Alabama's debts, interest payments and other obligations. Becoming interested in the industrialization of the South, it backed cotton mills in Alabama and Louisiana.

After Mayer Lehman's death in 1897 and Emanuel's retirement shortly afterwards, a second generation of Lehmans—Philip, Sigmund, Arthur, Meyer H. and Herbert—took over and directed the firm's activities toward investment banking. The young partners became interested in the country's new technology. Philip and Sigmund Lehman joined John Jacob Astor and P. A. B. Widener in launching the Electric Vehicle Company which contributed to the early development of automobiles. In 1899 they backed the Rubber Tire Wheel Company of Springfield, Ohio, makers of the Kelly-Springfield tire, the only pneumatic tire then on the market. Apparently the Lehmans had a hunch even then for the wave of the future.

After the Spanish-American War, Lehman Brothers and other bankers arranged the merger of several Cuban tobacco firms into the Havana Commercial Company. In March, 1899, the firm underwrote its first public offering—the preferred and common stock of an industrial combine that brought together the country's five leading producers of steam pumps, and later emerged as the Worthington Pump & Machinery Corporation.

At the beginning of the twentieth century, partnership in Lehman Brothers was limited by a family law to blood relatives bearing the name of Lehman. Philip (the son of Emanuel) and Arthur (the son of Mayer) were the senior partners. During the following decades, members of the Lehman clan married into other Wall Street banking houses of German-Jewish origin—Kuhn, Loeb; Loeb, Rhoades; Hallgarten; Wertheim; and Lewisohn Sons.

An indestructible myth claims that "Wall Street is dominated by a sinister conspiracy of international capitalism," and that America's Jewish banking firms began as branches of Europe's "international bankers." The emphasis is on the "international" character of the so-called conspiracy. The myth is indestructible because it has long been effective in the hands of political extremists. Goebbels's theory that a lie, often enough repeated, will eventually become accepted as the truth, is now a fact of political life and an instrument of psychological warfare. The myth of the "sinister conspiracy" was believed first by millions of people who listened to the Nazi and Fascist propaganda, and later by millions listening to Communist propaganda. It is still believed by many people all over the world.

These people don't know, or don't want to know, that there are almost no Jews in the command posts of Wall Street's big financial forces where the big money is concentrated—the insurance companies, pension funds, great commercial banks, and various "institutions."

The City of London is not exactly a hospitable place for newcomers, foreigners and Jews. Wall Street is even less so. In London, the leading Jewish merchant bankers are now accepted socially. In New York, they have never been accepted. Robert Lehman, whom *Fortune* called "a Wall Street patrician," is not a member of the Links, New York's leading "corporate establishment" club. At the Links, at the Bohemian Club and other august institutions the House of Lehman is respected as a "smart" Jewish firm, and represented by some of the firm's non-Jewish partners. Other Jewish houses, known as "not terribly smart," are also represented by their non-Jewish partners, together with the Gentile investment banks, some of which are known as "smart" and others as "not terribly smart."

The fact is that no Jewish-American banking house began as the offshoot of an "international" (read: European) house. The truth is far less glamorous. Nearly all of them began as peddlers and petty merchants in the United States of America, in rags-to-riches style. Nearly all of them made their first fortunes during and after the Civil War when they supplied much-needed goods. The Seligmans were clothing merchants and made uniforms. Goldman, Sachs was in the window-glass business, later became money-lenders and note-brokers. The Lazards got rich in New Orleans and California in the clothing business during the 1870 gold rush. Messrs. Kuhn and Loeb were successful clothing merchants in Cincinnati. The Speyers, the Guggenheims, the Hallgartens, and many others started out as merchants before they became bankers.

Clearly, the beginnings of merchant banking are similar on both sides of the Atlantic; Europe's merchant bankers too were merchants before they were bankers. The difference is that the old European banking dynasties have learned to live with their humble, colorful, exciting past. Americans, now only in the third generation, are not as relaxed yet about *their* recent history.

In the early years of this century, Lehman Brothers had close relations with another "smart" Jewish house—Goldman, Sachs & Company. Philip Lehman was a friend of Henry Goldman, the other firm's senior partner. Both shared an enthusiasm for merchant banking and art collecting. The Lehmans were richer, the Goldmans more enterprising. Between 1906 and 1914 the two houses jointly underwrote fourteen security issues. The first two, in 1906, were for the General Cigar Company and for Sears, Roebuck & Co. Julius Rosenwald, the guiding genius behind Sears, Roebuck needed money to expand but it wouldn't have occurred to him to go to the public for money. He told his friends Philip Lehman and Henry Goldman he wanted to privately borrow $5,000,000. There were no issues of mail-order houses on the market. The great Wall Street bankers avoided the retail business like the plague.

Goldman and Lehman took a deep breath and decided on a public offering. They had the vision of an America that some day might turn from a production economy into a customers' economy. A big mail-order house might yet become a profitable client. The issue was a success.

Six years later, F. W. Woolworth Co. needed money. J. P. Morgan wouldn't touch a five-and-ten cent store with a flagpole. Even Goldman and Lehman hesitated for a while but Woolworth sweetened the deal. As in the earlier case of Sears, Roebuck it was arranged that the bankers would buy twenty per cent of the common *and* preferred stock but the total price was less than the value of the preferred stock alone. Hence the bankers got the common shares "free" for bringing out the issue.

A soft, collective sigh is heard around the partners' room at One William Street when the Lehman partners reminisce about these deals.

"We could own twenty per cent of these giants today and be billionaires," a partner says. "Unfortunately, we did not keep the shares."

The First World War which ended so many things on both sides of the Atlantic brought the underwriting activities of

Lehmans and Goldmans to an end. After the war, new partners appeared in both firms. At Lehman Brothers, Philip's son Robert, born in 1890, joined the partnership. He was a third-generation Lehman, a grandson of senior founder Emanuel. He went to college, and served as an artillery captain in the First World War. He was only thirty when he joined the firm in 1920 but he had inherited the family's very special talent for the business.

Five other Lehmans were then in the partnership but Robert realized that some day there might not be enough talent left in the family to carry on and expand the firm. He brought in the first non-Lehman partners—John M. Hancock, a former naval officer; Monroe C. Gutman, a young business man; and Paul M. Mazur, a Harvard graduate.

At Goldman, Sachs the guiding spirit was then Waddill Catchings. There was also a gifted young man named Sidney Weinberg who had started in the firm as an office boy, and is now respected as one of the shrewdest investment bankers in Wall Street.

(Today many great investment banks are proud of having at least one former office boy among their partners, the young fellow who ran long enough and hard enough until he made it. In the official history of Kuhn, Loeb & Co. the admittance to the partnership of Jerome J. Hanauer "who had entered the employ of the firm as an office boy" is called "the recognition and rewarding of meritorious service, regardless of family connections.")

Disagreement arose at last between Goldman, Sachs and Lehman Brothers, as often happens when the sordid subject of money is concerned. The Goldman, Sachs partners didn't like to split profits with the Lehmans on deals originated by Goldman, Sachs—and you can't blame them. The younger Lehman partners didn't like to remain silent, invisible partners in some spectacular deals, involving more Lehman money than Goldman money, with the whole credit going to the other firm—and you can't blame *them*.

At last the differences became too painful to be ignored. Wall Street was talking. In 1925 a memorandum was drafted between Herbert and Arthur Lehman, and Catchings and Arthur Sachs. It listed sixty corporations that the two firms had jointly underwritten. The two houses agreed to respect each others' "rights" to certain corporations. Goldman, Sachs was granted the prime interest in forty-one companies and Lehman Brothers in nineteen. The Securities Act of 1933 forced the two houses to amend the memorandum. Old wounds broke open, and there was much bitterness on both sides. Only in 1956 was a permanent truce established. Sears, Roebuck had just set up its sales acceptance subsidiary and once more needed money. Sidney Weinberg called on Robert Lehman and suggested that the two houses jointly resume Sears financing.

Many people in Wall Street believe that the breakup of the comfortable relationship with Goldman, Sachs was the best thing that happened to Lehman Brothers. Alone, on their own, the Lehman partners had to roll up their shirt sleeves and go out for new business. They haven't let their sleeves down yet. It was the beginning of the new era of ingenuity —and of the phenomenal rise of the firm.

The partnership of Lehman Brothers has grown so fast in recent years that no one seems to be sure exactly how many partners there now are. Each of three senior partners I asked mentioned a different figure. At this writing, Lehman Brothers has thirty-one partners. The firm's legal counsel, Edwin Weisl, of Simpson, Thacher & Bartlett, an influential man in Wall Street and at the White House, sits in on many meetings. The partners range in age from seventy-nine to twenty-nine, in background from former office boy to ex-general, from liquor company president to former college professor.

Wall Street appears to some people as a soulless city district populated in daytime by faceless organization men, but conformity has not quite overtaken Lehman Brothers on the partnership level. One partner wears lavender-colored shirts; another owns an interest in prizefighter Cassius Clay and smokes cigars made by a non-Lehman company (though some do smoke cigarettes manufactured by a top Lehman account). Principal partner Robert Lehman owns a share in the Los Angeles Angels, a baseball club, and the Los Angeles Rams, a football club.

After Robert Lehman's arrival in the firm in the 1920's, its new economic philosophy was evolved, which turned out to be the foundation of its later success. At Lehman Brothers they realized—a little earlier than elsewhere—that the key to America's future prosperity was the size of consumption, not of production. It was a revolutionary thought at a time when most investment bankers were not interested in the distribution of consumer goods. As a result Lehman Brothers began to finance department stores, drygoods manufacturers, motion pictures and airlines. It did many other things that the more conventional bankers ignored. In the 1920's, when Hollywood was making wonderful one-reel slapstick pictures, Lehman Brothers financed B. F. Keith Corporation, Radio-Keith-Orpheum, Paramount, and Twentieth-Century Fox. Robert Lehman was so confident of the future of commercial aviation that he joined forces with W. A. Harriman & Co. in organizing the Aviation Corp., the first integrated unit in the new aviation business, which later became American Airlines. He was one of the early directors of Pan American Airways Corporation. Lehman Brothers also financed National Airlines, Capital Airlines and Continental Airlines.

Long before radio and television became foaming waves of the future, the Lehman people were mixed up with the new broadcasting industry and sponsored the first public underwriting of a television company, the Allen B. Du Mont Laboratories. They participated in the development of the electronic age by financing the Radio Corporation of America. They had their hands early in American Cable & Radio Co. and the Western Union Telegraph Co.

Lehman Brothers was investment banker for over half of the twenty leading American retailing enterprises. It financed both Macy's and Gimbels when the two department stores waged their mythical war. Macy's might not tell Gimbels, and vice versa, but Lehman Brothers talked to both, though never about the respective competitor, adroitly avoiding a conflict of interests. By keeping their own counsel and sticking to the ethics of their profession, Lehman partners advised at the same time Federated Department Stores, Allied Department Stores and Interstate Department Stores; Woolworth, Grant and Kress; Philip Morris and P. Lorillard Co.

Senior Partner Paul M. Mazur is credited for developing the firm's special knowledge of the distribution of consumer goods. Mazur, a reticent, gray-haired, slow-spoken man, the prototype of the dignified investment banker, had published as early as 1927 *Principles of Organization Applied to Modern Retailing*, which is still a basic textbook on the subject.

In 1931, when Prosperity was only a memory and a hope, when management and labor were fighting about the eight-hour day, Mazur wrote in "New Roads to Prosperity":

> The five-day week is simplicity itself in content. All labor in America would be limited to five out of the seven days of the week. . . . To the forty million adult workers of the United States there would be suddenly given one added day of leisure per week.

Twenty-two years later Mazur wrote that America's system of free enterprise would last only if industry gave more attention to consumption and the forces which bring it about. He was right again: today the customer is the uncrowned king in the United States. Mazur was one of the first people at Lehman Brothers who foresaw the future of automation. And at the antitrust investment banking trial in 1952, government lawyers called him "the most famous expert in the department store field."

Department stores had been Mazur's early interest. After graduation from Harvard, as a B.A. in economics, he worked at Filene's in Boston, later served as director of several department store organizations and adviser to chains. He organized Lehman Brothers' famous industrial department that would help the partners "to formulate judgment about prospective opportunities, particularly in the retailing field."

"Clothes and automobiles change every year," he said recently. "But because the currency remains the same in appearance (though its value steadily declines) most people believe that finance doesn't change. Actually debt financing changes like everything else. We have to find new models in financing, just as in clothes and automobiles, if we want to stay on top. In the old days most companies needed money and we had to find it. Today it's easy to find money but the question is what to do with it. More people want to buy companies than to sell them. There is our new job. And, besides, we must remain inventive architects of the money business."

The inventive architects show ingenuity in creating new vehicles for money and credit. Lehman Brothers, modern magicians without silk hats and tail coats, perform veritable money miracles. They talk of "senior" and "junior money," of "rolling over an old loan" and "coming up with a blended rate." They have discovered new ways of handling money.

"The main problem," says Partner Herman H. Kahn, "is not to get imitated right away." Kahn himself, who started at Lehman Brothers as a $15-a-week runner and landed in the partners' room, is a much-imitated American success story. A boy from the Lower East Side of New York, he had heard from his parents, poor immigrants from Europe, many wonderful stories about the Rothschilds. He read all the stories about the poor boys who had become millionaires in God's Own Country. He was sure he was on the right track when at the age of eighteen he got his $15-a-week job with Lehman Brothers in 1928.

A year later, after the Crash, Herman wasn't so sure any more but he hung on, enrolled at New York University, took all the available economics and finance courses and started to work on two theses—on the tobacco industry and on the public utilities industry. Before turning in his papers Herman asked the boss at Lehman Brothers' sales department to read them.

As a result Herman was promoted to the statistical department where he studied securities and portfolios in the daytime, continuing his university studies at night. By 1934 all employees of the statistical department had been laid off except Herman who became everybody's analyst. The next year he was promoted to be head of a newly established department that specialized in seeking out corporations in need of an investment banker.

Two years later, Herman persuaded the partners to enter the private placement field. Private placements have been known in Wall Street since the mid-1930's as a new, revolutionary technique. A company that wants to borrow long-term money may offer bonds to the general public or place its debt notes directly ("privately") with an insurance company, pension fund or another large institutional investor. The offering is not available to the general public. The borrowing company avoids the red tape and legal expenses of an SEC registration. Underwriting fees are smaller than in a public issue, and the deal can be closely tailored to the borrowing company's needs. The tailoring is done by the investment banker who acts as middleman.

By 1948 American corporations for the first time had

placed more debt privately than publicly. Today the big institutional lenders with their enormous resources look "aggressively" for new deals in which they can invest. The investment banker's job is to find and arrange such deals. Lehman Brothers is now able to raise a hundred million dollars just by making a few telephone calls.

For Lehman Brothers such private placements are less profitable than public offerings, but also less risky. Instead of buying bonds from a company which they offer for sale, hoping for a profit, they act as a catalyst, bringing together borrower and lender, and negotiating mutually acceptable terms and conditions. They get a fee which is smaller than that for a public sale. Lehman Brothers is now in second place, after the First Boston Corporation, among a small group of investment bankers handling this side of finance.

"Merchant banking," says Partner Kahn, "is the conversion of a dream into reality, with the help of money. Merchant banking is a vision. Investment banking is a technique."

Kahn speaks poetically of a company that wanted to diversify and go into financial services: a dream that had to be converted into reality. But the company had been growing fast and needed so much money that it didn't have the basic capital to raise more money. This didn't worry the magicians at Lehman Brothers. They happened to know just the company that had plenty of money and was looking for such an opportunity.

"We brought them together," says Kahn. "We blended them and recast the capital structure. We are a fountain of investment opportunities. An exciting deal, and we were the spark plug. Our commission was fifty cents a share, which would have cost them $1,750,000 in commissions. The chairman of the board came to see us. He was afraid his board might not approve the deal, it seemed just too expensive. I didn't blame him. I said, 'Now, how about a fee of $1,000,-000?' The directors approved and voted their appreciation to us."

And there was a good, not too well-known finance company which needed money, as much as could possibly be raised. Lehmans' industrial department examined the company under their ultramicroscopes, liked what they saw, and wrote a lengthy analysis. The partners agreed to endorse the company's credit up to $15,000,000. Sitting in his swivel chair in the partners' room, looking into the room and talking into the phone, Kahn began to raise the money. Within less than an hour he had raised $25,000,000. A great many people in Wall Street are delighted to lend millions of dollars as soon as Kahn drops a hint, on behalf of Lehman Brothers.

The following week the president of the finance company was invited to lunch in the partners' dining room. The final details were amicably discussed. All went well, until the president mentioned, quite casually, that the bonds of his company were not eligible for investment by life insurance companies. They were good bonds but for technical reasons they had failed to meet the strict requirements of securities which life insurance companies may take into their portfolios.

There was a stunned silence around the large table as the awful truth of the president's remark began to sink in. Kahn had raised the $25,000,000 from life insurance companies.

"It was like announcing that the wedding cannot take place after the invitations are sent out," Kahn says, with a shudder. "There was only one thing to do. I would have to make a full disclosure to everybody. If they wanted to quit, we would make good all damage. I went back to my phone and called the insurance companies, one after the other. I told them that these securities were eligible by the rules of reason but not by the laws that govern insurance companies. One by one, the companies said they would hold to their commitments and place the securities in a special reserve account. Only the last man said he wanted the previously accepted five per cent interest increased to five and a half per cent. In order to make amends, he offered us two million more than he'd first promised. They all trusted Lehman Brothers."

The divine element must not be ruled out of investment banking, according to Partner Harold J. Szold. He joined the firm in 1924 and helped to finance Brunswick, the Jewel Tea Company, General Cigars and Allied Stores—glorious chapters in the annals of Lehman Brothers.

"God has been good to us," says Szold. "Many unorthodox deals made money for our customers. When I started to work here, it was tough to find money. Today the economy virtually generates money, and we have to find opportunities for the money. But with prestige and vision one can still do all kinds of ingenious things. Like the Brunswick deal."

Szold became a director of Brunswick in 1953 when the situation of the famous, old company was "almost hopeless." The bowling alley business had been in bad shape. After the introduction of the automatic pinsetter Brunswick suddenly had plenty of orders, but neither the plant facilities nor the money to fill them.

"That's the worst thing," says Szold. "That really hurts. We had ten million dollars but needed almost ten times that much—for machinery, plant, buying out a partner. But there is always a lot of information at Lehmans and a traffic in ideas. Somebody happened to know of a company with the plant capacity for production. The bank said they would give us $24,000,000. Unfortunately we needed twice as much. We had to go to a finance company for the financing of customer purchases. They charged us 11½ per cent. People said we were making a mistake. I told them it was better to borrow quietly at 11½ per cent than to put out bonds. Maybe I was making a mistake. But the only way to avoid making mistakes is to do nothing. Like the fellow who joins the poker game and says, 'Now, boys, remember—if we all play carefully, we can all win a little.' "

Six years after Szold had joined the board of directors of the "almost hopeless" company, Brunswick was the talk of Wall Street. Anyone courageous enough to invest $10,000 in Brunswick's debentures in January, 1957, had $68,000 thirty months later, after a series of splits and stock dividends. No wonder Szold believes in the help of the Almighty.

"I'm getting skeptical about the so-called geniuses in merchant banking. Of course one has to know one's arithmetic but above all it's a matter of instinct and timing and—why not admit it?—of being lucky. In the careers of nearly all successful men there is always an element of luck."

Szold remembers the owner of an oil company who came to see him one day late in October. The tax laws were going to be changed, the man thought the country was going to the dogs, he was sick and tired of the business, and wanted to sell it. For cash. For thirty million. Not one penny less. Owing to taxation he would have to have the money on December thirty-first.

There was no time for a public offering or for any of the regular channels. But Lehman Brothers wanted to make the deal. Its oil department had carefully investigated the impatient customer and was certain that his business was worth much more than $30,000,000, but it didn't tell him *that*. Instead Lehman Brothers borrowed $20,000,000 from the Chase Manhattan. With the prestige of the Chase Manhattan and Lehman Brothers behind the deal it was child's play to raise another $10,000,000. By the end of December the syndicate had bought the man's oil business for $30,000,-000. The impatient customer had his check. He was very pleased. So was Lehman Brothers who later resold the business, at an undisclosed but considerable multi-million-dollar profit.

"It was the prototype of a nice, clean deal—for three good reasons," says Szold. "First, don't be afraid to look for irregular channels when you can't find a regular one. Second, be sure to know the oil business, or you'll get your fingers burned, as have so many other people. Third, you must have real prestige to get other people to put up the money for you. That's the most important element. It takes years of integrity and honest work to build up a good name. The rest is relatively easy. You find out all there is to know about a certain business and then you bring the right kind of financing to that certain business. No magic at all."

Many years ago Szold joined the board of directors of the ailing Jewel Tea Company. He soon realized that vision and courage would be needed to keep the company alive.

"They relied on wagon routes. The drivers going around with the merchandise didn't make enough money and didn't care. I said, let's give them a profit-sharing incentive. Somebody said, 'Sure, if they make a hundred dollars a week instead of eighty-five, they'll work harder.' I said, 'Why not let them make a hundred and thirty?' As easy as that. Suddenly the business improved. The rest was just shrewd financing."

A great merchant bank is a mirror of the country's economy. Monroe C. Gutman, the oldest senior partner, who entered the firm in 1922, remembers Lehman Brothers' first issue for R. H. Macy & Co.

"There was no SEC in those days and no red tape. The circular was written in twenty-four hours, and Robert Lehman wrote it himself. Now it might take several weeks. Early in 1933 we brought out the original issue of Schenley Distillers. The Eighteenth Amendment had just been repealed, and the Securities Act had not yet been passed. A most appropriate moment to finance a liquor firm with great expectations."

The prospectus quoted the price of a share at $16 but Schenley shares were briskly selling for $40 even before they were offered for public sale. (No wonder the merchant bankers speak wistfully about the old days.) There were problems at Schenley's, and a young Lehman associate, Joseph A. Thomas, was "lent" to Schenley as administrative assistant. Lehman Brothers always serves its clients well. Herbert Lehman once spent several months in Indiana helping Studebaker to straighten out its difficulties. Other Lehman partners went to Hollywood to give a hand to certain film companies. You've got to protect your investment.

Gutman shakes his head about the young people who speak of the "peaceful" old days. Peaceful, indeed! When Lehman Brothers negotiated the purchase of the Gaumont theater chain for Twentieth-Century Fox, Lehmans kept the lines open to Paris for several hours. The money was raised in New York, and payment was made minutes later in Paris.

But no one is infallible—not in Wall Street. Partner Thomas unhappily remembers the Flintkote deal, known around the partners' room as "Thomas's Folly." As an eager if somewhat inexperienced banker he had looked over some statistics and noticed that Flintkote was owned by the Shell Union Oil Corporation and N. V. de Satoopsche Petroleum Maatschappij of Amsterdam. Perhaps Shell and the people in Amsterdam would be interested in liquidating Flintkote? Thomas contacted them. The two companies were interested in making a deal. After protracted negotiations Lehman Brothers formed a buying group that offered 330,614 shares of Flintkote at $47.25 a share, in March, 1936. The stock broke at once. By the end of the year Flintkote's shares were down to $11.50. Thomas's mood was lower than the shares' market value. He had to wait twenty-two years until the Flintkote shares reattained the original offering price.

When something goes wrong, Lehman Brothers spends blood, sweat and tears to make it right again. It has toiled for years on some companies before giving up. It is less worried by financial losses than by the loss of reputation; it feels it can afford some mistakes, but not too many.

Sometimes it merges or sells a company before it becomes a total loss. Sometimes it loses clients whom it helped to build up and expand. Sometimes it has bad luck with clients (such as Fruehauf Trailer and Underwood Corporation). It turned down Revlon because it didn't trust the firm's dependence on a television program, and refused to handle Korvette which later became the success story of the discount houses, because it was afraid to offend some old friends in the department store business who take a dim view of discount houses.

Lehman Brothers has been criticized for "pushing glamor stocks" and "getting a bite" of situations it sponsors.

"True," a partner admits. "But when we sponsor the stock of a little-known company, our sponsorship often becomes more important to the company than its past record. If Lehman Brothers approves of a company, Wall Street will almost automatically fall in line."

Such is the prestige of a great investment bank.

Lehman Brothers' partners are considered star performers on the battlefields of high finance and they behave exactly like star performers in the arts, music, science or sports. They have different viewpoints and sharp disagreements. The prima donnas of finance have their cliques and feuds too. But there is unanimous agreement about Robert Lehman, the firm's principal partner, a soft-spoken, shy man of seventy-three who is credited by his associates with the firm's postwar growth. Quiet and unassuming, he is always in command of the house. His partners call him "the great catalyst," "a natural leader of men," "one of the country's most important bankers," "a great collector of people and paintings."

The lonely dissenter in this chorus of praise is Robert Lehman.

"Robert Lehman is very much Lehman Brothers, but Lehman Brothers is not Robert Lehman. I've built the team but I'm doing little myself. Lehman partners are members of the Lehman banking family. They are young. The partners' average age is forty." Youth, the great American fixation. You can't be young enough.

"I would rather have fifty per cent of an active firm than one hundred per cent of a dull one," says Robert Lehman. He probably owns over fifty per cent of an extremely active firm. Most of the partners are always somewhere else, in search of "special attitudes," looking for deals, on their way to board meetings. They are members of over two hundred boards of directors, performing services, giving advice, protecting Lehman Brothers' investments. All of them were brought in by Robert Lehman who realized early that non-Lehman partners would give the firm vigor, initiative, new life. Robert Lehman calls himself a "nontechnical banker" but he doesn't fool his partners.

"He absorbs everything by osmosis," a senior partner says. "He walks through the third floor and feels what goes on."

Generals don't fire guns. Robert Lehman brings in an important client and hands him over to a younger partner who is a skilled "technical banker." Robert Lehman is particularly pleased when he walks into the partners' room and finds it empty. That means that the partners are elsewhere. Working.

I once asked him what he thought was the basic aim of his firm.

He was silent for a long while, and then he said, "To continue the good traditions and to build its reputation. To preserve its good name, and show ingenuity, and do constructive things for the banking community and for the country." He sounded very much like the great merchant bankers in London.

Lehman partners have a time-honored record of contribution to civic and national affairs. There was Grandfather Emanuel Lehman who performed important missions for the South. Herbert H. Lehman was Governor of the state of New York, later member of the United States Senate. His brother Irving served as Chief Justice of the New York State Court of Appeals. A Lehman associate, Alex Sachs, acted as intermediary between Albert Einstein and Franklin D. Roosevelt, and interested the President in nuclear fission as early as 1939. A Lehman partner, the late John M. Hancock, drafted with Bernard M. Baruch the first United Nations plan for control of the atom. Other partners perform less obtrusive services as trustees of philanthropic organizations.

Lehman Brothers is the right place for people with the right competitive spirit. "Wall Street is a competitive community," says Robert Lehman. "Our people were brought up to compete since their school days. Our method of doing business is different from the English method. Americans don't resent high pressure in business, on the contrary, they expect it. They are receptive to salesmanship. We use salesmanship even in the distribution of securities. We have to do more paperwork than the English because we have more government controls. Competition, legal restrictions and the urge to get there earlier than the next fellow are always with us. We cannot afford the leisurely ways of the great London bankers."

Memories of the government's antitrust action in the early 1950's linger on, and there is widespread aversion to putting anything in writing. Everybody is constantly aware of the uncomfortable commitment of the written word. Don't write a memorandum that might someday become a source of conflict.

Lehman Brothers' partners are very independent; once a man is made a partner, he is very much on his own. He is not told where to go or what to do, though he may have certain duties to perform. He reports to his partners what he deems worth reporting. Disagreement is inevitable when thirty star performers work under the same roof but disagreement often creates achievement. Postwar growth has changed the style, though not the basic character, of the business.

"Individuals now count less than before," Robert Lehman says. "In the early years of the century when something went wrong, the elder J. P. Morgan would call in a few people, and the matter was quickly settled. Far-reaching decisions were made in a few minutes. To be a member of that small, exclusive group was a distinction, like being a Baring or Rothschild in London. This respect for a few 'great names' is gone, but respect for a few great firms has remained. I like to think that we are one of them. I feel that a mutual affection exists between our partners and our employees. I believe most of them are glad to be in a firm which is still run like a very large family—a family of seven hundred people. Some might not feel that way, as in every large family. But on the whole I think we've preserved the early spirit of Lehman Brothers . . . *Plus ça change, plus c'est la même chose.*"

The spirit is evident the moment one enters One William Street, a triangular, eleven-story corner building with a pseudo-baroque façade. On the ground floor, clerks behind old-fashioned cages take in and hand out stock and bond certificates. On the upper floors there is an air of dignity and a tangible sense of purposeful activity. Despite its size Lehman Brothers is not a banking bureaucracy. In 1941 a four-story annex had to be added. The building is located next to the New York Cotton Exchange but Lehman Brothers, which made its early fortune in cotton, is no longer in the commodity business.

The partners' room on the third floor has ancestral paintings and a fireplace, deep rugs and paneling. But there are no grandfather clocks as in London, the patina is missing, and the atmosphere is different. Everybody walks a little faster and talks a little louder than in a London merchant bank. People are always on the go, even when they sit at their desks. Bankers resemble one another all over the world—so do salesmen, cello players, politicians, bartenders and doctors —but American merchant bankers look more American than bankers, while British merchant bankers look more bankers than British.

Compared to London everything is on a big scale. The large oval walnut table in the main dining room on the eighth floor seats the entire partnership but they are rarely all there at the same time. There are also several small, private dining rooms. A staff of ten serves the food, and a famous chef works in the kitchen; it seems a mixture of Bishopsgate and Hollywood. On the top floor is a gymnasium where the partners are kneaded into condition by an able masseur. Rows of slippers are on the floor, each with a name. Some Lehman partners claim there is a connection between a good massage and a successful deal. An investment banker needs *mens sana in corpore sano*.

On a "typical" day when Robert Lehman asked me to lunch, the atmosphere in the partners' dining room was quite different from the mood in London's old merchant banks. There was no alcoholic or conversational protocol. People had their drinks—the sort of drink most London bankers would decline with an invisible shudder—at the table. There was no seating protocol. Robert Lehman sat at the head of the table, flanked by his two guests. (At his right side sat an old, cultured Chinese banker, formerly in Shanghai, now in Hong Kong.) Usually the seats at Robert Lehman's sides are reserved for senior partners. Everybody else sits where he likes.

The food was indifferent, and there was a pleasant sense of informality—the natural American informality, not the carefully practiced informality of understatement and half-sentences which London's bankers like so much. In New York everybody talked about what was on his mind. In London, they would talk about everything *except* what is really on their minds.

The guests in William Street were "assessed," as always when bankers are around, but not in the casual way of London where one must never become aware of being X-rayed. On the contrary, it was an oral examination, with questions and answers. The conversation ranged far and wide, from international affairs ("When will Red China become an important industrial power?") to national politics, from currency problems (the clouded future of the pound sterling) to the lively arts. Jokes were told, and everybody laughed. No one disclosed any inside information; no hot tips on the market were divulged. It wasn't at all what many people would have expected. Most would be disappointed.

Looking around the large table I was reminded of what Jocelyn Hambro, the London merchant banker, once told me of his early experiences in the United States. "I'd thought I knew Americans because they speak the same language but I was mistaken. It's much harder to distinguish the differences among Americans than among Frenchmen or Scandinavians because we English are apt to think that Americans are like us. They are not."

The partners' faces reflected the fascinating human kaleidoscope that exists nowhere outside the United States. People's ties and suits may reveal a certain uniformity but not their faces. The patterns and types are much more evident in London. I thought there were quite a few individualists among the men around the large table. Extrovert wheeler-dealers and reticent economists; a former attorney, a former CIA man, a former civil servant; an enthusiastic super-salesman and a thoughtful professor; men who preferred to listen in silence, and men who seemed exhilarated by the sound of their voices; liberals and conservatives, Democrats and Republicans, well-read intellectuals and men who never read anything but the *Wall Street Journal* and the *New York Times;* wise old men and brash younger men; quite a few Harvard graduates. A financial chamber orchestra, performing with enthusiasm and virtuosity under the benevolent, invisible baton of Robert Lehman.

Every Monday there is the ritual partners' lunch (no guests) when projects under way are discussed, urgent topics are brought up, and after discussion a vote may be taken. Partners serving on the boards of corporations bring up problems confronting these companies. Another company needs new capital for expansion; there is talk about a private placement. And there may be "new business," that might raise the status of younger partners and give the older ones a pleasant sense of anticipation. Who knows, maybe there will be a spectacular success—such as the Litton or Hertz deals.

At two-thirty everybody is back on the third floor, which is headquarters, command post and nerve center of the House of Lehman. It is very quiet there. On the fourth floor planned chaos is the rule: the syndicate department prepares the distribution of a new issue, attorneys are wrestling with SEC requirements. But on the third floor the talk is quiet, the rugs are deep, the surroundings serene and the paintings beautiful. Robert Lehman has a small, unpretentious private office there, with a few Impressionist and Fauve period paintings.

On the third floor the general policies are evolved and the basic decisions are made. Day-to-day routine happenings are of no interest there. No ticker disturbs the rarefied atmosphere of *haute finance*. The only ticker in the house is in the sales department. Old Lehman hands remember a day in the fall of 1939 when everybody stood around the ticker. War had broken out in Europe; in New York stock prices tumbled. Then the markets closed and Philip Lehman (whose portrait in the partners' room shows a man of quiet authority and great warmth) turned to his partners and said, "Well, there's nothing to be done today—let's go home and have a good dinner."

Everybody went home; there was no panic. There has never been any sign of panic on the third floor. Lehman Brothers has learned to live with disaster as with the common cold. There is no remedy against either one, but life goes on. It has been like that for the past one hundred and fifteen years. Today the front page of the *New York Times* affects Lehman Brothers much more than the financial page.

"Merchant banking is never upset by peripheral things," says Partner Frank Manheim with a historian's detachment. "At the heart things always go forward."

Philip Lehman, Robert's father, had the merchant banker's sixth sense for people. One day Ivar Kreuger came in and asked Lehman to be his banker. Kreuger talked and talked, while Lehman made a few notes on a piece of paper.

When Kreuger had finished, he sat back and looked at the banker. Philip Lehman shook his head and said the answer was no.

"I have a rule, Mr. Kreuger. If I cannot understand something by reading my notes on the subject, I won't buy it. You are too complex for me, Mr. Kreuger."

Mr. Kreuger left and a few months later shot himself.

The partners of Lehman Brothers don't agree on how a great banking house should be organized. Some think that an "active" firm should remain somewhat disorganized. There should be the daring that comes "from hunger," a powerful, permanent force of drive and initiative. Others worry about the danger of getting rich and successful; there is always the temptation of slowing down after reaching the top. One heretic claims that some of the best ideas are born under chaotic conditions. And there are conservatives who believe that a merchant bank should function like a funnel whose holes are covered by screens. Ideas are filtered through, and the distillate that comes out is usually pretty good. A certain house is mentioned that was organized like a pyramid, with all reports being channeled to the top. The house went broke. Bankers now deal in such huge sums that a couple of mistakes may be fatal. And a single man is bound to make more mistakes than a group of people.

Since Lucius DuBignon Clay joined Lehman Brothers in 1963—as a senior partner, though the newest partner in the hierarchy—he has been, in the words of Robert Lehman, "of invaluable service to the firm in his organizational ability, in his leadership, and in his success—creating and securing new business." General Clay embarked upon the arduous task of bringing order and organization into the "organized confusion" of Lehman Brothers. Long before Clay became famous as the organizer of the Berlin Airlift that broke the Soviet blockade in 1948, he had shown his special talent in the Army Corps of Engineers when he supervised the construction of a hundred and ninety-seven national airports. He was used to dealing with huge corporations and legions of executives.

At Lehman Brothers, the General (as he is still called by most people) instituted management by committee. Some partners expressed doubts whether this is the "ingenious" way of running an "active" investment-banking house. Will the spirit of unrestrained enterprise remain alive in committee meetings?

Clay's organizational chart, the bank's order of battle, is topped by the executive committee made up of six to eight older partners, with some of the younger ones coming in on rotation. The committee meets once a week, sets down "the fundamental [strategic] policies," makes "the operating [tactical] decisions."

On the level below the executive committee is the underwriting committee which deals with all issuing operations and provides capital for all sorts of ventures. This committee supervises several of the firm's famous service departments. The retail-sales department studies all planned issues, tests the market, assesses the prospectus and does the complicated technical job of issue that has made Lehmans famous for its efficiency. The firm relies on hundreds of independent broker-dealers all over the country who move the securities. There is the industrial department whose experts keep in touch "with developments and dynamics," formulate the firm's judgment of business opportunities, banking situations, consolidations, mergers—a super-research department. Members of the large legal department act as guides through the underbrush of regulations and jungle of restrictions. And the syndicate department deals with large issues that are being floated in cooperation with other investment firms.

Working directly under the top executive committee is the investment committee, which makes the policy decisions for the firm's two investment funds. A special economics department submits the American economy as a whole "to a broad and continuing analysis," and interprets the vital economic data relating to the nation.

Lehman Brothers' investment advisory service, said to be the largest in Wall Street, controls, directly or indirectly, two billion dollars. A special institutional investment service seeks new ways of attracting money from the institutions for "special attitudes." This should not give anybody the idea that Lehman Brothers solicits accounts. Individuals with less than half a million dollars needn't apply. In the early 1950's the firm turned down some people no matter how much money they had. Some of them were show people.

No Lehman employee must benefit from premature hot tips on the market. Anybody in the house caught trading in a stock that was recommended by the advisory services will be instantly dismissed. Partners may buy such shares—*after* the investment funds have bought them, and *after* individual clients have been advised. By that time the shares may no longer be an interesting buy. The partners must make all dealings through Lehman Brothers. They must not give advice for a fee on the securities of a company whose board they joined as directors. The research staff of Lehman Brothers' advisory service is completely independent from the research staff of the Lehman Corporation. They often disagree.

Finally, there is a special committee in charge of commercial-paper operations, and an administration committee. Obviously they have everything at Lehman Brothers except a committee on committees.

"We have to take substantial risks," says General Clay, who wastes no words. "Management by committee is expected to minimize the risks. Next year we shall make a big step forward. We'll be completely computerized."

The Lehman Collection has no connection with Lehman Brothers except its owner, Robert Lehman, the bank's principal partner—and the fact that it was created by money that came from the banking business. There are many good paintings at the bank, probably more than in any other merchant bank on earth, and under Robert Lehman's influence many partners have become collectors on their own.

The Lehman Collection is probably the greatest private collection in the United States. Robert Lehman is one of the last collectors in the classic tradition of collecting. Taxation and inflated prices, undignified haste and objectionable profit-making have brought an end to this elusive activity.

The Collection was lovingly created by people with taste, time and money. They never hurried; never tried to make a "killing" in the art market; they collected for the sake of collecting—for the joy it gave them.

Robert Lehman inherited the love of beauty from his parents. His father, Philip Lehman, started the Collection in 1911, during the golden era of collecting. The Lehmans chose with discrimination and understanding, acquired with taste and enthusiasm. Investment bankers at heart, they never collected art only as an investment. When they saw something they liked very much they bought it—which is the only way of collecting.

In his teen-age years, Robert Lehman would accompany his father and mother to Europe where they went to buy paintings, tapestries, furniture. It was a great indoctrination. They would visit Bernard Berenson in Italy and would tour the small museums in the sleepy hill towns. They talked with curators, restorers, collectors, experts. Robert started out with drawings and illuminated pages of medieval manuscripts. Gradually he worked his way up to Old Master drawings, then to Old Master oils. From there he proceeded to modern masters, particularly the French Impressionists. In the spring of 1956, when the Lehman Collection was shown at the Musée de l'Orangerie, a branch of the Louvre, in Paris, it was the first private American collection ever exhibited in Europe, and created a sensation. French connoisseurs who were in the habit of saying that American collectors had "more money than taste" were astonished by the impeccable standards that ruled the selection of the art works. More than seventeen thousand people saw the show during its first two weeks.

Robert Lehman lives with his treasures. He keeps some, which are particularly close to his heart, in his Park Avenue apartment—paintings, sculptures, porcelain, other rare *objets d'art*. The Collection itself is domiciled at Robert Lehman's town house on Fifty-fourth Street, which was built by John H. Duncan, the architect of Grant's Tomb. (Duncan was in a more cheerful mood on Fifty-fourth Street.) Robert Lehman grew up in this house, among the paintings, tapestries, drawings, furniture. Living close to the works of art he established an easy, first-person relationship with them. This was never a collection to him; it was a beautiful home.

The house, no longer inhabited, is occasionally shown to people, usually for the benefit of New York University's Fine Arts Institute, of which Lehman is a trustee. He was able to raise the enormous inheritance taxes after the death of his father but it is doubtful how long the Lehman Collection will remain in the family.

Friends and a few lucky people are taken through the house by Lehman or his curator. I was asked to come there one evening when only an armed guard and the curator were present. The guard opened the entrance door cautiously, watching me through a slit, until I identified myself, and then he let me in. The curator switched batteries of lights on and off, as we walked through the house. From the outside came soft, swishing sounds of tires on the wet pavement. Inside the house it was very quiet and peaceful. The walls of the ground floor were covered with olive-green velvet. The house had been redecorated in 1961 by Serge Royaux, a French interior designer who in 1957 redecorated the Musée de l'Orangerie.

Two rooms downstairs are filled with fourteenth- and fifteenth-century paintings from Siena and Florence—Lippo Vanni, Giovanni di Paolo, Barna da Siena, Spinello Aretino, Sano di Pietro, Andrea Vanni, Neri di Bicci. The oldest paintings are two oils attributed to Duccio di Buoninsegna who was active in Siena from 1279 to 1319. There is also a beautiful majolica collection. Many items came from the former Hearst Collection. W. R. Hearst had bought them, in turn, from merchant banker J. P. Morgan and Clarence Mackay. Many of the Hearst items were sold by Gimbels. Robert Lehman is a director of Gimbels.

Some of the finest paintings are displayed in beautifully furnished rooms on the second floor, enhanced by tapestries, rugs, furniture, chandeliers, a perfectly orchestrated symphony for the eyes. One room is still paneled in sixteenth-century red velvet which formerly covered most of the walls. Sitting down in an armchair, one is surrounded by beauty and much closer to it than in the large, cold halls of most museums.

I still cherish the memory of these intimate moments spent near Botticelli's *Annunciation*, Bellini's *Madonna and Child*,

Velasquez's *Portrait of Maria Theresa*. Two magnificent El
Grecos (particularly *Christ Carrying the Cross*), two somber
Rembrandts, and Goya's lovely *Countess Altamira and Her
Daughter*. I could sit here forever. Time stands still in this
room.

Other Florentine and Sienese masters are on the stairway
that leads to the third floor. There are Venetian drawings—
Tiepolo, Piazzetta, Canaletto—in the hallway. In a third-floor
room the Flemish School is represented by Hans Memling's
Annunciation and Petrus Christus's *Legend of Saint Eligius
and Godeberta*. On this floor are the French masters—Renoir,
Boudin, Degas, Monet. A Signac, a Derain, a Vallotton, a
Petitjean. The stairway leading to the fourth floor is dominated by Canaletto's *A View of Santa Maria della Salute*, done
with the same loving care that Antonio Canale applied to all
his paintings, in Venice, Warsaw and Dresden.

The front room on the fourth floor contains rare drawings
by Rubens, El Greco, Pisanello, Bellini, Dürer, Rembrandt,
da Vinci, Goya, and Van Dyck. The lights can't be left on for
a long time in this room, or the old drawings might fade. And
in the back room there is a profusion of beauty—Guys,
Moreau, Barye, Millet, Bazille, Bonnard, Segonzac, Modig-
liani, Degas, Renoir, Matisse, Signac, Boldini, Seurat, Utrillo,
Cézanne, van Gogh, Sisley, Pissarro, Picasso. And many
others.

Robert Lehman remembers how each of the paintings was
acquired, and he remembers the paintings he couldn't get.
The collector's joys and disappointments, and his mistakes.
He offered too little for Ugolino da Siena's *Last Supper*, and
ended up paying four times the original asking price. The
value of the Collection is hard to assess; some experts think
it's worth more than a hundred and fifty million dollars. Some
of Robert Lehman's best investments are, ironically, in art.

An investment banker's success rests on his perfect batting
average. Lehman Brothers needs at least 550—otherwise no
one will be interested in the firm in ten years, or in twenty.
Every day the research departments work through massive
amounts of facts and figures. But in the final analysis everything depends on whether the partners will make the right
decision on the fair price of a business. Sooner or later they
must bypass the facts and figures and get down to the

intangibles—the whims of popular taste, management, trends, and, above all, people. This is what makes investment banking an occult art rather than an exact science.

A while ago, Lehman Brothers and a large brokerage house competed for a large corporation issue. Lehman Brothers offered to underwrite the issue at 14. The competitors offered 16, and got the business.

"We didn't mind," a partner says. "They were very eager to get the business, to acquire the prestige of an investment bank. Perhaps they will sell the issue at 16½ and make a profit. But there might be weakness in the market and the stock would start with the handicap of a bad reputation. We don't like such a risk. Lehman Brothers can afford to take the long-term view. One has to offset long-term selfishness against immediate selfishness. The great thing in this business is to say 'No' to certain propositions. People ought to get a bonus at the end of the year because they had the foresight to turn down a deal that later went sour."

Lehman Brothers feels confident about the future of investment banking in America. The nation is getting more prosperous; consumer industries are expanding with the growing population. The iceman no longer cometh, he is replaced by the refrigerator salesman. The small radio is replaced by the large television set. Automation creates small and big machines which have to be produced—and financed. The capital requirements of America's industries are growing. And the customers keep borrowing more money. Everybody has learned to live on his future earnings. Billions of dollars have to be raised to finance the production of goods, and their consumption.

Lehman Brothers knows where to find the billions and how to channel them from those who have the money to those who use it most profitably. Hand in hand with the new technological developments, Lehman Brothers invents new techniques for raising, buying and selling the most common merchandise of all—money.

8

Rothschilds: The Young Generation

*"Money is the God of our times,
and Rothschild is his prophet."*
Heinrich Heine

WHAT is it like to be "a Rothschild," to walk around
as a living legend, to bear the proudest name in international *haute finance?* Millions of people have asked themselves the question. In America a boy wants to become
President. In Europe he would rather be a Rothschild. The
very name is synonymous with wealth. To be "a Rothschild"
is to be a modern Croesus, a twentieth-century Midas.

It's good to know that the Rothschilds are still around.
They are proof that our way of life prevails. Capitalism has
often been buried but isn't dead yet. Merely by surviving, the
Rothschilds have symbolized the continuity of dynasty and
wealth, of integrity and Western civilization. If the Rothschilds didn't exist, one would have to invent them. But they
do exist; let's hope they will be here forever. The family
company owned by the British Rothschilds is aptly called
Rothschild Continuation Limited. In 1961, a second corporation was formed, Second Continuation Limited, in which the
French Rothschilds have an interest.

The legendary "Rothschild"—neither first name nor title
required—is the knight of many myths, the hero of affectionate jokes, the protagonist of the World's First Jewish
Family. You may have heard of the poor Jew who sees a
small Rothschild being helped by a butler into the elegant
coach, and exclaims wistfully, "So small—and already a
Rothschild!" Today people need such fairy tales as much as
food. And there is the story of another poor Jew—God

really must have loved them, he made so many of them—who cries bitterly at the funeral of the mythical "Rothschild." A bystander asks him whether he happens to be a relative. "No," the poor Jew says, wiping his tears. "That's why I am crying."

To be a Rothschild means many things to many Rothschilds. To some it means the possession of money and a supreme ability of enjoying it. To others it is a challenge to outdo the spectacular achievements of their ancestors. To almost all it means devotion to their faith, a sense of dynasty, a feeling for responsibility. Rothschilds have been financiers, scientists, legislators—and also sportsmen, collectors, playboys. It's a big family which has its eccentrics and black sheep, like any other family.

Paradoxically, the Rothschilds—symbol of wealth—are not the world's wealthiest people. But the wealth of the wealthier Middle Eastern oil billionaires is culturally meaningless. The Rockefellers, the Fords, the Carnegies, the Vanderbilts made more millions, but it was only money.

The wealth of the Rothschilds means more: history, pride, power, charity and, above all, integrity. Is there another family on earth whose members outsmarted Napoleon and outlived Hitler, built railroads in Europe and factories in South America, developed oil fields in the Sahara and water power in Newfoundland, financed uranium mines and the tunnel under the Channel, supported enormous philanthropies, helped to create countries and toppled dynasties, owned art collections, castles and great vineyards—and have triumphantly overcome the dangers of decadence that are said to be inevitable after eight generations?

THE WATERLOO COUP

The Rothschild legend has long ago outrun the facts. This is the Rothschilds' own fault. They are even more reticent and aloof than other merchant bankers when family matters are concerned. They developed the technique of absolute discretion to perfection. Their family labyrinths are complex, dark and mysterious. Bertrand Gille, the French historian, has been working twelve years on a history of the Rothschilds, and hasn't finished yet. Significantly, no Rothschild-approved history of the family has yet appeared. A whole library of books exists about the Rothschilds. All were written without their blessing, often against their wishes, mostly without their cooperation, and sometimes they have protested in court against them.

No one has ever gone through all the family archives. Perhaps once a Rothschild will be permitted to do it but certainly not an outsider. The family has produced many diversified talents in the past two hundred years. Someday there will be a historian named Rothschild and he will write *the* book.

Until then the same tales are being told and retold, often embroidered with amusing bits of fiction, tales of "foresight, imagination, daring." Inevitably, the tales begin in the ghetto of Frankfurt am Main where Meyer Amschel Rothschild, born in 1743 or 1774, began as a merchant in cloth and old coins. He became a money-changer, moved from the humble "Red Shield" (in German: *Rot Schild*) house to the larger five-story "Green Shield" house, and sent four of his five sons to the citadels of finance in Europe. Jakob (later James) went to Paris, Salomon to Vienna, Kalmann to Naples, Nathan to England.

Amschel stayed at home with Father, who landed his first coup when he helped Prince William of Hesse Cassel (who had to flee from Napoleon) to save and invest his vast funds. Father, an early, skilled investment adviser, sent the talers to London where son Nathan Meyer multiplied them by shrewd speculations. After Prince William returned, he was given back the money, plus interest. He was very pleased. So was the family, who made a profit and won a reputation. Ever since the Rothschilds have stuck to the reputation-*cum*-profit formula.

All spectacular coups have increased the Rothschilds' fortune *and* their prestige. During the Napoleonic Wars the British asked Nathan to get large amounts of gold to Wellington's army trapped in Spain. Nathan shipped the gold to France where brother James took over and smuggled it straight through the enemy lines. It was a costly operation, since ministers and local police chiefs had to be bribed, but entirely successful.

When smuggling takes on heroic dimensions, it becomes part of history. So does successful speculation on a gigantic scale. The post-Waterloo coup is retold in all the books on the Rothschilds; a legend has been repeated so many times that it is now accepted as fact. Nathan did get advance information about Waterloo—not through the legendary carrier pigeon but through a courier who brought him a Dutch newspaper with a report of Napoleon's defeat. Thereupon he used a technique at the London Stock Exchange—later practiced by other Rothschilds with special advance knowledge—in order to make a killing in the market. Instead of buying shares upon hearing the good news, which the average little speculator would do, Nathan dumped some of his shares. There had been rumors of a British defeat, and when word spread that "Rothschild is selling," the rumor was accepted as fact. Everybody began to sell, and prices broke "sharply."

At this point Nathan issued fast orders to his agents who began to unobtrusively buy back the shares at cut-rate prices, just before the news of Waterloo became public. Timing is always essential in such delicate operations. Prices rose "sharply," and Nathan made a fortune.

What the books fail to say—either because their authors didn't know it or thought it might spoil a good story—is that Nathan did not keep his advance information for himself but immediately passed it on to the Prime Minister, Lord Liverpool. In an article, "The Waterloo Despatch," first published in 1962 in the *Quarterly Review* and later reprinted by Her Majesty's Stationary Office "as a small but romantic commemoration of the 150th anniversary of the Battle of Waterloo," Reginald Colby writes:

[Wednesday, June 21st, 1815] had been a day of rumour and counter-rumour in London, the uncertainty rousing the Englishman's traditional sporting instincts, and bets had been laid on the result. At Brooks's in St. James's Street members had been betting on a French victory, as there was a general feeling that Napoleon would emerge the victor in the great struggle. One person in London, however, knew that this was not so, and that not Napoleon, but the Allies had won a great victory. That man was Nathan Rothschild, the banker, who had established his business in London ten years before, and had excellent connections with the continent through his brothers in Paris, Frankfurt, Vienna and Naples.

He had returned from the continent only a few days before the fighting broke out and being deeply involved financially in the fortunes of the restored French monarchy (he had arranged through his brother James in Paris for Louis XVIII to draw a bill for £200,000 when the King returned to France in April 1814) he was extremely anxious to know the outcome of the fighting since the future of the Rothschild Bank depended on it, and had left instruction with his agents to bring word to him in London at the earliest possible moment. One of his agents, Roworth, arrived on Tuesday evening (June 20th), a full twenty-four hours before Percy (Major The Hon. Henry Percy, of the 14th Light Dragoons, A.D.C. to the Duke of Wellington, and bearer of the famous Wellington Despatch), with a Dutch paper giving the news of a great English victory, but with confusing details. Nevertheless, early in the morning [of Wednesday, June 21st] Rothschild hurried round to his friend John Herries, the Commissary-in-Chief who had been with him on the continent, and Herries took him to Downing Street to see the Prime Minister, Lord Liverpool.

But Rothschild's good news was scouted. Despondency reigned in Downing Street, too, as no word had come from Wellington, and this lack of news was considered a bad sign.

It is often said that Nathan Rothschild kept the news of Waterloo to himself and made use of it in speculations on the Stock Exchange. He is supposed to have watched the battle himself and as soon as he saw that Napoleon had lost galloped off the battlefield and brought the news to London.

And Colby repeats the often repeated report that Nathan made straight for the Stock Exchange, where he stood by his favorite pillar, "adopting an appearance of great gloom," which depressed the market. Stocks "tumbled" and when they had fallen low enough Rothschild's agents stepped in and bought them up cheap.

It is a dramatic way of explaining the rise of the fortunes of the Rothschilds [continues Colby], but it is disproved absolutely by Nathan Rothschild's call at Downing Street, and his communication of the news to the Prime Minister. He was a trusted man of affairs, working closely with the government, as he had not only arranged the loan to Louis XVIII, but had provided the much-needed gold for the paying of the British army in Spain, and other war expenses. It is true that the Allied victory over Napoleon greatly strengthened his financial position and Waterloo may be said to be the foundation on which he built up his colossal fortune, but that fortune was not built up through speculation on the Stock Exchange by keeping the news of the victory to himself. Stocks certainly rose between Tuesday, 20th June when London was still without news of the battle, and the following Thursday, 22nd June when the victory was in everyone's mouth. If Rothschild bought stock on the morning of Wednesday, 21st June, having already communicated the news to the Cabinet, it was his own business, but it was not sharp business.

A list of stock-market prices during these days disproves the fictional claim that prices "tumbled" and "rose madly." For instance, four per cent consols stood at 70½ on June 12. The battle of Waterloo was fought on June eighteenth, a Sunday. Two days before, on Friday, June 16, consols reached a low of 69 1/16. On Wednesday morning, June 21, when Rothschild first sold and then bought, consols were quoted at 70. Three days later they were traded as high as 71½. By present-day standards, these fluctuations are hardly sensational.

But the Waterloo coup did give the Rothschilds enormous prestige. Emperors, kings, prime ministers came to New Court for advice or money, or both. When slavery was abolished in 1833, it was Rothschilds who arranged the West India Loan of $75,000,000 by which the British government compensated the Jamaica slave owners for their losses. In Paris, James's loans helped France to establish herself in Algeria. (James's present-day descendants in France now help to develop oil in the Sahara.)

After the American Civil War, the English Rothschilds shared with a few other merchant bankers the honor of providing the gold cushion for the new United States cur-

rency. In 1875 Disraeli and the British government waited
breathlessly for Rothschilds, "the only firm which could do
it," to lend them at shortest notice, and at the patriotic
interest rate of three per cent, four million pounds to buy the
majority holding in the Suez Canal.

Loyalty to their rulers has always been a Rothschild
trademark. In Vienna, Salomon was loyal to the Habsburgs,
named his first railroad venture "Kaiser Ferdinand Nord-
bahn," and was rewarded by huge profits, a title with an
escutcheon—coronets, lions and eagles—and a rather reluctant
nod of acceptance from the Kaiser's anti-Semitic court. In
Naples, Kalmann floated loans for the Papal States and the
King of Naples. And in Paris, James supported first the
Bourbons, then Louis Philippe, and finally Napoleon III who
even paid a state visit to "the King of the Jews" a few years
before he lost his empire and was deposed.

"Money is the God of our times, and Rothschild is his
prophet," Heinrich Heine wrote in Paris.

HOW RICH ARE THEY?

The supremacy of the Rothschilds in international banking
lasted a hundred years, from the Napoleonic Wars to the
beginning of the First World War. During these hundred
years the English Rothschilds brought out eighteen government loans amounting to £1,600,000,000—a nice, round
figure. The family's financial genius was Nathan Meyer who
had started as a cotton merchant in Manchester, and in 1804,
when he was twenty-seven, founded N. M. Rothschild &
Sons in London.

Before N.M. had come along, foreign bonds in London had
been issued in pesos, francs or talers. British investors were
never sure at what rate of exchange they would receive their
interest payments. N.M. had the simple and brilliant idea of
issuing his bonds himself and paying the interest, in due
time, in pounds sterling, acting as an agent for the foreign
government. It was an early, private sort of Marshall Plan.

Suddenly foreign issues became attractive. When Mr.
Rothschild let it be known that he would be at his "counting
house" on a certain day, people would queue up for the new
Austrian, French or Russian bonds. Mr. Rothschild had

prudently purchased a considerable slice for his own account which he would dispose of later when the bonds had gone up. More profit and more prestige.

Under his son Lionel, the family home in New Court, St. Swithin's Lane, "a sovereign's throw from the Bank of England," became the most famous address in international finance. It still is today. And the Paris house has achieved a spectacular renaissance since the end of the Second World War. The other family branches have disappeared—Naples in 1861, Frankfurt in 1901, and Vienna in 1938. Baron Louis de Rothschild was arrested by Himmler's Gestapo, and released only after the family had raised approximately $20,-000,000 as ransom.

The Nazis did all they could to exterminate the First Jewish Family. The Rothschilds prevailed. They had their ups and downs, on a monumental, Rothschildian scale: subtle rivalries and bold coups, huge profits and huge losses. After 1914 the Rothschilds didn't always live up to their exalted name. Wars, Nazi persecution and taxation depleted their wealth. Between the two world wars the British and French houses continued the business which they already had without expanding. One of the few high spots was the floating of Woolworth on the London market in 1931. In these years the Rothschilds lost millions—but never their integrity. They came out of the battles with their prestige enhanced.

Almost to the day, a hundred and fifty years after the Battle of Waterloo, N. M. Rothschild & Sons moved into its new, modern headquarters. It stands on the old site in St. Swithin's Lane, a shortcut between Lombard Street and Cannon Street Station, a six-story structure, described by the *Sunday Times* as "a discreet aluminium, glass and black marbled building." It has a floor area of 50,000 square feet (the old building had only 19,000 square feet) and it is the only building in London which was planned and built entirely as a merchant bank, with all the departments where they belong, a partners' floor, several dining rooms and, naturally, a computer. The annual rent—the freehold of the land belongs to the City Corporation—was £1000 in 1925 and has since gone up to £43,000. Before rebuilding, the Rothschilds renegotiated an eighty-year lease which should take them into the tenth generation.

The modern façade shows the firm's old symbol, a small oval sign embossed by five gold arrows, and the old family paintings and panelings which ancestor Nathan Meyer enjoyed are still there, but most of the old trappings have vanished. Gone is The Room, as the partners' room was called. It has become obsolete in these days of efficient merchant banking. A pity, really, for The Room was one of the last, authentic settings of genuine financial grandeur: rugs and paneling, ancestral portraits and framed old accounts, including a receipt for two million pounds, payment to the Duke of Wellington, memorabilia on the mantel shelves—a very special atmosphere that will never be recreated.

Members of the staff would enter the partners' room by a door whose upper half was glass. They never knocked. They would wait outside until a partner saw them and pressed a bell on his desk. Sometimes they waited there for a long time. A senior member of the staff who recently retired estimates that he spent a year of his life waiting outside the glass door.

The disappearance of The Room has a subtle touch of irony which the Rothschilds can well afford. N. M. Rothschild & Sons is the only merchant bank that remains a true partnership, with no "Ltd." after its name. They are real partners who *ought* to have a partners' room. Death duties and taxation have forced all other financial dynasties to become either a private or public limited company.

The Rothschilds remain superbly unlimited but even their days may be numbered. A banking partnership in England is legally allowed to have no more than ten partners. Counting the two Continuations there are now nine partners. The bank itself has seven partners. In the last few years they have taken on a number of bright young men with great talent. If they cannot make the grade as partners, they may leave for other banks where they can become directors. People cannot be really useful without being able to make important decisions, and such decisions are still made by the partners. Clients prefer to deal with the partners in a merchant bank. Seven is a thin layer of principals. Unless the law is changed, it is possible that the partnership of N. M. Rothschild & Sons will go the way of all other merchant banks.

Today the bank is—still—owned by the family and doesn't have to publish statements. This keeps one of the world's great financial parlor games alive: how rich are the Rothschilds? Are they worth a hundred million dollars? Five hundred million? A trillion?

One of the Rothschilds who was recently asked the question, smiled. "I know how much I am worth," he said. "But the others . . ." He shrugged diplomatically. Perhaps even he didn't know, down to the last ten million. The London house is said to own acres and acres of London real estate and shares in a multitude of mining companies, controls insurance and finance companies.

Most merchant bankers say little but the Rothschilds say even less. In the past fifteen years they have extended their traditional acceptance and foreign-exchange business but in other fields—new issues and advice to big companies on take-overs and mergers—they have reaped less glamor than some of their younger rivals. There are certain indications that the younger generation will remain less aloof than their predecessors. It can be said that the Rothschilds now back perhaps more than a hundred different business enterprises all over the world. They are involved in transactions going back to the great past, and in projects extending into a perhaps even greater future.

From the past there are the fruits of the empire-building exploits of Cecil Rhodes whom the Rothschilds backed to the hilt: enormous holdings in gold mines and De Beers Co. (diamonds). From the past derives their influence in Rio Tinto, the giant corporation that began in Spain's rich copper mines and has since acquired a stake in the Rhodesian copper belt. There is the Sun Alliance life insurance company, most aristocratic of all insurance companies, founded by Nathan Rothschild in 1824, with a Rothschild on the board; it has elegant clients and ducal estates but occasionally takes a spectacular risk in the great Rothschild tradition; it was the first company that insured radioactive isotopes.

The future is dramatically symbolized by Brinco, the British Newfoundland Corporation. Its shareholders are the British and the French Rothschilds—the company was organized in 1952 by Edmund de Rothschild, the senior partner of the London house—and Anglo American Corporation, Bowater and Rio Tinto. Brinco owns exploratory rights to 60,000 square miles in Newfoundland and Labrador, with enormous resources in timber, minerals and hydroelectric power, an area larger than England and Wales combined.

The English Rothschilds remain official gold broker to the Bank of England, are still the most important bullion broker in the country, the hub of London's gold market. N. M. Rothschild & Son is the only bank on earth with its own Gold Fixing Room. On the walls hang the portraits of some of their former clients—the Emperor of Austria, the Czar of Russia, the Kings of Prussia, Portugal and Holland. Every morning the quaint ritual of fixing the day's price of gold takes place in this room. A Rothschild man is in the chair. The dealers take their places; each has a telephone—with a direct line to his office—and a small British flag in front of him. When the flag is down, the verbal dealing must be honored, but when a man says "Flag up!" everything stops, and the man has time to think it over, whereupon he says "Flag down!" or changes his mind. No one knows exactly the origin of the ritual; the idea is the dealers will indicate whether they want or don't want to buy gold. As a rule, they are buyers. The Rothschild man in the chair says "Figures, please!" and the dealers make their offers, which are passed on by the Rothschild man to the bank. The bank may either accept the offers or say "No gold," which means the dealers have to offer a higher price if they want the gold. Like much ritual in the City of London, gold-fixing has become outmoded and superseded by harsh reality: more gold is now traded outside the gold-fixing room than inside, at different prices. But the tradition is maintained.

And the Rothschilds still make gold bars, in the family's private refinery near the Tower of London. It is called the Royal Mint Refinery and was once part of Great Britain's Royal Mint. Don't hesitate to accept Rothschild gold bars. They are of standard size and "good delivery fineness," containing 995 parts of fine gold or better.

A YOUNG ROTHSCHILD PARTNER

On July 1, 1960, N. M. Rothschild & Sons made a historic announcement. For the first time in the bank's history, a non-Rothschild, non-Jew was admitted to the partnership.

It was an inevitable development. In the past, almost all male Rothschilds would "go into the bank." Some of them were not born to be bankers, didn't work out, and had to be carried along. Today there are only nineteen men bearing the name of the Rothschild family. The family's great problem between the two world wars was that the banks in London and Paris, which traditionally were run only by Rothschilds, were short of able Rothschild bankers. The titular head of the British family, Victor Lord Rothschild, is a "nonbank" Rothschild, a prominent philanthropist, a Socialist peer, a don at Cambridge and a distinguished zoologist and biophysicist. He was chairman of the Agricultural Research Council, is now chairman of Shell Research and on the board of Shell Chemical. He is still director of research in the Department of Zoology at Cambridge and very interested in problems of fertilization. Not so surprising; an earlier Rothschild, Charles, was fascinated by rare butterflies. Lord Rothschild's cousin Lionel Nathan was always more interested in gardening than in banking. Lord Rothschild's sister Miriam is coauthor of a volume titled *Fleas, Flukes and Cuckoos*. His youngest sister, Kathleen Nica Rothschild de Koenigswarter, lives in Weehawken, New Jersey, and patronizes serious jazz and jazz musicians, among them Thelonius Monk. Lord Rothschild himself is a swing man and disciple of Teddy Wilson.

What with all these extracurricular activities, there was no talent available for the bank, which was run by Anthony de Rothschild in the not-so-gay thirties, forties and fifties. After the last war he was joined by two nephews, Edmund and Leopold. Today the clan can no longer afford unable partners in the bank. Only born-and-bred merchant bankers will stand up to the tough demands of this competitive age. Of the seven partners of N. M. Rothschild & Sons, four are Rothschilds: Mr. Edmund (as he is called on the bank's telephone card), Mr. Leopold, Mr. Evelyn, Mr. Jacob. The other three partners are David Colville, who created the historical precedent when he was admitted to the exalted partnership in 1960; Michael Bucks, who had spent all his life in the bank, proof that even at Rothschilds a man now can work his way up from the bottom to the partners' room; and Philip Shelbourne, a complete outsider, a brilliant barrister specializing in taxation. It was obvious that the Rothschilds wanted to end their self-created, splendid isolation in the City and were going out to compete with the younger, more vigorous merchant bankers. They've done that ever since.

The bank's youngest partner is the Honorable Jacob Rothschild, Lord Rothschild's son, who will one day inherit the title. I met him in City Gate House shortly before the bank moved into its new home in St. Swithin's Lane. Assorted busts and ancestral paintings seemed to have been perfunctorily placed in the entrance hall, almost like stage props, to convey the authentic atmosphere of a venerable merchant bank. Blue-clad Rothschild couriers sat on benches, waiting to make routine errands in the City. No longer do they dash off to Nairobi or to the Continent. No more carrier pigeons. Their function was taken over by two tickers in inconspicuous mahogany casings, one for the stock market, one for the races.

Jacob is a very British Rothschild: quiet and relaxed, reticent and soft-spoken, elusive and very sure of himself. He is a first-rate salesman in a city where the soft sell is at a premium. He is not a flamboyant Rothschild, rather modest and businesslike. But in spite of his academic shyness he is respected among merchant bankers as a man who has quickly learned the business. He and Philip Shelbourne developed the firm's new, successful Finance Department which advises industrial companies and deals with new issues.

With his longish face, the typical "Rothschild" lower lip, the melancholy, slightly ironical expression of the eyes, Jacob resembles the portraits of ancestor Amschel (1773-1855) of the late, lamented Frankfurt bank, half a dozen generations ago. The Rothschilds are fine material for students of genetics and chromosome researchers. The family resemblances are very strong.

Behind Jacob's desk was a famous Rothschild painting, showing Nathan Meyer's son Lionel entering the House of Commons, on July 26, 1858, on his way to the Table where he took the oath with his head covered, according to Jewish tradition. He had been elected three times before to the House. Parliament had refused him because he had turned down "the form of words" and desired "to be sworn on the Old Testament." At last Parliament gave in, and Lionel was a Member until 1874.

Next to the painting hung a framed account—the Rothschild gold shipments made to Wellington in 1815. Not many merchant banks can display such proud paraphernalia of the past.

I asked the obvious question. "What is it like to be 'a Rothschild'?"

Jacob hesitated. "I don't think it's very different from being someone else. One is, of course, acutely aware of bearing the name. My upbringing taught me to respect it. And one is left with a strong wish to sustain and enhance its traditions."

Rothschilds always speak of other members of the family as "Rothschilds," a tribe unto themselves. Historians have claimed that intermarriage is the main reason for the family's continuing wealth and identity. Of the family's fifty-nine weddings in the nineteenth century half were between male and female Rothschilds. James, one of the founding brothers, married his cousin Betty. Of their five children four married Rothschilds. Of Kalmann's five children four married Rothschilds. And of N.M.'s seven children four married Rothschilds.

Many outsiders claim—and many Rothschilds deny—that this systematic inbreeding was a dynastic policy instituted by ancestor Meyer Amschel. The Rothschilds say that their men happened to find their cousins and second cousins more attractive than other women. Maybe. At any rate, the money has remained "in the family." In spite of the obvious risks the process turned out well. It also explains the Rothschilds' devotion to their family and to their faith.

I asked Jacob, "What is, in your opinion, the merchant banker's most important single requirement?"

This time he didn't hesitate.

"If you ask for one requirement only, it must be integrity. Without complete integrity there cannot be complete confidence. This confidence, our good will, is our most important asset."

Jacob was made a full-fledged partner only a few years after he left Oxford. Such a decision is never lightly made; the older partners must have thought well of him. Even today almost every male Rothschild "goes into the bank," but how far he gets once there, depends largely on his ability. The family assessment is confirmed by prominent merchant bankers in London, Paris and New York who call Jacob a coming man of the younger generation.

Jacob's father, Lord Rothschild, was educated at Harrow and Cambridge, but Jacob went to Eton and Oxford. (Rothschilds have traditionally gone to Harrow and Trinity College,

Cambridge.) He specialized in history, an apt preparation for merchant banking, and graduated with first-class honors in 1959. He never so much thought of an academic career. He wanted to be a banking Rothschild though he is not a merchant banker by environment.

In Jacob's home no one ever talked about finance but there was always talk about other Rothschilds, without the exalted undertone that princes of royal blood are used to. Jacob was not taught that being a Rothschild is a terrible burden. Instead he formed a feeling of quiet pride in the family.

"We are especially proud that the bank has remained in the family for six generations. The Rothschilds must have had ability—and the good fortune to produce in each generation a few first-rate bankers. The degree of success achieved by any merchant bank cannot for long exceed that of the people responsible for running it."

Jacob was not the small Rothschild whom the butler lifted into the elegant coach, as the story goes. His family never lived on the opulent scale of the French Rothschilds. The English are quieter anyway. Having been born in 1936, he grew up during the Second World War. And there were his father's Socialist ideas.

After graduating from Oxford, Jacob went into the bank. It might have been difficult not to go into the bank, but he actually liked it from the very beginning. He learned a few basic things but didn't stay there very long. He decided to leave N. M. Rothschild & Sons and go elsewhere for a while. He worked in the City, and later went to New York where he got more training at Morgan, Stanley. There, says Jacob, he felt "almost at home" in the dignified blue-chip atmosphere of Wall Street's *haute finance* investment bank.

"There is no school of merchant banking," he says. "No one teaches a course. I suppose the Harvard Business School provides some of the necessary background knowledge. The rest is common sense, experience, the ability to judge people and provide ideas. The subject has great fascination for me. And one learns from the standards and methods of one's competitors."

Jacob Rothschild lives in a house in Knightsbridge. By former Rothschild standards it is a rather modest place but it suits him well in this age which is an age of computers, not an age of footmen. He is married to the former Serena Dunn, the English-born daughter of Canadian steel-entrepreneur Sir Philip Dunn. They have two children, Hannah and Beth, eighth-generation Rothschilds.

We reminisced about the great days of a bygone era when the very name of Rothschild carried enormous power on the international scene—the days when kings, ambassadors and ministers waited patiently for an appointment at the bank.

"Yes, I believe the house had greater power once. Today though we have a more varied and greater scope. The spectacular deals are not as frequent as in the old days. Merchant banking has become more professional and more service orientated. Some people have said that our bank is mainly concerned with looking after the Rothschild investments, but anyone who is well informed will tell you that this is not true. We offer a full range of the functions of the merchant bank of today: financial advice on mergers and amalgamations, the underwriting of capital as well as commercial banking. We manage large investment funds. And I doubt if anyone would dispute our particular strength and scope in foreign exchange and bullion."

Government and foreign bonds, historically the great specialty of the house, became almost extinct in the 1930's but in the last few years there has been a revival. In cooperation with other merchant bankers, Rothschilds has successfully floated loans for Japan, Austria, Portugal, and leading undertakings in Denmark and Sweden. The London Rothschilds claim there is no special "Rothschild territory" on the merchant-banking map of the world but admit to being "especially strong" on the Continent, in Brazil and the eastern half of Canada.

N. M. Rothschild & Sons performs a dual function. Privately the partners, using their own money, act as investment bankers. The general bread-and-butter business provides "an ordinary and reasonable living." Rothschilds, like everybody else, go through extended periods of ordinary times. As a modern merchant bank Rothschilds now offers all services expected from a modern merchant banker. It didn't do so well in one of its first take-over battles, as adviser to Odhams which attempted unsuccessfully to shake off the take-over bid of the *Daily Mirror*, advised by Warburgs. Two years later it proved its skill by its ingenious handling of the take-over of

Whitehead for the state-owned Richard Thomas and Baldwins. Acting as quickly in the market as some of their nineenth-century ancestors, the Rothschilds snatched victory from Stewarts and Lloyds and outdid their rivals Morgan Grenfell and Schroder Wagg.

Rothschilds has played an important role recently in raising dollar loans through London. It helped in the raising of finance for the European Coal and Steel Community with Warburgs, and is leading the loans for the sixty-million-pound Transalpine Pipeline, a truly international project, the financing of which was sought by the world's leading bankers. Among those who did not get the business were some of the greatest names in international banking.

N. M. R. recently floated a new issue and introduced two American companies, Hertz and the Buckingham Corporation, to the United Kingdom. It showed its new talent for mergers when it advised Carreras, fixed up the 88-million-pound Charter Consolidated merger, acted in the bloodless insurance fight for a nonindustrial client, Sun Alliance. Old Nathan Meyer would be pleased: the firm that he started a hundred and forty years ago has become a thriving 105-million-pound business for his heirs.

AN AURA OF ROMANCE

And there are still the "top deals," the icing on the cake, great transactions with the aura of romance. Brinco, above all. The concession, granted by the Provincial Act of May, 1953, embraced the right to explore for minerals in 50,000 square miles in Labrador and 10,000 square miles in Newfoundland; the right to develop "all unalienated water power potentials" in these regions; a timber concession of black spruce covering an area of 1450 square miles along the shores of Lake Melville in Labrador. One area, the Baie d'Espoir in southern Newfoundland, has a possible potential of 500,000 H.P., utilizing certain lateral rivers, and is currently being developed for the Newfoundland government. But the greatest potential lies in Labrador where the Churchill River, when harnessed, can produce nine million h.p., more than twice as much as the Grand Coulee Dam, and the biggest hydroelectric operation outside the Soviet Union. Sir Winston Churchill called the project "a grand imperial concept but not imperialistic."

It is not a get-rich-quick project, and the Rothschilds proceeded with traditional caution. They employed costly experts who testified that there was no danger of earthquakes in Labrador and surveyed the possibilities of losses through lightning, landslides and avalanches. An early report calls the Hamilton Falls (now Churchill Falls) scheme "inevitably a long-term project with little hope of immediate reward." Reports to the shareholders are usually written by experts in gloom. Rothschilds feels that one has to wait patiently for a good thing. It can afford to take the long-range view.

But it has a different attitude in competitive merchant-banking operations.

"We have tried to learn that the merchant banker must not wait for an opening, an opportunity," says Jacob. "He must create them. People should seek our advice because they can expect to be provided with creative ideas. We have a nucleus of ability here at the bank. We must try and make ourselves as much a bank of brains as of money. That's our strength and our weakness. We can never have enough of them. We must be the catalyst who helps the development of trade. We must never remain static, always attempting to maintain our initiative."

The new psychological attitude in merchant banking is reflected by the new, functional style of the six-story New Court, so different from the Victorian palazzo of the past. Of the old traditions only the daily eleven o'clock partners' meeting remains, and the quaint ritual of the one o'clock lunch. Even there things have changed. The conversation is no longer limited to philanthropy, gardens, politics, the arts, music. Most lunches nowadays are concerned with tough business matters.

"No doubt this trend has been accentuated by the inelegance of our present luncheon facilities," says Jacob. He doesn't seem to regret it.

THE ELEGANT FRENCH COUSINS

Between the English Rothschilds and their French cousins there is "genuine affection and real friendship." Until a few years ago it was more a personal than a business relationship. Today there is constant communication by telephone and telex. The cousins on both sides of the Channel are fond of each other because they are so different. N. M. Rothschild & Sons in London is more a service bank, while De Rothschild Frères in Paris is more a large private bank.

There is a difference in temperament and attitudes. The English cousins are financiers and sportsmen; Edmund likes fishing, Leopold prefers sailing, Jacob plays tennis and Evelyn, the British family's leading extrovert, plays polo, sometimes with Prince Philip. By comparison, the French cousins are more colorful—elegant, artistic, *sportif*. They definitely make good copy (although no Rothschild would ever think of himself in terms of "copy").

Head of the French *maison* is Baron Guy de Rothschild—slim, urbane, charming, a brilliant financier, collector and connoisseur of many good things. Guy has dramatically broken with many staid traditions, showed great diplomatic skill in creating close relations with his English cousins, displays the blend of imagination and courage that is a typical Rothschild heritage.

Guy does things on a big scale. He has a nine-thousand-acre estate and château at Ferrières, which is *the* Rothschild showplace, nineteen miles east of Paris, famous for its art collection and its shoot. Even the late, unlamented Kaiser Wilhelm was impressed when he was invited to a party at Ferrières. Not long ago Guy and his wife had a little dance there for fifteen hundred people. The whole château was covered with a sort of luminous material that glowed like a fairy castle when it was properly illuminated. No English Rothschild would ever think of giving such a party. Besides, they could hardly afford it. The French Rothschilds are probably richer than their English cousins who were badly hit by British taxation in the past decades. When James de Rothschild died in London in 1957, his heirs had to pay over twenty million dollars in death taxes. That hurts—even a Rothschild.

Guy has something of the Midas touch. He raises and races famous horses. The most famous was Exbury, who had a glorious career and after retirement earned $240,000 a year at stud. Big money always attracts big money. Guy broke another precedent in 1956 when he divorced his Jewish wife and married Catholic Marie-Helene van Zuylen Nicolai. He had to resign as president of the Jewish Community in France.

Guy and his three cousins—Elie, Alain and Edmond—own the celebrated vineyard of Château Lafite in Pauillac, Bordeaux, which ranks first among the *Premiers Crus* of the Gironde since the still-valid Classification of 1855. Separated by a narrow footpath are the just-as-celebrated vines of Château Mouton-Rothschild, classified as the first among the *Seconds Crus*, much to the indignation of the owner, cousin Philippe de Rothschild, who is one of the English Rothschilds and lives in Paris but is not a partner in the French bank. Philippe commissioned Cocteau and Braque to design labels for his wine and promoted it on such a magnificent scale that the people in the Médoc call Mouton-Rothschild "le vin Hollywood," perhaps owing to the elegant banquet rooms, the impressive coat of arms and the beautiful cellars lit up by huge reflectors. Philippe has the satisfaction of selling his *Second Cru* in certain years for a better price than the cousins across the footpath get for their *Premier Cru*. One of the pleasures of being a Rothschild, or of working for them, is to get very fine wines at wholesale prices.

Guy's partners in the family bank, at 21, Rue Laffitte, are Alain, prominent philanthropist and president of the Paris Jewish Community; and Elie, polo player and expert vintner, who not long ago bought an interest in Divonne-les-Bains, a gambling casino conveniently close to the French-Swiss border where rich Swiss from Geneva, often stingy at home, become optimistic plungers, comforted by the absence of neighbors and tax collectors.

Finally, there is cousin Edmond of whom even the Rothschilds say that he is "the richest Rothschild." He inherited a terrific estate from his father Maurice, a celebrated Rothschild black sheep. From an anonymous-looking building at 45, Rue de Faubourg St. Honoré, Edmond manages a private empire called Compagnie Financière which finances developments in Israel (among them the Beersheba-Eilat pipeline and luxury resorts in the Gulf of Caesarea), housing projects in Paris, banks and factories in Brazil, supermarkets and mutual funds in Europe, Pan American's Inter-continental Hotels, the French Alpine resort of Megève. With his French cousins he develops sites around the new Mont Blanc tunnel, builds bungalow villages in Majorca, developments in Martinique and Guadeloupe. Another vintage Rothschild, Edmond is said to have a sixth sense for Opportunity Unlimited.

These are just the well-publicized small hobbies. The top deals are much less conspicuous. De Rothschild Frères set up two real-estate investment trusts, Société de Promotion (UFI) and Société d'Investissement (IFI), and a construction company, Société Nationale de Construction; formed a consortium to explore for oil in the Sahara; controls Penarroya and Le Nickel in New Caledonia; Miferma, the iron ore producers in Mauretania; and Cie. Française des Minerals d'Uranium, the biggest French uranium mining company; and has even reached into space with GESPA, which is Société des Etudes et des Réalisations pour le Génie Spatial. De Rothschild Frères has outdistanced its former competitors in the private banking fields—Neuflize, Lubersac, Worms, Hottinger—and is now in the big league with Banque de Paris et des Pays Bas, and Banque de l'Union Parisienne.

All this, and much more, has been achieved since the end of the last war. De Rothschild Frères, known in Paris as *La Grande Dame des Banques Privées*, is less a merchant bank than is N. M. Rothschild & Sons. Merchant banking is based on persuasion, and Frenchmen are not easy to persuade. Also, Paris will never rank as a financial center with New York or London.

Among the rather recent projects of the French Rothschilds is the draft of the original plan for financing the tunnel under the Channel that will connect France and Britain. President de Gaulle is very much in favor of the project. And de Gaulle's right-hand man (and one of the men mentioned as de Gaulle's successor) was Georges Pompidou, Prime Minister, who was formerly Baron Guy de Rothschild's right-hand man and general manager.

Plus ça change, plus c'est la même chose.

Between the two branches of the family there is endless curiosity about each other. The Rothschilds' favorite topic of conversation is the Rothschilds. They never get tired of talking about each others' adventures, achievements, hobbies, affairs, deals, victories and conquests. The French discuss the English eccentricities and the English agree that the French cousins are even more fascinating than all the gossip about them.

Their war exploits, for instance. Guy was trapped in Dunkirk, escaped, arrived in New York one day in 1941 with a million dollars' worth of diamonds in his briefcase, enlisted with the Free French, was torpedoed on his way to England, swam several hours in the icy North Atlantic until he was rescued by a British destroyer, and carried out secret missions for General de Gaulle.

Or Philippe (of Mouton-Rothschild) who escaped from German-occupied Paris to Morocco, was arrested by the Vichy government, organized gymnastic sessions in prison, was brought back to France, escaped by joining some smugglers across the Pyrénées (possibly walking some of the footpaths where the audacious smugglers working for his ancestors had carried French napoleons, British guineas and bills on certain Spanish banks to Wellington), reached Lisbon from where he sailed to England, joined General de Gaulle in London, and was billeted at the French Officers' Club at 107, Piccadilly, which happened to be the former mansion of his Grandaunt Hannah.

The English Rothschilds had their war heroes too. Edmund, an artillery major in the Italian and North African campaigns, distinguished himself repeatedly, and often acted with the superb assurance of a field marshal, ignoring the entire chain of command. Lord Rothschild, a noted bomb removal expert, was awarded Britain's George Medal and the U. S. Legion of Merit. Once he set up a laboratory in the treasure-filled mansion of his cousin Robert on Avenue de Marigny in Paris and began to experiment with high explosives, almost blowing up some priceless works of art.

ONCE UPON A TIME

When the Rothschilds run out of conversation about living members of the family, they can always fall back on the colorful exploits of their ancestors. Suppose your great-granduncle had traveled in his private train from his castle to the bank, had entertained the Prince of Wales (later King Edward VII), Cecil Rhodes, the Prime Minister, Lord Kitchener and Nellie Melba at dinner, with the food served on solid gold plates? The great-granduncle also conducted his private philharmonic orchestra, acted as ringmaster in his own circus, always presented his guests with gifts before they departed.

Great-granduncle Alfred de Rothschild attended synagogue punctiliously, was the first Jewish director of the Bank of England, was active in philanthropy, and was a skilled diplomatic catalyst. He foresaw the specter of the First World War as early as 1912, when he wrote to von Eckardstein, a prominent German diplomat, who thought the letter important enough to forward it to Count Bülow, the Kaiser's Chancellor:

> of recent years Germany's policy toward England has been a kind of "pinprick" policy, and, although a pin is not a very impressive document, repeated pricks may cause a wound ... I hope and pray with my whole heart that no serious wound may result. I have done everything possible over such a long period of years, and I feel now that you do not fully appreciate the great advantage of a genuine understanding with England ...

When war came two years later, as Alfred had expected, he wrote to the Prime Minister and offered "so many fine trees in my woods at Halton" as timber for pitprops in dugouts. It was a symbolic act. Nothing has ever been the same since, in Halton and elsewhere, for the Rothschilds. Their mansions were razed to ease traffic congestion in the cities. Their country estates became public parks. In 1937, Baron Lionel's town house at 148, Piccadilly was closed. It was there that he and Disraeli had discussed the purchase of the Suez Canal. The catalog of its contents, which were to be auctioned off, contained two hundred fifty pages with sixty-four colored plates.

Alfred de Rothschild's great manor at Halton became a training center for the Royal Air Force. In Buckinghamshire the second Lord Rothschild sold his collection of a quarter of a million birds to the New York Museum of Natural History. The former Rothschild mansion in Kensington is now part of the Embassy of the Union of Soviet Socialist Republics. *Non sum qualis eram.* Another family mansion is now owned by the National Trust. And in Paris some former Rothschild palaces have become the headquarters of the United States Mission to NATO and the Cercle Interallié.

The truth is that only great governments can now afford to live on the former Rothschild scale.

CREDO

Historians, economists, sociologists and novelists have tried to explain the Rothschild phenomenon, the secret of survival of the dynasty and its power after eight generations. They have searched for dark secrets, mysterious laws governing the family conclaves, for sinister links with governments, dictators, kings. There is always speculation about the Rothschilds. Last year, the French family brought court action against a French novelist who was said to have portrayed some Rothschilds in a *roman à clef*. The defense claimed, characteristically, that the Rothschilds were in the public domain, and "like all the greats of this world, are open to public criticism." Justice Rouanet de Vigne-Lavit agreed with the defense.

The worldwide, century-old search for the Secrets of the Rothschilds has remained unsuccessful. There is no secret. The family has had its good and bad days, like any other family. But they have always understood how to live with the changing times. After the golden epoch came the inevitable decline, between the two world wars. The previous generation failed to foresee the great opportunities in the United States. They were Europeans through and through, didn't understand America, missed active participation in the greatest industrial expansion in history.

The younger generation well realizes the tremendous possibilities in America but today the family doesn't have enough members to actively disperse on both sides of the Atlantic. The renaissance of the House of Rothschild which began twenty years ago in Paris and later caught up with the more conservative branch in London is a European renaissance. Still, nothing has really changed. The Rothschilds' greatest asset—the name and its prestige—does not show up on the balance sheets.

"A Rothschild," says a member of the young generation, "will always be hypothecated by the family's past. One could try to have a good time enjoying the fruits of one's predecessors' labors. Or one tries to work even harder and do better than they did. This has become very difficult in an age of increasing competition. The name naturally helps—but the name is not enough today. One needs ability and foresight, imagination and daring."

The credo of a Rothschild—and of a merchant banker.